**rock**climbing

Design and production
Vertebrate
Graphics
info@v-graphics.co.uk

# rockclimbing

## ESSENTIAL SKILLS & TECHNIQUES

The official handbook of the
**Mountaineering Instructor** and **Single Pitch Award** schemes

Written by **Libby Peter**

**Rock Climbing –**
**Essential Skills & Techniques**
**The official handbook of the Mountaineering Instructor**
**and Single Pitch Award schemes**

Copyright © 2004   Libby Peter

Published by Mountain Leader Training UK
www.mltuk.org

Mountain Leader Training UK
Hyfforddi Arweinwyr Mynydda y Deyrnas Unedig

First printed 2004

ISBN 0-9541511-1-9

Cover photo: Caroline Hale making delicate moves on Valkyrie VS 4c,
The Roaches, Derbyshire
by Ray Wood

All photography by Ray Wood unless otherwise credited

Vertebrate
Graphics

Designed, typeset and illustrated
by **Vertebrate Graphics**, Sheffield
www.v-graphics.co.uk

Printed in the UK by Clearpoint Colourprint, Nottingham

**While every attempt has been made to ensure that the**
**instructions in this book cover the subject safely and in**
**full detail, the authors and publishers cannot accept any**
**responsibility for any accident, injury, loss or damage**
**sustained while following any of the techniques described.**

# Contents

# Author's acknowledgements

Embarking on this project when I was five months pregnant felt rather like a race against time and needless to say I wouldn't have seen it through to the end without considerable technical, practical and emotional support. I would like to say a very special thanks to everyone who offered advice, criticism and help so willingly.

John Cousins of MLTUK 'held my hand' and displayed endless patience, utter confidence and co-ordinated the editorial assistance of Sue Doyle, Malcolm Creasey, Allen Fyffe, Andy Newton and Andy Say. The team at Vertebrate Graphics was equally patient and helpful throughout.

George Reid and Clare Bond contributed greatly to the environment section. Dawson Stelfox added an Irish perspective to the historical section, which proved to be the most controversial and debated chapter in the whole book. My apologies to those who feel it is still not right! On matters technical and involving kilonewtons Fred Hall, Neville McMillan and Andy Perkins were invaluable. Staff at the BMC, particularly Ian Hey and Stuart Ingram, were always helpful. The finer details of bouldering were made clearer by Ray Wood and Simon Panton, while Mike Robertson took the time to read through and comment on the deep water soloing chapter.

Gill Lovick of the Beacon Climbing Centre and Mike Smith of Bear Rock had useful comments about the use of indoor walls. Anne Salisbury and Marcus Bailie from AALA gave valuable insights into risk management and Paul Debney checked the legal section for obvious errors. Berwyn Evans and Dave Smith helped me greatly with information on high ropes courses, while Jamie Holding and George Smith gave me a better understanding of sea-level traverses and tyroleans. Martin Doyle, Louise Thomas, Bob Timms and Tim Neill found time from busy work schedules at Plas y Brenin to make up-to-date comments and answer random questions.

The outstanding photography of Ray Wood undoubtedly adds a professional quality to the book and thanks to Jo Maclaren, Ric Potter, Jude Spancken, Tania Scotland, Nathan Jones and Lou Wilkinson for giving up time to be 'models'. Thanks also to Sprayway and DMM for their support with the photography. Additional photos were kindly supplied by Allen Fyffe, Mark Richards, Mike Robertson, Nigel Shepherd, Ken Wilson and MTT.

Lastly I would like to thank my family and friends for so much help with the little 'uns and to my two gorgeous daughters themselves for their tolerance of my hours at the computer and for sleeping so soundly through the night!

*Libby Peter*
Dinorwig, 2004

# Editor's note

It is with a mixture of pleasure and pride that I write the final words for this fantastic book. Libby Peter is a very impressive author and I hope that *Rock Climbing* isn't the last time that she puts pen to paper. Not only did Libby produce fifty thousand wise words but she also turned out a great set of diagrams and has sourced an impressive collection of photographs. With these basic components the staff at Verterbrate Graphics have done a great job illustrating and compiling the book. Libby has also been very receptive to a group of editors who themselves have made a considerable contribution. In particular I would like to thank Malcolm Creasey, Allen Fyffe, Andy Newton and Andy Say for their technical editing and Stephen Gapps and Sue Doyle for their proof reading. As well as all the staff within *Mountain Leader Training* there are a great many volunteers who have assisted with this project and I would like to thank Brian Griffiths, Doug Jones and Anne Salisbury for their help. Finally I want to thank the chair of Mountain Leader Training UK's publication group, Allister McQuoid. Without his business acumen and enthusiasm I believe the whole project might have foundered and I hope climbers everywhere appreciate our collective efforts.

*John Cousins*

# Foreword

Some three years ago *Mountain Leader Training* discussed the need to upgrade and improve the quality and appropriateness of its supporting literature, with the added aim of sharing this good practice with the wider public. This resulted in the formation of a sub-committee, notionally referred to as the *Mountain Training Publications* (MTP) group, which was blessed with abundant enthusiasm and relevant experience, particularly on the complexities of successfully matching a publication to market criteria. Through a momentary lapse in concentration I was appointed Chairman of the MTP and we were charged with creating a series of definitive handbooks on behalf of *Mountain Leader Training*.

The first book, *Hill Walking*, published in 2003 and written by Steve Long was considered to be a major undertaking both in terms of investment and in the design of a high quality, informative handbook for hill walkers, Mountain Leaders and Walking Group Leaders. By March 2004, however, *Hill Walking* had sold 10,000 copies, well ahead of our best expectations with a reprint necessary two years earlier than planned. This underpinned not merely the market demand for the subject but the ability of the MTP to work with an author to achieve the correct chemistry for commercial and technical success. With this initial hurdle having been passed and the very evident new levels of collaboration amongst the national bodies the MTP progressed quickly towards its next publication with increased impetus and motivation.

*Rock Climbing* is the second book of this series and from the outset was considered to be a challenging topic to cover. In the first instance the sport and associated instructional techniques are constantly evolving and therefore, while in need of material, it warranted a writing style that would be advisory rather than prescriptive. Secondly there is a significant number of publications in existence ostensibly dealing with the subject of technical rock climbing and this book needed to differentiate within these and still cater for the general climbing public. This balance has been carefully and diligently met from our initial author selection, through the contents design, the superb application of the author and finally the editing.

This book should find a place on many bookshelves and in many rucksacks. While fashioned to the MLTUK criteria it was also shaped by our enthusiasm for the sport of climbing and by Libby Peter's impressive experience and specific skills. Libby has consulted widely throughout the development of the book and has met or surpassed all our aims for ensuring that it is inclusive in its style. As one of only two resident female Mountain Guides in the UK, her technical knowledge is beyond reproach and is balanced by her readiness to listen to others and incorporate their ideas. When you learn that Libby wrote the entire book in six months and for the last two months of this was looking after her new born baby you can see that the author is a very special character. Climbing has been a special part of my life for over thirty years and continues to be so. Having read this book I can assure you there is something in here for everyone, whether you are an enthusiastic novice or a gnarled old timer

Credit for this excellent publication is difficult to apportion and I trust that it is obvious from the quality of this book that Libby and the editorial team have much to be praised for. Libby deserves special recognition for maintaining her sterling

sterling family dedication and her professionalism in meeting our demanding timetable and requirements right through pregnancy. From a personal point of view I have to note how impressed I have been with the MTP group who claim to be solely mountaineers with limited industry or commercial experience and yet they have once again completed a complex publication on time, on budget and in specification. I must also single out John Cousins for his catalytic ability within the team to ensure that we keep our collective energy focused and for harnessing the best of all our inputs. Finally the publication remains a statement of success for the training boards and the MLTUK committee who have encouraged and endorsed this effort.

*Allister McQuoid*

**August 2004**

This book is published by Mountain Leader Training UK, which is a registered charity. Revenue from the sale of books published by MLTUK is used for the continuation of its publishing programme and for charitable purposes associated with training leaders.

# Introduction

## The essence of rock climbing

**For some people rock climbing is about a journey to a summit on a sunny day; for others it is an intense physical and mental challenge requiring training, discipline and effort. Many people make climbing their life, whilst for others it is a recreation or sport to be enjoyed sociably with a group of friends. Climbing can also be used as a vehicle to develop confidence and interdependence within groups or simply as a fun activity for youngsters, organised by both voluntary and commercial parties. Rock climbing takes place on boulders and outcrops, in quarries and indoor walls, on sea cliffs and sea stacks and on remote mountain crags. All these various approaches to and styles of climbing, though diverse, are equally valid and share a common ground which forms the subject and content of this book.**

### About this book

At the heart of this book is a desire to communicate the simple delights of climbing. Its main aim is to unlock some of the mysteries for those who are just getting started, whilst providing a comprehensive resource to competent climbers keen to improve their technical skills, safety and confidence.

The book considers all aspects of rock climbing in the UK and Ireland; it is divided into six parts beginning with a look at the climbing environment and historical background in order to put the subsequent chapters into a context. In Part II, movement skills and basic techniques are covered; these are the building blocks for going climbing, whether indoors or outdoors. Climbing at single pitch venues, multi-pitch climbing and scrambling are the subjects of Parts III, IV and V. This division allows for a progressive introduction of techniques rather than suggesting that it is necessary to go single pitch climbing before attempting multi-pitch routes or scrambling. Indeed it is hoped that readers will dip in and out of the book as and when they need some technical information. The final section considers information on how accidents happen and how they can be avoided or dealt with; in particular by considering strategies for managing risk.

Those looking for definitive statements about how things must be done or how to become an instructor will be disappointed, the aim is to outline a number of options and highlight good practise without prescribing one particular method. Experienced climbers and instructors pick and choose from a repertoire of skills and techniques

---

**NOTES FOR INSTRUCTORS** ## Notes for Instructors

This book contains valuable information for those taking others climbing whether as friends, fellow club members, leaders, instructors or guides; throughout the book information on looking after others is boxed separately and indicated by the symbol shown above.

according to the situation. No reference book can short cut the development of judgement skills; these must be acquired in the time-honoured fashion of 'getting out and doing it', for which there is no substitute.

## Looking after yourself

Rock climbing is perceived by some as a high-risk activity. In fact the actual number of accidents are few but the potential for those to be serious or fatal is great. Everyone has a different perception of acceptable personal risk but this book assumes that most individuals want to make things as safe as possible in any given situation. Knowledge underpins sound judgement and decision making. Rehearsed technical skills allow for efficiency and flexibility, which ultimately makes climbing more relaxing and enjoyable. It is hoped that this book will provide the foundation for a lifetime's safe and rewarding climbing.

## Looking after each other

The interdependence of a climbing team is one of the fascinating aspects of the sport. Climbers should understand not only their own strengths

## Participation statement

**Mountain Leader Training (MLT)** recognises that climbing, hill walking and mountaineering are activities with a danger of personal injury or death. Participants in these activities should be aware of and accept these risks and be responsible for their own actions. MLT provides training and assessment courses and associated literature to help leaders manage these risks and to enable new participants to have positive experiences while learning about their responsibilities.

and weaknesses but those of their partner too. 'Trust is earned' is an oft used but appropriate phrase.

For those climbing with novices or less experienced climbers, whether for fun or financial gain, the relationship is more complex and there is no escaping the fact that it is a huge responsibility. Introducing others to the world of climbing can be immensely rewarding but it should not be undertaken lightly. Leaders, supervisors, instructors or guides should first be highly experienced climbers themselves before considering taking novices under their wing.

CLIMBERS ON THE FINAL PITCH OF **OCTO** HVS 5b, CLOGWYN D'UR ARDDU, NORTH WALES

Part

# Environment & history

# The climbing environment

ADAM WAINWRIGHT ON **THUNDERHIPS** E1 5b, FAIRHEAD, NORTHERN IRELAND          Photo: Mike Robertson

Climbing takes us to some of the most
beautiful, special and fragile corners
of our land.

FIGURE 1.1   THE REMOTE AND ATMOSPHERIC AM BUCHAILLE, NORTH WEST SCOTLAND          Photo: Mark Richards

We are fortunate in the UK and Ireland to have one of the most diverse selections of climbing venues anywhere in the world. From roadside limestone crags to gritstone edges on windswept moors; from lonely and ancient volcanic cliffs in high mountain corries to remote sea-washed stacks of sandstone. We have an enviable choice of rock types in special natural environments surrounded by breathtaking scenery. Many climbers claim they would never venture further afield for rock climbing, if it wasn't for the weather! Our climate, typified by unsettled cyclonic weather patterns, adds unpredictability and a certain amount of frustration to climbing trips. However, mildness is also a characteristic that allows for year round climbing, especially in the south of England, for those keen to capitalise on the dry spells.

## 1.1 Coasts

At coastal venues alone there are cliffs of granite, basalt, limestone, quartzite, sandstone, chalk, gabbro, shale and slate, some can be accessed by a friendly beach stroll whilst others require committing abseils or intimidating sea-level traverses at low tide. The birds and plants that inhabit coastal environments thrive in these inaccessible and therefore unspoilt niches of our busy shores. Many of these are unique species, such as Portland sea lavender and the sea cabbages of Lundy and the Ormes. Kittiwake, guillemot, puffin, chough and razorbill are regular sea-cliff nesters along with the more aggressive and common fulmars. Fulmars often remain on their nests as climbers try to pass, coughing up and projecting a foul smelling oil in defence, while skuas defend their ground nests with fierce and accurate dive bombing. Protected or not, nesting birds should be avoided for the wellbeing of both bird and climber!

FIGURE 1.2   CLIMBER CAREFULLY AVOIDING A UNIQUE "ORME CABBAGE"

The habitats at the margins of the land are fragile and depend on a delicate balance, which careless climbers could easily upset. Soil substructures are weak and vulnerable to erosion, often irrevocably, once vegetation has been damaged. Rock quality varies enormously; from the clean wave-washed zone at the base of a route to a finish on tottering loose blocks. Climbing above the sea almost always has an additional 'grip factor' instilled by the ever present threat and noise of crashing waves.

## 1.2 Mountains

A great number of the wilder climbing venues are found in the mountains. Many of the routes most prized by climbers are located in the hills of Snowdonia, the fells of the Lake District, the peaks of Ireland and the remote mountains of Scotland. The weather and climbing conditions are seldom perfect on mountain cliffs, with a touch of dampness here and there, a sprinkling of moss or lichen and maybe some loose rock. Yet it is just this unpredictability that adds to their appeal, along with a high commitment factor and the reward of spending time in the heart of the mountains.

The upland cliff environment, perhaps surprisingly, hosts a large number of plants and

birds. The conditions suit many arctic-alpine plants which don't grow anywhere else; some are quite rare such as the elusive Snowdon Lily found only on a few sites in Snowdonia, yet others are fairly widespread, particularly in Scotland. The purple, mossy and starry saxifrages (saxifrage literally meaning rock breaker) regularly colonise cliff-side nooks and crannies and the scree below, whilst cushions of purple moss campion are often glimpsed along with many species of fern and moss. The base rich rocks

FIGURE 1.3   MOSS CAMPION

FIGURE 1.4   PARKING AND FOOTPATH EROSION BOTH NEED CAREFUL MANAGEMENT AT POPULAR VENUES

like dolerite support the greatest variety of species, whilst on acidic rhyolite and granite cliffs far fewer will be found. Many of these plants prefer damp and shady cliff habitats which, though not attractive to rock climbers, are also the haunts of ghyll scramblers and winter climbers.

A few tenacious rowan, juniper, birch and holly trees survive on mountain cliffs, remnants of our once heavily wooded landscape, surviving centuries of deforestation by virtue of their inaccessibility. Unfortunately, a proportion of these survivors have since met their demise at the hands of careless climbers.

Ravens, peregrine falcons and golden eagles are some of the more spectacular species that may be spotted circling mountain crags. Conflicts between climbers and birds on mountain cliffs are not common, as nesting sites are few and easily avoided. Nowadays climbers have a good reputation for keeping away from threatened nesting birds. Sadly birds are still at a far greater risk from egg thieves and long-term ecosystem changes than they are from climbers.

## 1.3  Other environments

The coast and mountains may provide our most spectacular climbing environments and longest routes, but escarpments, gorges, outcrops and quarries offer accessible and often sheltered venues. Many of these lie within National Parks or designated protection areas due to their setting amidst a unique landscape. Others are on the fringes of towns and cities where they provide a convenient recreational asset. Moorland sites are often home to ground nesting birds such as the merlin and plover whilst the ring ouzel prefers steeper rocky ground at the base of crags. Sheer volume of climbers on some of the more accessible crags is a real problem in many places and may require them to work closely with landowners and managers to ensure continued use.

## 1.4  Where can we go?

In the UK and the Republic of Ireland the access laws vary but considering that the majority of the cliffs we climb on are on privately owned land there are surprisingly few access problems. There are a limited number of notable exceptions where access has been denied, normally after the venue has reached a state of such popularity that conflicts such as parking problems, excessive noise and damage to property have arisen.

The three Mountaineering Councils; **British Mountaineering Council** (BMC), **Mountaineering Council of Scotland** (MCofS) and **Mountaineering Council of Ireland** (MCI) play an important role in access and conservation

FIGURE 1.5 CLIMBERS AND LANDOWNERS IN CONFLICT

work. Council staff and volunteers liaise with landowners and conservationists where conflicts arise. In the UK and Ireland the Access and Conservation Trust (ACT) supports this process by providing resources for erecting sign posts or stiles and for footpath erosion control work.

The Mountaineering Councils provide information about climbing sites where there are restrictions or problems. For example the BMC Regional Access Database (RAD) found on its website contains details of over 500 crags in England and Wales. Current access issues are also reported in the climbing press and on climbing websites, see *Appendix 5: Useful Contacts* on page 218 for details.

# 1.5 Legislation

Climbers should be aware of legislation and designations that protect the UK's natural heritage. The website www.magic.gov.uk can be searched to find out which areas are covered by specific designations; however all areas should be treated with respect and care – designation or not. *The Wildlife and Countryside Act 1981* is the legislative basis for natural heritage protection in the UK. This act protects all birds, their nests and eggs, some animals and some plants and it makes it an offence to injure, kill or take such specimens from the wild. Birds listed in *Schedule 1*

FIGURE 1.6 THE BMC'S REGIONAL ACCESS DATABASE

of the Wildlife and Countryside Act are generally the most rare breeding birds and therefore afforded higher protection.

The Wildlife and Countryside Act has been amended, not least by the *Countryside and Rights of Way (CRoW) Act 2000*. In respect of nesting birds the CRoW Act has amended the wording of the Wildlife and Countryside Act in relation to disturbance of Schedule 1 birds from 'intentionally' to 'intentionally or recklessly'. This inclusion of the word 'recklessly' is a subtle but potentially significant change for climbers. The

FIGURE 1.7   BIRD RESTRICTION NOTICE AT GOGARTH

amendment is designed to increase the effectiveness of the legislation in protecting Schedule 1 birds from persecution and egg thieves, although climbers have faced prosecution in the past. Schedule 1 birds are monitored carefully and climbers should avoid known nesting sites and be sensitive if they find themselves in the vicinity of a protected nesting bird. Peregrine falcons, chough and golden eagle are the Schedule 1 species climbers are most likely to encounter. They are particularly vulnerable to disturbance just after laying and hatching, which normally takes place between late February and early May. If the parent birds are scared off the nest for too long, excessive cooling can damage the eggs or the feeding of chicks can be disrupted.

The CRoW Act has also amended the Wildlife and Countryside Act to increase sentences for wildlife crime, including increased protection of *Sites of Special Scientific Interest* (SSSI). Harm to wildlife is now a criminal offence with an increase in fines and imprisonment for up to six months. It is worth noting that the CRoW Act 2000 passed through parliament after the devolution of Scottish legislative powers, and the amendments to the Wildlife and Countryside Act described only cover England and Wales, although it is likely that similar amendments will be made in the *Nature Conservation* *(Scotland) Bill*, which is currently before the Scottish parliament.

Access was also addressed by the CRoW Act which outlines a statutory right of access on foot to specific mapped areas of open, uncultivated countryside, defined as mountain, moor, heath, down and common land. This is in addition to the access currently provided by public rights of way and local access agreements as often exist in national parks and on National Trust land. The new legislation is due to be in place by 2005. Climbers and commercial organisations in particular should seek information, available from the BMC, Countryside Council for Wales, the Countryside Agency and English Nature. (See *Appendix 2: Access legislation* on page 212.)

A different situation exists in Scotland where the *Land Reform (Scotland) Act 2003* has secured a more generalised right of access to land and inland water, which should result in fewer problems for climbers and other outdoor recreational users. This is accompanied by the *Scottish Outdoor Access Code* to clarify access details. The MC of S and Scottish Natural Heritage (SNH) provide up-to-date information.

Recent legislation has not affected Ireland where most conflicts arise when farmers restrict or deny access and which are dealt with locally. The MCI is a good source for details of problem

FIGURE 1.8   MOD ACCESS RESTRICTION NOTICE, MRS WESTON'S, PEMBROKE

areas in both the Republic of Ireland and Northern Ireland. In Northern Ireland, the Countryside Access and Activities Network (CAAN) is a useful information source. (See *Appendix 2: Access legislation* on page 212.)

## 1.6  Access restrictions

Seasonal access restrictions to allow birds to nest undisturbed form an important and widely accepted part of the balancing of conflicting interests. First introduced in the 1970s these restrictions are agreed between the mountaineering councils and conservation bodies and are respected by climbers as a positive balance between access and conservation. In England and Wales over 160 crags have some form of restrictions between 1st February and 15th August. Information about restricted areas and periods are contained in guidebooks, the Mountaineering Council websites and leaflets such as the BMC's 'Access and Seasonal Restrictions'. Local, temporary changes are also posted on boards near the climbing site.

The Ministry of Defence restricts access to a few climbing areas most notably in Pembroke where certain areas are regularly closed. In recent years the MOD has been open to negotiation for improved access for climbers although these remain tightly managed.

A number of mountain crags on Scottish estates are affected on certain days during the red deer stalking season (July–October for stags, October–February for hinds). Though this is rarely a cause of conflict for climbers it is important to check the situation beforehand. The Hillphone leaflet, available from SNH, the MC of S and various shops, provides phone numbers to get details of some of these preferred access routes during the stalking season via recorded messages.

## 1.7  Minimising impact

The majority of climbers value their climbing resource and would never knowingly exacerbate an access problem or cause environmental damage. However, most climbers could occasionally be accused of taking a poorly thought-out short cut such as abseiling from the last remaining tree on a crag. Even seemingly innocuous acts of laziness or poor practise contribute to the bigger picture. How long would that tree survive if every single climber were to belay and abseil from it,

**FIGURE 1.9**  ADRIAN BAXTER TOP-ROPING CLASSIC BOWLES SANDSTONE

trampling around its roots and wearing through its bark as the ropes are pulled? Walking off is possible on the majority of crags even if it takes a little longer and is less convenient than abseiling.

## 1.8 New routing and guidebooks

Developing new crags often involves cleaning to unearth climbable rock, which can be devastating for the plants and lichens growing there. Climbers should be aware that it is an offence to intentionally pick, uproot or destroy wild plants listed in *Schedule 8* of the Wildlife and Countryside Act, or to uproot any wild plant intentionally, except on your own land, or with permission of the landowner. Some habitats are afforded higher

protection (see *1.5 Legislation* on page 7), and climbers should check the status of sites and keep gardening and brushing to a minimum. Recently the extent of brushing has resulted in degradation of the rock itself and as a rule it should not be undertaken

Some crags have not previously been developed for a reason, such as a historic access conflict or special conservation value; this should be investigated beforehand. The placing of fixed equipment or bolts on climbs has always been contentious, which is why the mountaineering councils promote policies to minimise and contain the spread of fixed equipment guided by local ethics and the consensus view; these are available on the councils' websites.

Climbers of new routes have long struggled with the conflict of whether to publicise new areas or keep them a closely guarded secret. Crags featured in articles and selected guides or mini topos become honey-pots and recommended routes become focal points for higher numbers and therefore greater damage. Definitive guide-books give the broader picture, not only provid-ing more venues and routes to choose from but also imparting valuable historical, access and conservation information to promote a wider appreciation of the climbing environment. Some guidebooks have recently omitted the traditional star system of indicating quality routes to avoid overcrowding on certain climbs.

Specific information on new routing and gar-dening is available from each of the moun-taineering councils.

## 1.9  Parking

Many venues have limited parking facilities lead-ing to badly parked vehicles, which can cause friction with local residents, land managers and other climbers. This is a common cause of access problems, so if parking places are limited users should consider alternative parking with a longer walk in, public transport or an alternative venue.

## 1.10  Style and structure of activity

*Bottom-roping* and abseiling can cause consid-erable damage; without the appropriate protec-tion for the rocks or the trees, loaded moving ropes erode vegetation and cut grooves in soft rock. Sandstone is the most extreme example of this and the popular southern venues including Harrisons and Bowles now have very strict guidelines to keep further damage to a minimum.

Leading routes and belaying from the top gen-erally cause less damage. *Top-roping* is prefer-able to bottom-roping (see *Appendix 1: Glossary* on page 210) as is moving to different routes through the day to spread the load. Of course such methods are time consuming and difficult to implement with large groups but this is no excuse for taking the easiest option that causes the most damage. An 'every little helps' attitude is essential in this respect.

### 1  NOTES FOR INSTRUCTORS  Putting something back

Taking the time to explain good practise to novices and involving groups in small acts of looking after the venue, such as litter removal, fosters the idea of environmental responsibility. If the leaders don't do it who will?

Many groups find that contributing to local repair projects is of great value. Organisations such as the British Trust for Conservation Volunteers (BTCV) or the John Muir Trust (JMT) can facilitate this.

## 1.11  Sanitation

This delicate but everyday subject requires com-mon sense and some management to avoid the dreaded unpleasant discovery under a rock close to the crag. It may be a good idea to explain to groups beforehand that crags don't have toilets and schedule a toilet stop shortly before arriving at the cliff. Urination and defecation close to the crag is smelly, unsightly and a potential hazard to health; it is also unnecessary. Going to the toilet should take place well away from the crag and at least 50m from any watercourse or footpath. Caves, shelters and boulders should not be used as toilets; the smell will linger in enclosed places.

Many youngsters may not have been to the toilet in the open before and the instructor may need to designate an appropriate area that is safe but private.

Defecation at crags is to be avoided but in an emergency current advice encourages burying excrement in a 15cm deep hole rather than hiding it under a rock and carrying out toilet paper, tampons and sanitary towels. A lightweight trowel and some strong plastic bags are therefore crucial items of a leader's kit.

Those responsible for introducing others to the magical world of climbing have an added duty of imparting environmental awareness and wisdom to tomorrow's climbers. It is only with a committed approach to minimising damage that these fragile environments will survive intact.

on maximum group size, small groups are preferable all round; better for the quality of experience for the group and other users and healthier for the venue. Other countries do stipulate numbers in groups as a measure to minimise their impact such as in Canadian parks where they limit groups to a maximum of ten.

## Group size

Bigger groups, however well supervised, make a greater impact; more noise, more pairs of feet walking in, more needing to go to the toilet and so on. Any opportunities for splitting groups to different venues or at least different sections of the same venue should be sought. The size of group one instructor is asked to look after has steadily grown through commercial pressure and financial necessity. Adapted climbing techniques, such as bottom-roping systems, have made this possible and though there are no specific restrictions

## Choice of venue

Sensitive and busy crags can be avoided by researching and seeking out lesser-known venues. Leaders should avoid returning repeatedly to the same venue for the same activity; a break from the routine and thus a break from the trampling pattern is healthy for the ground. Indoor climbing walls or alternative activities should be considered in very wet weather when greater damage occurs, or when the activity is not linked with the outdoors such as in some types of management training exercises.

FIGURE 1.10 A BUSY DAY AT THE GRITSTONE CRAG, ALMSCLIFF, YORKSHIRE

# A brief history of
# UK and Irish climbing

KERN KNOTTS CRACK, WASDALE, LAKE DISTRICT C.1920          Photo: Bâton Wicks collection

Understanding something of the history of rock climbing allows an insight into the ethos of the sport that we recognise today. It is the story of adventurous individuals and colourful characters for whom exploring new cliffs and making first ascents became a focal point of their lives.

Interwoven with the history of climbers is the development of increasingly refined climbing and rope techniques together with a growing sophistication in the equipment used. Harder routes required better protection, and developments in gear allowed more difficult climbing; the two are inextricably linked.

The rich legacy of climbing tradition and ethics also contributes an important backdrop to the role of the climbing instructor, who while ensuring safety has to impart a sense of the exhilaration, freedom and adventure that is intrinsically part of climbing.

## 2.1 In the beginning

The story of rock climbing began over 200 years ago with the botanists, shepherds, quarrymen and miners who scaled precipitous cliffs in search of plants, minerals and stray sheep. One of the earliest recorded ascents was in 1798 when the Reverends Bingley and Williams clambered up the Eastern Terrace on Clogwyn D'ur Arddu in search of botanical specimens. In a similar era men from the crofting communities on the Scottish island of St Kilda climbed difficult sea-cliffs to collect sea fowl and eggs following a tradition that was as much a rite of passage as a necessity to supplement their diet or to pay rents in kind. Early recorded adventurous explorations in the Lake District include the poet Samuel Taylor Coleridge's short cut on Scafell in 1802, descending what is now known as Broad Stand, and the ascent of Pillar Rock in 1826 by a Lakeland shepherd, John Atkinson.

Throughout the later years of the 1800's numerous mountaineering and rock climbing routes to summits via gullies and ridge lines were climbed, often by Alpine Club or Scottish Mountaineering Club members in training for the Alps. The alluring peaks of the Cuillin on Skye were obvious objectives and it is here that the first professional guide, John Mackenzie, was based. In Wales, early activity was concentrated on Lliwedd, the first recorded ascent being West Buttress (1883) by A.H. Stocker and T.W. Wall. By 1909, when the first Climbers' Club guidebook was produced, there were over 40 routes on the cliff, mostly by J.M. Archer Thomson.

In Cornwall, Sir Leslie Stephen was responsible for the earliest recorded sea cliff climb in 1858 and Aleister Crowley, also well known for his interest in the occult, was pioneering routes on the crumbly chalk cliffs of Beachy Head in 1894.

In Ireland, although there was one recorded ascent on Luggala in 1908, climbing didn't develop in earnest until the 1930s in the Mourne Mountains.

The origins of pure rock climbing and bouldering also lie in the 19th century. Cecil Slingsby born in 1849 was climbing at Yorkshire's Crookrise crag from the age of 15 and exploring Almscliff in the 1870s. By the end of the century Jim Puttrell had discovered the potential of a number of Peak District crags. His tour de force was leading the **Downfall Groove** (c.1900) on Kinder Downfall. At a grade of Hard Very Severe, although barely known to many people then, it was well ahead of its time in terms of difficulty.

Despite considerable earlier activity, it is the ascent of **Napes Needle** (Hard Very Difficult) in the Lake District by W.P. Haskett Smith on his own in 1886 that is often cited as the 'birth of rock climbing', as a sport distinct from mountaineering.

## 2.2 1900–1950

Owen Glynne Jones was one of many to be inspired by the Napes ascent and adopted a modern attitude towards difficulty, famously top-roping **Kern Knotts Crack** (VS) prior to a lead in 1897. The turn of the century saw climbers continents apart experimenting with protection and aid techniques in order to make progress on harder ground. In Austria, Hans Dulfer developed the tension pendulum and Hans Fiechtl used the first piton, whilst on Scafell in 1914 Siegfreid Herford was standing on G.S.Sansom's shoulders to gain height up the Great Flake on Central Buttress.

In the late 1920s Fred Piggott and Jack Longland utilised both pitons and stone chockstones to climb the East (**Piggott's Climb**) and West (**Longland's Climb**) Buttresses on Clogwyn D'ur Arddu. Traditionalists in the UK were vehemently opposed to the use of pitons and ensured they did not become widely used, as was the case in Europe. The most famous piton episode came in 1936 when visiting Bavarian climbers placed two for aid on Tryfan's **Munich Climb** (VS), piquing national pride and prompting great scorn. A free ascent by Menlove Edwards and Colin Kirkus quickly followed, along with the removal of the pitons. So ingrained in our climbing history is the fixed protection debate that it rages as fiercely nearly 100 years on.

Longland was responsible at Idwal in 1930 for one of Britain's earliest Extremely Severe gradings, when going off-route he established **Javelin Blade**, now given E1 5b. Another step forward, also at Idwal, came just after the war in October 1945 with Chris Preston's bold lead of **Suicide Wall Route 1** after top-rope inspection. Still graded E2 5c today, it is worth remembering it was done wearing a pair of gym shoes.

The likes of Colin Kirkus, John Menlove Edwards and Arthur Birtwistle left a legacy of technical and bold free climbs. Kirkus climbed a phenomenal volume of routes including **Great Slab** (VS, 1930) on Clogwyn D'ur Arddu, **West Rib** (HVS,1931) on Dinas Mot and **Mickledore Grooves** (VS,1931) on Scafell. Birtwistle's boldness is evident in his ascent of the remarkable **Diagonal** (HVS) on Dinas Mot in 1938. It didn't see another ascent for ten years. Edwards' **Central Gully Direct** (HVS, 1938) and **Eliminate 1** (E1 5b, 1928) at Helsby were among his outstanding achievements.

Two climbers who set standards in the Peak District were Ivar Berg at Laddow Rocks with **Cave Arête Indirect** (E1 5a, 1916) and Harry Kelly, whose gymnastic struggle at Stanage produced **Kelly's Overhang** (HVS 5b, 1926).

In the Lake District Jim Birkett made a psychological breakthrough on Castle Rock with **Overhanging Bastion** (VS, 1939) while his **Harlot Face** (HVS, 1949) on the same crag ten years later was the hardest lead in the Lake District.

With the focus in Scotland mainly directed towards winter climbing, along with fewer climbers and poorer weather it's easy to see why hard free climbing didn't develop as fast as south of the border. Johnny Cunningham's **The Gallows Route** (E2 5b,1947) on Buchaille Etive Mor was a definite exception that looked to the future.

The Irish Mountaineering Club was formed in 1948 and this marked the start of significant development in Ireland. Dalkey Quarry outside Dublin, Luggala and Glendalough in Wicklow, along with the Mournes were the first crags to be developed.

FIGURE 2.1   THE LAKELAND GUIDE, JIM CAMERON, GUIDES A CLIENT ON SCOUT CRAG, LANGDALE IN C. 1962.          Photo: Ken Wilson, Bâton Wicks collection

## 2.3  1950–1970

Social change following the Second World War meant that climbing, which had previously been mainly the preserve of the professional middle classes, now experienced the involvement of a growing number of the proletariat; climbers used to tough conditions from less privileged backgrounds. The hegemony of Joe Brown and Don Whillans typified this, setting the pace in North Wales and the Peak District. Together they added **Cemetery Gates** (E1 5b,1951) and **The Thing** (E2 5c, 1956) to the Cromlech. Here Brown was also responsible for one of Britain's most famous climbs, **Cenotaph Corner** (1952) using two points of aid; now E1 5c free with a polished crux. It was not unusual to use the odd piton or sling around a chockstone to help get past a particularly tricky section in this period. Brown's **Elder Crack** (E2 5b, 1950) and **Right Eliminate** (E3 5c, 1951) at Curbar and Whillans' crossing of the huge overhang at the Roaches to establish **The Sloth** (HVS 5b, 1954) along with the uncompromising **Extol** (E2 5b, 1960) in the Lake District are further examples of the huge contribution they made to British climbing.

In his short life, the talented Robin Smith had a huge impact on climbing in Scotland pioneering such classics in Glencoe as **Yo-Yo** (E1 5b, 1959) and **Shibboleth** (E2 5b, 1958/59). Glasgow climbers formed the formidable Creag Dubh club, whose members were responsible for climbing many outstanding lines.

The development of Gogarth, probably Britain's finest sea cliffs, was a major theme of the sixties led by Pete Crew, Baz Ingle, Martin Boysen and of course Joe Brown. Meanwhile at Stoney Middleton, a traditional aid venue, Tom Proctor showed the direction climbing was taking with his emphasis on free climbing and in particular by establishing the difficult test case **Our Father** (E4 6b, 1968). Two years later he came up with the frightening **Green Death** (E5) at Millstone Edge.

The late 1960s also saw the 'discovery' of Fair Head on the north coast of Ireland, set to become a major climbing venue until the present day.

## 2.4  1970s

Steve Bancroft and John Allen were synonymous with technical brilliance during this period in the Peak District. Allen was responsible for routes including **White Wand** (E5 6a, 1975) at Stanage and Millstone's **London Wall** (E5 6a, 1975) while Bancroft in 1976 established **Strapadictomy** (E5 6a) and soloed the audacious **Narcissus** (E6 6a), both at Froggatt. Another bold offering from 1976 was the first free ascent of **Linden** by Mick Fowler (E6 6b) on Curbar.

It was a period of applying the free-climbing ethic to previously aided routes, although the growing use of chalk provoked criticism from some climbers on ethical and environmental grounds. The names of Pete Livesey and Ron Fawcett came to the fore; both embraced a scientific approach to training on the newly developed climbing walls. Livesey applied his stamina to great effect in 1974 with first ascents of **Right Wall** (E5 6a) in the Llanberis Pass and **Footless Crow** (E5 6b) in Borrowdale. On Yorkshire grit Fawcett made his mark with **Slip 'n' Slide** (E6 6a, 1976) and the unprotected **Desperate Dan** (E7, 1978). On the Bowderstone Crag he freed an aid climb to give **Hell's Wall** (E6 6c, 1979) and muttered, "c'mon arms, do your stuff" while being filmed making the first ascent of **Lord of the Flies** (E6 6b, 1979) on Dinas Cromlech.

That same year Scotland got its first E5, thanks to Dave Cuthbertson's **Wild Country** (E5 6b) on the Cobbler. Mick Fowler produced **Stairway to Heaven** (E4 6a, 1976) on Skye and made the first free ascent of **Titan's Wall** (1979) on Ben Nevis, now given E3 5c.

On Clogwyn D'ur Arddu, a little-known route of note is **Quiver**, climbed in 1974 by Phil Bartlett and today considered as E5/6 making it a candidate for the most fearsome route of its day.

During the mid-seventies the prolific Pat Littlejohn was at the heart of the action that got under way to develop Pembroke's extensive limestone sea-cliffs.

In Ireland new crags were being discovered such as Ailladie in Clare and Muckros Head and Malinbeg in Donegal. Fairhead gained its first E4 with **Wall of Prey** by visitor Arnis Strapcans in 1979 but after a rockfall it was re-climbed by Calvin Torrans at E5 6a.

## 2.5  1980s

In 1980, John Redhead's first ascent of the sparsely protected **The Bells! The Bells!** (E7 6b) on Gogarth's friable North Stack Wall was considered the most serious pitch in Britain. The big grit breakthrough of the early eighties was Johnny Woodward's desperate **Beau Geste** at Froggatt; at the time graded E7 7b it has now settled to E6 6b. In 1983 Scotland's Dave Cuthbertson completed the crack-line of **Requiem** at Dumbarton Rock resorting to many 'yo-yos' and leaving the ropes in place. Given E7 7a it is nowadays thought to be E8 by some and given F8a+ for a redpoint with the wires in place (see the sidebar *To bolt or not to bolt* on page 18 for an explanation of redpoint). The following year the first bolt protected F8as were climbed with Ben Moon's classic **Statement of Youth** at Pen Trwyn and Jerry Moffatt's **Revelations** at Raven Tor, although the latter is now considered even harder after some holds disintegrated.

On Clogwyn D'ur Arddu in 1983, Moffatt, wearing the first pair of 'sticky-soled' rock boots in the UK, climbed John Redhead's attempted line up the right hand side of Great Wall, taking the 'easiest way' to finish and producing **Master's Wall** (E7 6b) in the process. Redhead's **Margins of the Mind** from 1984 on the same cliff although

FIGURE 2.2   NEIL GRESHAM ON **REVELATIONS** F8a+, RAVEN TOR, DERBYSHIRE

## To bolt or not to bolt

Bolting was on the increase at the start of the '80s, prompting passionate debate about where it should and should not take place. The Mountaineering Councils developed fixed equipment policies to keep bolts largely confined to quarries and certain limestone cliffs. There were frequent episodes of bolts appearing and then being chopped with particular scorn levelled at retro-bolting of lines previously climbed without bolts.

The sport climbing ethic, imported from the continent, of relatively safe, well-protected bolt lines became popular, readily allowing climbers to push their grades and improve their fitness.

Sections or moves of a route are often 'worked' first before trying to link them in preparation for a *red-point* ascent – climbing the route in one push from the ground, clipping the already placed quick-draws on the way with no falls or rests to the lower-off.

originally graded E7 is now considered a contender for the first E8 in Britain pre-dating Nick Dixon's **Doug** (E8 6c, April '86) at the Roaches. Cloggy's 'Great Wall Saga' culminated in 1986 in "the hardest lead in the country even after practise" with Johnny Dawes' **The Indian Face** (E9 6c). Dawes was also responsible in 1988 for the impressive totally on-sight first ascent of **Hardback Thesaurus** (E7 6b) at Gogarth. On the gritstone Andy Pollitt was **Knockin' on Heaven's Door** (E8/9 6c, 1988) at Curbar but it was John Dunne's **New Statesman** (E8/9 7a, 1988) at Ilkley and **Parthian Shot** (E9 7a, 1989) at Burbage that captured the headlines.

## 2.6 1990s–2003

When Ben Moon climbed **Hubble** (F8c+) at Raven Tor in 1990, it was the hardest sport route in the world. A little while later Ruth Jenkins was the first British woman to climb F8b with her ascent of **Zeke the Freak** at Rubicon in 1995. Another British first was **The Big Bang** at Lower Pen Trwyn hesitantly given F9a by Neil Carson in 1996 but still unrepeated.

Nick Dixon made the second ascent of **The Indian Face** eight years after Dawes' 'voyage' had shown the way and Neil Gresham made a further repeat a few days later. Both ascents, like the first, involved top-rope practise. Leo Houlding held a clear vision of the adventure of climbing even as a 17-year old, with his on-sight of **Master's Wall** in 1997.

John Dunne raised standards with his ascent of **Divided Years** in the Mourne Mountains in Northern Ireland, the UK's first E10.

The art of *bouldering* has always been dear to the hearts of British climbers; a cherished sub-culture of the bigger game of climbing. Its popularity as a sport in its own right grew dramatically in the 1990s with the introduction of crash pads from the US and the publication of specific guidebooks to the Peak and Yorkshire. Many of the top sport climbers of the late '80s and early '90s, such as Jerry Moffatt, Ben Moon and Malcolm Smith, abandoned roped climbing altogether, choosing to focus their not inconsiderable talents upon increasingly difficult boulder problems. A proliferation of bouldering videos and websites, increasing magazine coverage and yet more guidebooks, drew rapidly escalating numbers to appreciate the simple art of bouldering, either as a core activity or as an essential base for the broader aspects of route climbing. The UK bouldering scene grows ever stronger with burgeoning grass roots support and truly world-class standards being achieved by scene leaders, John Gaskins and Malcolm Smith.

*Head-pointing*, where a route is practised on a top-rope prior to being led, became a fashionably acceptable means of climbing for a minority trying the most challenging routes, particularly poorly-protected grit routes. The zenith of this approach was Neil Bentley's **Equilibrium** (E10 7a) at Burbage in February 2000. Neil Gresham's repeat two years later made it the only route of this standard to have had the grade confirmed.

Repeating established routes in a 'purer style' has always been an important challenge for cutting-edge climbers. While a handful of E8s have been 'flashed' including **Carmen Picasso** (Gorple) and **Countdown to Disaster** (Ilkley), courtesy of Ben Bransby and Ryan Pasquil respectively, it probably wasn't until the summer of 2003 that Dave Birkett made the first true on-sight of an E8, repeating James McHaffie's **Fear of Failure** on Dove Crag in the Lake District.

MARK REEVES TAKING ON THE **RED BARON** V7, SHIPLEY GLEN, YORKSHIRE

# Part II

# Getting moving: indoors and outdoors

# Warming up

A SIMPLE FOREARM STRETCH

Warming up before any sport or physical activity is important to avoid injury, increase efficiency and enhance performance. Climbing is no different, yet climbers often fail to warm-up adequately.

The basic principles of warming up are more important than a prescriptive routine, as these can be varied and adapted according to the situation and setting.

# 3.1 Comprehensive warm-up

A comprehensive warm-up should include the following elements:

### 3.1.1 Five minutes of low-intensity aerobic activity

Anything that gets the heart and lungs working harder, such as running, cycling, walking fast with a rucksack or boulder hopping, is beneficial. The increased blood flow to muscles and connective tissues makes them more elastic and injury-resistant.

### 3.1.2 Loosen up joints

Move all joints through their full range of motion to lubricate them. Work systematically around the body, opening and closing fingers, circling wrists, bending elbows and rotating shoulders, then carry out similar movements to neck, spine, hips, knees, ankles and toes.

### 3.1.3 Stretching

To be done properly this should include all the major muscles used in climbing, and stretches should be done slowly, gently and held for about 20 seconds. Bouncing and rapid stretching is counterproductive and can often be damaging, as is stretching without being warmed up. A full stretching session is not always practical but key areas can be focused on such as forearms, shoulders or any injured muscle.

### 3.1.4 Easy climbing

Easy climbs, problems or moves prepare the muscles for pulling harder later but also get the body used to the feel of moving on rock again. It is virtually impossible to jump on to a hard route 'cold' and climb it smoothly.

Bouldering is a popular warm-up activity and is dealt with in more detail in *7 Bouldering* on page 73.

### 3.1.5 Mental preparation

Climbers preparing for a hard route, training session or competition use the warm-up time to prepare psychologically for what is coming. Novice climbers shouldn't need to 'psyche up' for their first moves but are likely to have anxieties that can be allayed by knowing what to expect.

# 3.2 Shortened warm-up

When a comprehensive warm-up is not practical or necessary, a shortened version that includes the key elements can be completed without much interruption to the day. This should include:

- Walking to the crag or around the block before going into a wall
- A few loosening up exercises
- A little gentle stretching of key muscles
- Some easy climbing

# 3.3 Injury avoidance

This section considers soft tissue injuries sustained during climbing or training, commonly through over use. Acute injuries that occur suddenly involve tears or ruptures to muscle, tendon or ligament. A small partial tear, although painful at the time, should recover by itself in about ten days, whilst a serious rupture requires immediate medical attention.

Over-use injuries result from accumulated micro damage that occurs within the muscle or connective tissue creating a weakness that eventually gives way. Early symptoms such as mild pain or aching subside quickly and are easy to ignore, hence the pattern is repeated until a tear occurs or more serious inflammation has developed.

Any minor soft tissue injury can be treated initially by the *RICE* method (see page 24). If a more serious injury is suspected medical advice is essential.

Warming up is the most effective protection against injury but it is also important to train or climb harder progressively to allow the body time to adapt to new stresses. Climbing and training should be avoided when ill or over-tired;

FIGURE 3.1    LEG RAISE STRETCH ON A HANDY BOULDER

Taking a group through a warm-up routine at a busy wall or crag may not be appropriate. It may make them feel uncomfortable and self-conscious unless there is a warm-up area or quiet corner to use. In these situations ensure a gentle and progressive start to the session.

For example, youngsters can be captivated by a structured imaginative session that incorporates all the elements of warm-up without being called one.

Introduce a theme like a sunny beach and start by stepping or jumping over small then bigger waves. Mimic swimming arm strokes first slowly and then with urgency as a shark approaches. Sit in imaginary canoes and paddle slowly then quickly then slowly as a storm approaches then passes (heart rates will be increased and joints loosened). At walls play coloured hold 'twister' by nominating a colour to touch for each hand and foot whilst standing on the ground (stretching and gentle pulling).

recovery following a big effort may take up to 72 hours. Listening to the body is the best measure as it knows when enough is enough. Varying climbing or training regimes spreads out the stress and helps achieve muscle balance, which in itself reduces the chance of injury. Minor aches and pains should not be ignored otherwise a chronic injury could develop which may take months or even years to heal.

## The RICE method

### REST
Rest immediately and for at least 48 hours.

### ICE
Ice or something cold to reduce bleeding and swelling, applied for 10–15 minutes and at regular intervals for the first 24 hours.

### COMPRESSION
Strapping or an elastic tube bandage helps reduce bleeding and swelling by applying an even pressure from well below to well above the site. Seek advice if unsure.

### ELEVATION
Elevation to drain fluid away from injury.

FIGURE 3.2   INNER THIGH AND HIP FLEXIBILITY – GETTING THE CENTRE OF GRAVITY CLOSER TO THE ROCK

# Movement
## skills

BEN MOON ON THE **BUCKSTONE DYNO** V9, STANAGE, DERBYSHIRE

Moving gracefully and effectively over rock is amazingly satisfying. How best to use holds and move the body is partly instinctive, yet also requires considerable practise. This chapter identifies the essential movement skills and how to improve them.

Moving over rock should be the most natural part of climbing. Children are the best example of this; point them in the right direction and they'll work out the rest. Somewhere along the way, many adults lose the ability to move without inhibition due to irrational fears and imagined constraints. Reading the rock and applying effective body position, style and technique enable the climber to make tricky moves efficiently. This is achieved partly by doing what feels right, but also by understanding and improving movement skills. This includes how best to use hand- and footholds, optimising body position and refining particular climbing techniques.

## 4.1 Handholds

The biggest holds are often referred to as *jugs*, or jug handles, where all the fingers can be curled over the lip or side of the hold (see *Figure 4.1*). A hold used by pulling sideways becomes a *layaway* or *side pull*, while an *undercut* allows the climber to pull outwards and upwards (see *Figure 4.2*). Hanging off big holds with a relaxed grip and straight arm is the least strenuous way to use them as some of the weight is taken on the skeleton and, in certain situations, affords something of a rest.

FIGURE 4.2  SIDE PULL OR LAYAWAY AND UNDERCUT

Fingerholds vary in depth from the second finger joint size to tips only and widthways may accommodate all four or just one finger. Finger strength takes time to develop and most new climbers will adopt a *closed crimping technique* where the fingers make a tight angle at the second joint and the thumb pushes over the index finger (see *Figure 4.3*). This is strong but puts considerable stress on the ligaments and tendons and can result in injury.

*Open crimps*, where the second joint is at about 90 degrees and the thumb is redundant, put less stress on the fingers but is slightly weaker (see *Figure 4.4*). Whilst an *extended grip* utilises the first joint and recruits forearm strength, this is often used with finger pockets and *smears* where the hold is indefinite (see *Figure 4.5*).

Larger rounded holds, or *slopers*, require an open-handed position to enable maximum friction between skin and rock. An extended arm keeping the body below the hold is crucial (see *Figure 4.6*). *Palming* also makes use of indefinite holds using the palm of the hand to push down whilst getting body weight over the hand to ensure maximum friction and security (see *Figure 4.7*).

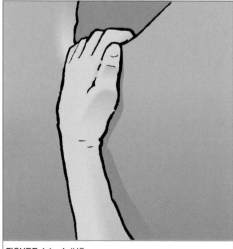

FIGURE 4.1  A JUG

**FIGURE 4.3** CLOSED CRIMP

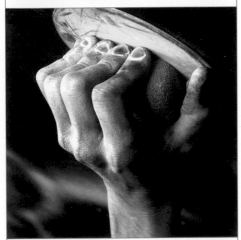

**FIGURE 4.4** OPEN CRIMP

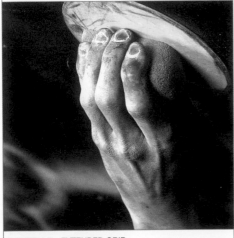

**FIGURE 4.5** EXTENDED GRIP

**FIGURE 4.6** USING AN OPEN-HAND POSITION

**FIGURE 4.7** PALMING

# 4.2 Footwork

Good footwork involves not only precise use of a foothold but also optimum use of the lower body to take weight off the arms.

Climbers frequently find that focusing on footwork improves their climbing considerably. Edges, smears, pockets and cracks all require different and subtle positioning of the foot and application of pressure to make the foot stay in place. Pressing a specific part of the foot on the hold with an appropriate amount of force is more successful than merely stepping on to it.

*Edges* require the toe or side of the foot to be used (see *Figure 4.8*) whilst **smears** require the ball of the foot or under toe area (see *Figure 4.9*).

An unlikely but effective way to use the feet is in **heel hooking**, which helps the climber move the body around bulges, roofs and overhangs. The heel of the foot is placed on a high hold, possibly around the bulge itself, allowing much weight to be taken off the arms while new handholds are found (see *Figure 4.10*).

**Toe hooks** around edges can be used as a type of layaway enabling the climber to make longer reaches without overbalancing (see *Figure 4.11*).

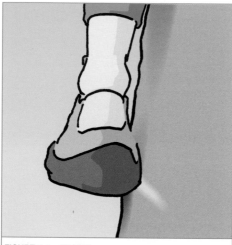

FIGURE 4.8   EDGING

FIGURE 4.9   SMEARING

FIGURE 4.10   HEEL HOOK

FIGURE 4.11   TOE HOOK

## 4.3 Body position

Slabs require the body to be held away from the rock in order to keep the centre of gravity over the feet; this position suits any low-angled climbing so that the feet can be seen, lifted and placed easily. Most of the climber's weight is on the feet with the hands used for balance and pulling lightly on holds (see *Figure 4.12*). 'Hugging' the rock makes climbing slabs considerably harder and less secure.

On near vertical walls keeping the body close to the rock reduces outward pull on the hands making it less strenuous. Flexibility is an advantage here as it allows hips and feet to turn out in a frog-like position whilst keeping the centre of gravity over the feet.

A face-on technique becomes strenuous and inefficient on overhanging ground. Instead, turning sideways and using the outside edge of the foot enables greater reach and makes *locking-off* more efficient. A lock-off involves holding the body close to the rock with a bent arm and contracted muscles. For example if a high reach is required with the left arm, a lock-off position is

FIGURE 4.13   CLIMBING AN OVERHANGING WALL

held by the right arm and the torso turns towards this arm. Using the outside edge of the left foot makes this twisting action possible. The right foot can be placed on a hold, flag or simply dangle (see *Figure 4.13*). A *dropped knee* or *Egyptian* is also commonly used on overhanging ground to facilitate this high reach whilst keeping the body close in to the rock (see *Figure 4.14*).

FIGURE 4.12   CLIMBING SLABS

FIGURE 4.14   DROPPED KNEE

## 4.4 Climbing techniques

*Bridging* is most commonly used in corners and wide chimneys where both walls can be pushed against to bridge the gap. With one foot on each wall it is possible to find a balanced and even restful position. Flexibility is once again an advantage here (see *Figure 4.15*).

Opposing pressure between arms pulling on an edge and feet pushing against the rock is the essence of *laybacking*. It requires body tension to hold the position and momentum to make upward progress. This is achieved by walking the feet and moving the hands up at the same time. Corner cracks, flakes and arêtes can all be lay-backed (see *Figures 4.16* and *4.17*). If there is nothing obvious to push the feet against there is a danger of 'barn-dooring' or swinging off; subtle positioning of the feet can be used to counteract this tendency.

Gaining flat ledges or holds involves pressing down on them with the hands and arms whilst propelling the body up. This technique is known as *mantelshelving* and is often done without

FIGURE 4.16   LAYBACKING A CORNER CRACK

FIGURE 4.17   LAYBACKING ON AN ARÊTE

FIGURE 4.15   BRIDGING

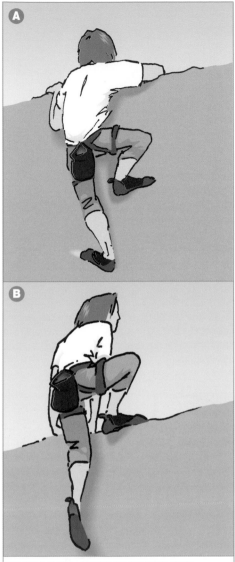

FIGURE 4.18A&B   MANTELSHELVING TO GAIN
A FLAT LEDGE

FIGURE 4.19   FINGER JAMMING

and leaves scars. Once mastered, however, jamming is a valuable addition to a climber's repertoire of techniques.

When using **finger jams** (see *Figure 4.20*), the width of the crack dictates how far the fingers can be inserted, anything from tips to knuckle. Natural constrictions can act as a wedge; otherwise the fingers are twisted to lock them in place. A thumb-down position usually feels more secure but the crack will dictate the best position.

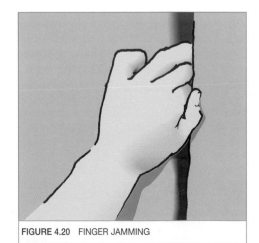

FIGURE 4.20   FINGER JAMMING

footholds by running the feet up as the arms are straightened until one foot can be placed on the ledge. It requires a dynamic approach and a certain amount of explosive power (see *Figure 4.18*).

Climbing cracks requires a combination of techniques; the bottom edge of horizontal cracks can be used as handholds and the sides of vertical cracks create side-pulls. **Jamming** uses the crack itself but few climbers find this a natural or easy technique to learn (see *Figure 4.19*). Poorly placed jams are likely to slip; this feels insecure

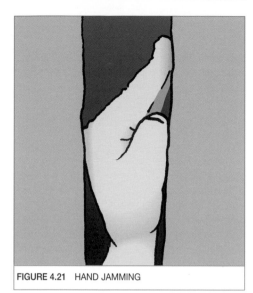

FIGURE 4.21   HAND JAMMING

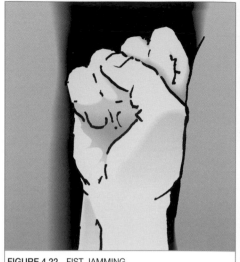

FIGURE 4.22   FIST JAMMING

The narrowest **hand jamming** cracks accept the hand with the thumb resting next to the index finger. The hand is cupped slightly to fill the crack and opposing pressure between the tips, fleshy part of the thumb and knuckles hold the jam in place. As the crack widens, the thumb drops into the palm or slides forward and pushes against the fingers (see *Figure 4.21*). Keeping the hand still once the jam is placed will help to keep the skin intact.

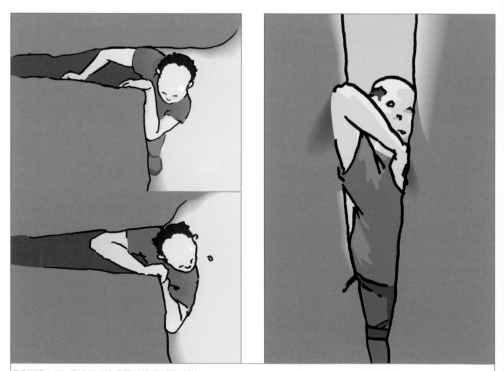

FIGURE 4.23   TACKLING OFF-WIDTH CRACKS

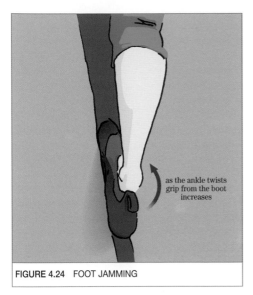

as the ankle twists
grip from the boot
increases

FIGURE 4.24  FOOT JAMMING

*Fist jams* (see *Figure 4.22*) make use of the sides of the hand which are wedged in the crack with the fingers squeezing into the palm of the hand to increase the size of the fist slightly.

*Off-width cracks* are wider than fist but narrower than body and require ingenuity to fill the gap. Stacked hands such as a hand next to a fist, arm bars and locks which rely on opposing pressure between shoulder and palm create a wedge enabling the feet and legs to be moved up and wedged before the arms can be moved up (see *Figure 4.23*).

When there are no footholds the feet are jammed by placing the toes or foot into the crack at an angle with big toes uppermost. The foot is then twisted downward to increase the wedging effect (see *Figure 4.24*). In off-widths the foot can be jammed with it toe to heel across the crack. As with hand jams this is painful but secure.

Gaps that are body width or wider require a combination of techniques referred to as *chimneying*. Forget elegance – this is about wedging the body and squirming upwards. Body tension helps maintain the wedge, which is released from one part of the body to allow an *udge* upwards before another wedge is resumed.

*Back and footing* (see *Figure 4.25*) is the most comfortable technique to climb chimneys, with the back pressed against one wall and the feet pushing against the other. As the chimney widens it can be *bridged* with a hand and foot on each wall (see *Figure 4.26*).

FIGURE 4.25  CHIMNEYING: BACK AND FOOTING

FIGURE 4.26   BRIDGING A CHIMNEY

FIGURE 4.27   DYNOING

## 4.5 Static and dynamic movement

Many climbers move statically using three points of contact at all times which is secure but limits fluidity. Children are naturally dynamic climbers using body thrust and momentum to reach the next hold without worrying about consequences. A happy balance can be found somewhere between these two approaches, using the momentum of the body dynamically to cover distance.

A *dyno* is a controlled launch for a hold out of reach. Whilst few climbers dyno willingly many make lunges which are less controlled. A practised dyno makes use of the *deadpoint* at which upward momentum has died and the body is temporarily motionless before falling. At this point the hold is latched with minimum energy and maximum precision. Dynoing requires commitment, co-ordination and a willingness to gamble that the hold will be as good on arrival as it looks from below (see *Figure 4.27*).

# Training & improving technique

LUCY CREAMER TRAINING ON AN INDOOR BOULDERING WALL

Often the most effective way to improve at climbing is to go climbing. This is true for novice and experienced climber alike. Mileage on the rock works miracles on technique and strength but more importantly builds confidence. At times though this improvement is too slow or a plateau is reached; this is when some form of training is required.

Training does not necessarily mean going off to the gym for a winter of pushing weights; in the first instance a long hard look at what is lacking is required. Becoming a better climber is a highly personalised process. For some it may mean getting stronger muscles but for others it may be placing better runners or learning to use footwork more effectively.

The following elements are all crucial to successful climbing and those wanting to improve their performance must analyse their own strengths and weaknesses in order to prioritise where to concentrate training effort.

1  **Physical skills**
   - Strength
   - Technique
   - Flexibility

2  **Practical skills**
   - Route finding
   - Placing good protection.
   - Rope work

3  **Psychological skills**
   - Controlling anxiety
   - Motivation

# 5.1  Physical skills

## 5.1.1  Strength

Most climbers at some point believe they could or should be stronger and this is probably true but what many climbers fail to do is determine the type of strength that is required. Maximum strength (how much force is produced by a muscle) is central; strong fingers are required to hang on small holds and stronger arm muscles make it easier to lift body weight. Equally important, however, is how the strength is used.

Power combines strength and speed; explosive movements carry climbers through moves that would be incredibly strenuous if attempted statically or slowly. Powerful moves require short bursts of near-maximum strength. It is possible to have very strong muscles but lack power.

Power endurance is required to link a number of powerful moves in a fairly sustained single push.

Endurance or stamina (not to be confused with general endurance needed for running) is required to make successive moves using moderate levels of strength on long routes.

Even without training individuals have a natural preference for a type of route that reflects the characteristics of their body and muscle type. By specifically targeting the type of strength lacking with a particular goal in mind, a climber will see better results from training. Training for climbing forms the subject of a number of books and articles (see ***Appendix 6: Bibliography*** on page 220). The basic principles of training for climbing are outlined here for general guidance.

## 5.1.2  Improving technique

Many climbers focus on strength-training regimes and fail to address weaknesses in technique which may be equally or even more important. A simple way to get better at a particular technique is to seek out appropriate routes; so, to improve jamming, climb cracks and lots of them. Unfortunately this is not always effective, especially if the climber is more concerned about falling off.

In stressful situations it is common to regress to first-learned behaviour or the most ingrained movement patterns. When trying new techniques or improving old ones it is important to remove distractions on awareness, like the fear of falling, in order to focus on feeling the movement. Exercises or games that highlight a technique where success, failure and falling are irrelevant are a good way of achieving this.

### Climbing style

The best climbers draw from a wide range of styles and switch between them as required, at times climbing slowly and deliberately, at others fast and aggressively for example. The following exercises and games emphasise a particular style and help climbers acknowledge their own preferred style and recognise when it is appropriate to make a conscious switch. The ideas below are aimed at individual climbers or instructors and coaches working with groups. They can be adapted to boulders, crags or climbing walls, routes or problems.

# Training basics

## 1 Warm-up and cool down
This is the most effective way to avoid injuries. See *Chapter 3: Warming up* on page 21.

## 2 Specific and personalised
Regimes should target specific areas of weakness with particular goals in mind.

For example, if lack of power is the biggest weakness there is no advantage doing high volume endurance training. Training should concentrate on the muscles, plus their antagonists, used in climbing and mimic how those muscles are used.

## 3 Frequency
Rewards don't come without effort, a minimum of two but preferably four sessions a week are called for. If time is short increase the density and intensity of sessions by reducing resting time and pushing harder.

## 4 Progressive overload
A gradual approach works best remembering that tendons take about six weeks longer than muscles to make similar gains in strength.

## 5 Variety
Introduce as much variety as possible to enhance training benefits and reduce boredom. This is especially true for new climbers who will benefit from a broad approach.

## 6 Basic aerobic fitness
30 minutes of running, cycling or other aerobic activity three times a week will enhance a training regime by improving the efficiency of the body's oxygen supplying mechanisms.

## 7 Rest
Listening to the body is the best way to ensure adequate recovery and is an essential component of a successful regime.

## 8 Stay healthy
All the benefits of training are lost if injuries are picked up. Pay attention to painful twinges, general health and nutrition.

## 9 Partner
A training partner will help maintain motivation and make training more fun.

## 10 Go climbing
Don't forget the reason for training in the first place!

### Quick and slow
*Speed climbing* forces quick decision making and a dynamic style. Climbing in slow motion emphasises body awareness and footwork and highlights the subtleties of weight transfer that are often missed when climbing at speed. Alternating between the two on the same problem or route makes for an interesting comparison.

### Static and dynamic
Climb with three points of contact at all times, rest on each move with time to 'shake out' and 'chalk up'. Contrast this with climbing in a series of mini-dynos using only one hand.

Other contrasting styles can be paired and compared such as climbing close in to the rock versus climbing with arms outstretched or climbing noisily and clumsily compared with quietly and precisely. The list is endless.

## Climbing animals

'Climb like an animal' is a game that amuses children and adults alike. The focus is still on movement style but in a light-hearted way. Apes for dynamic climbing, cats for stealth, lizards for sticking in to the rock, snakes for slinking around moves and so on.

## Assisted moves

Get a partner to take some weight or hold a slipping foot to practise succeeding rather than failing on harder moves. Once the correct movement pattern has been experienced it can often be repeated unaided.

## Closed eyes

Shutting out visual information forces a shift of focus to other forms of feedback by feeling what is happening and improving kinaesthetic and spatial awareness. In conjunction with a partner who describes the moves, it also becomes an exercise in trust and communication.

## Improving balance and footwork

Climb a slab gripping tightly to holds then compare how this feels with using fingertips only or no hands and lots of momentum. It encourages awareness of centre of gravity which is crucial to improve balance whilst at the same time forcing the climber to trust feet rather than hands.

## Climb like a world champion

By mimicking the style of an impressive or admired climber it is sometimes possible to trick the body into making harder moves or to climb more elegantly or dynamically.

## Beating *sewing-machine* leg

Insecure climbing requires a relaxed and deliberate confidence. Trembling, often called ***sewing-machine*** or ***disco leg***, sets in when the mind is freaking out. It may be possible to override the panic by faking confidence; acting as though success is expected can sometimes relax the body.

## Point and go

A partner nominates hand and/or footholds by pointing with a stick. It can be used to push a climber into longer or harder problems, to coach technique by using particular types of holds or parts of holds specifically, or as a fun way of creating problems.

FIGURE 5.1  "CLIMB TO TEDDY", A FUN TRAINING EXERCIS

## Games for children

Climbing with children should above all else be about play and having fun in safety. It's a great opportunity for the imagination to run wild and a few ideas include:

- Climb to teddy
- Collect treasure, letters or clues from holds that spell words and unlock mysteries
- Holding hands on an easy traverse
- Sharing holds: make room on a foothold or handhold for a friend
- Musical statues: hold the position when the music stops
- Climbing wall twister (see ***Warming up with groups*** on page 24)

## 5.1.3 Flexibility

Many climbers overlook the importance of flexibility but in reality it is an integral physical attribute that reduces injuries, increases reach and improves efficiency of movement. Good all-round flexibility gives a climber access to a greater selection of techniques and can be a

OR CHILDREN

greater asset than strength on many climbs. For example, flexible hips facilitate wide bridging on routes where holds for pulling or standing on are few and far between. Flexibility is improved by regular careful stretching in addition to the light stretching recommended as part of a warm-up or *cool-down*.

## 5.2 Practical skills

Much of the content of this book aims to improve the technical and practical skills of climbing. These skills are acquired gradually with time but the process can be speeded up by specific practise. For example, clipping the rope into a quickdraw smoothly with one hand can be practised repeatedly just off the ground or on a top-rope.

## 5.3 Mental/psychological skills

Climbers are regularly disappointed after a winter of hard training to discover that gains in strength do not translate to climbing harder routes, often because the 'head' or mental attitude has not moved on.

The perfect mental state for optimum climbing performance is difficult to achieve; it involves a number of factors that often seem elusively hard to control. Psychological skills, however, can be trained just as effectively as the others.

### 5.3.1 Anxiety
All climbers experience anxiety; it takes place in the mind but with real physiological responses. disco or sewing-machine leg is a common result as are increased heart-rate, sweating hands, dry mouth, knots of tension in muscles and needing to go to the toilet. Mild anxiety has a positive effect on climbing performance; the mind is focused and alert to dangers and the body can respond quickly to physical demands. Overanxiety impairs decision making and muscle function and causes a narrowing of attention. Climbers that are gripped with fear often fail to see obvious holds or runners and either can't move at all or make moves in a blind panic.

FIGURE 5.2   FLEXIBILITY

**FIGURE 5.3** MENTAL REHEARSAL

starting point and climbers are often seen taking a few slow deep breaths before embarking on a tricky section of climbing.

Self-confidence at the outset of a climb is vital for avoiding anxiety and being successful. Most climbers find that gaining experience gradually, building up skills and trying harder climbs progressively, rather than launching in at the deep end, help their self-confidence.

Positive thinking can help turn aspirations into reality and avoid the downward spiral that anxiety causes. This can take place beforehand through mental rehearsal and picturing success or it can be used to avert a negative moment during a climb.

Climbers often give themselves a talking to, either in their heads or out loud; "come on", "I can do this", "the runner is good" and so on. Negative thoughts, "this is too hard for me" or "I'm going to fall off" must be banished as they only undermine confidence and increase anxiety further.

Appropriate goal setting enables a climber to have faith in strategies outlined above and to push on rather than back-off a route or problem. If the goal is unrealistic then it is difficult to relax and impossible to be confident because there is real possibility of falling off. Goal setting can be general, such as "I want to climb harder routes", but it is more effective when it is specific and attainable. An example of this would be "I want to lead my first E1, well and in control, by the end of the summer".

Strategies to avoid anxiety or cope with its negative effects include:

- Relaxation
- Self-confidence
- Positive thinking
- Goal setting

Relaxation techniques are based around controlling breathing and re-focusing attention to calm the mind, slow the heart rate and relieve muscle tension. Individuals must find a method that suits them and that is practical to achieve on the rock face. Focusing on breathing is a good

### 5.3.2 Motivation

Drive and ambition fluctuate regularly, almost cyclically, and this is quite normal. Without motivation it is difficult to get fired up to train hard or make a great effort on a particular route. So rather than have a negative experience it is better to recognise the pattern and acknowledge that it is time for a rest or a change. Visiting a new area, climbing with a different partner, trying another type of climbing or training can rekindle inspiration and boost motivation.

MARTIN BURROWS-SMITH ON **TERRACE CRACK** VS, BIG ROOF BUTTRESS, ARDMAIR CRAG, NORTH-WEST SCOTLAND

Photo: Allen Fyffe

This chapter explains the basics or 'nuts and bolts' of rock climbing including terminology, rope-work systems, how climbs are graded, the best equipment to choose and how to use it, selecting safe anchors and essential knots.

6

It is useful to have a grasp of the terminology and jargon used in climbing, some of which is very obvious and self-explanatory but other terms are rather confusing.

# 6.1 Terminology and jargon

A good example of this is the use of ***belay***. The belay is the ledge, anchors and attachment system at the top of a climb, while the ***belayer*** is the person who safeguards the rope for the climber in order to hold a fall. ***To belay*** or ***belaying*** is how the belayer safeguards the rope while another person climbs but it is used to describe the process of setting up the belay.

***Top-roping*** and ***bottom-roping*** describe climbing systems which normally take place on single pitch crags and are set up from the top of the climb without someone first having led up the route. They are systems commonly used by groups of climbers wanting to climb the same route and by instructors taking novices climbing.

During top-roping the belayer is attached to one or more secure anchors at the top of the crag and belays the climber up the route (see *Figure 6.1*). For more on top-roping see *8.2 Top-roping*, page 81.

In a bottom-rope system the belayer is positioned at the base of the crag and belays the climber up the climb and lowers them back down from here (see *Figure 6.2*). Bottom-roping is described in detail in *8.4 Bottom-roping*, page 90.

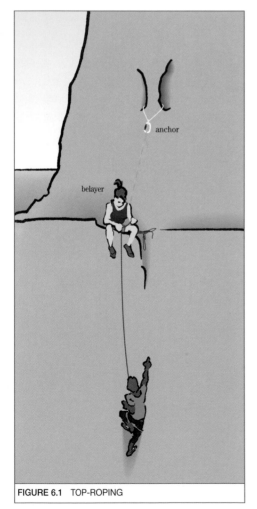

FIGURE 6.1  TOP-ROPING

FIGURE 6.2  BOTTOM-ROPING

In both these systems the climber is protected by a rope from above at all times and they are relatively safe styles of climbing.

A climber who is leading a route is protected from below by tying to a rope and clipping it at intervals to **anchors** or **runners** on the climb. In the event of a fall the belayer controls the rope using a belay or friction device and the falling leader is (hopefully) held by one or more of the runners (see *Figure 6.3*). A runner may already

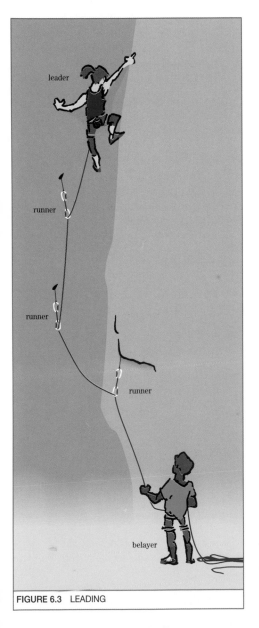

FIGURE 6.3   LEADING

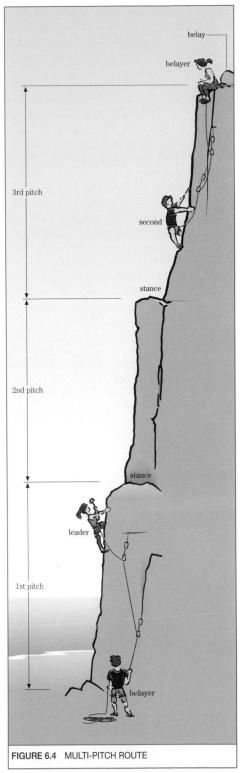

FIGURE 6.4   MULTI-PITCH ROUTE

be *in-situ* such as a metal peg or bolt, otherwise a gear placement is arranged by the leader who makes use of spikes and flakes or cracks and pockets in the rock. Leading climbs is covered in *Chapter 10*, page 111.

Climbs on which the protection is placed by the leader are referred to as traditional or *trad routes*, while those with bolt protection are known as *sport routes*. *Free climbing*, which can take place on trad or sport routes, uses only the natural holds and is the normal climbing style. *Aid climbing* is yet another branch of climbing that involves placing gear to use as hand and foot holds. Many early ascents of hard routes were achieved using *points of aid*, such as a sling to stand in to reach past a hard move, which have mostly now been eliminated. Although it is now rarely practised in the UK, aid climbing is still a popular style in which to make ascents of long, difficult rock walls. *Soloing* refers to climbing without rope protection.

*Multi-pitch routes* are climbed in stages or *pitches*, normally from one good ledge or *stance* to another. The pitches may be anything from 10–50m long and a climb (in the UK) may consist of 2 –10 pitches (see *Figure 6.4*).


# 6.2  Climbing grades

Rock climbs are graded according to difficulty in order to allow climbers to select appropriate objectives. Worldwide there are a number of different systems and these are compared in *Table 6.1* opposite. There are two systems used in the UK and Ireland, one for trad routes and one for sport routes. The trad system combines an *adjectival grade* that describes the overall difficulty of the climb, taking into account how sustained or well-protected the climb is, with a numerical *technical grade*.

The technical grade describes the hardest individual move or sequence of moves. For example, a grade of VS 4c describes the overall difficulty of the climb as Very Severe and the hardest individual move as 4c. The combination of the two grades gives an insight into the nature of the route. A 'standard' VS has several moves of 4c, but if every move on a route is 4c, or if the protection is scarce, the climb should have a

higher overall grade (Hard Very Severe, HVS) but retain the technical grade of 4c. Likewise, if a route has only one well-protected move of 4c and the rest is easier it should have an easier overall grade (Hard Severe, HS 4c).

Technical grades are not normally given to routes easier than 4a, while at the other end of the scale it is open-ended. The number ascends every three letters: 4a, 4b, 4c, 5a, 5b, 5c and so on. Adjectival grades are also open-ended and run from Easy, Moderate, Difficult, Very Difficult, Severe, Hard Severe, Hard Very Severe to Extremely Severe. The Extreme or 'E' grades then take on a number system: E1, E2 and so on, up to E10 (currently).

*Sport grades* (also called French grades) are a numerical technical grade describing how hard the climb is but without any reference to the nature of the protection. They run from 5a, 5b, 5c and so on, up to 9a and include + or – sub-divisions. Sport or French grades are not the same as UK trad technical grades so it is necessary to 'translate' from one grading system to the other in order to make a comparison. *Table 6.1* opposite compares a number of grading systems but it should be noted that any comparison is approximate and it is equally important to get a feel for the nature of the climbing and the grades when a new area is visited.

The grade of the route is suggested by the person who makes the first ascent, but it is not until a few other people have climbed the route that the grade becomes accepted. It should be remembered that grades are subjective and tend to vary slightly from area to area and according to rock type. A HVS on a Lake District mountain cliff will feel very different from a HVS on a Peak District gritstone edge for example. Over time the grade of a route may be altered by holds breaking off, the rock becoming excessively worn or 'polished' or the runner placements being worsened by overuse. This normally makes a route harder but it may take a while before the grade is updated accordingly. Grades should be used as a guide and climbers new to a venue or particular rock type should be aware of these local variations.

In some guidebooks, climbs are given a rating of one to three stars to denote quality. This is a purely subjective system but takes into account quality of the rock, elegance of the line, position and atmosphere, as well as the quality of the

**TABLE 6.1** A COMPARATIVE TABLE OF CLIMBING GRADES

| UK adjectival grade | UK technical grade (approx) | UIAA (alpine) grade | European equivalent | USA equivalent | Australian equivalent |
|---|---|---|---|---|---|
| Moderate | | I, II | 1 | 5.1, 5.2 | 4, 5 |
| Difficult | | II, III | 1, 2, 2+ | 5.2, 5.3 | 5, 6, 7 |
| Very Difficult | | III, III+ | 2, 2+, 3– | 5.2, 5.3, 5.4 | 6, 7, 8 |
| Hard Very Difficult | | III+, IV, IV+ | 2+, 3–, 3, 3+ | 5.4, 5.5, 5.6 | 8, 9, 10 |
| Mild Severe | | IV, IV+ | 3–, 3, 3+ | 5.5, 5.6 | 10, 11 |
| Severe | | IV, IV+, V– | 3, 3+, 4 | 5.5, 5.6, 5.7 | 10, 11, 12 |
| Hard Severe | | IV+, V–, V | 3, 3+, 4, 4+ | 5.6, 5.7 | 12, 13 |
| Mild Very Severe | 4a, 4b, 4c | IV+, V–, V | 3+, 4, 4+ | 5.6, 5.7 | 12, 13, 14 |
| Very Severe | 4a, 4b, 4c | V–, V, V+ | 4, 4+, 5 | 5.7, 5.8 | 13, 14, 15 |
| Hard Very Severe | 4c, 5a, 5b | V+, VI-, VI | 4+, 5, 5+, 6a | 5.8, 5.9 | 15, 16, 17, 18 |
| E1 | 5a, 5b, 5c | VI, VI+ | 5+, 6a, 6a+ | 5.9, 5.10a | 18, 19, 20 |
| E2 | 5b, 5c, 6a | VI+, VII–, VII | 6a+, 6b, 6b+ | 5.10b, 5.10c | 19, 20, 21 |
| E3 | 5c, 6a | VII, VII+ | 6b, 6b+, 6c | 5.10d, 5.11a, 5.11b | 20, 21, 22 |
| E4 | 6a, 6b | VII+, VIII–, VIII | 6c, 6c+, 7a | 5.11b, 5.11c, 5.11d | 22, 23 |
| E5 | 6a, 6b 6c | VIII, VIII+, IX– | 7a, 7a+, 7b | 5.11d, 5.12a, 5.12b | 23, 24, 25 |
| E6 | 6b, 6c | IX–, IX, IX+ | 7b, 7b+, 7c, 7c+ | 5.12b, 5.12c, 5.12d, 5.13a | 25, 26, 27, 28 |
| E7 | 6c, 7a | IX+, X–, X | 7c+, 8a, 8a+ | 5.13a, 5.13b, 5.13c | 28, 29, 30 |
| E8 | 6c, 7a | X, X+ | 8a+, 8b, 8b+ | 5.13c, 5.13d, 5.14a | 30, 31, 32 |

**Source:** *Lake District Rock*, FRCC

**TABLE 6.2** BOULDERING GRADES

| USA V grades (Used in the UK) | French Fontainebleau system |
|---|---|
| V0– | Font 3 |
| V0 | Font 4 |
| V0+ | Font 4+ |
| V1 | Font 5 |
| V2 | Font 5+ |
| V3 | Font 6a/F6a+ |
| V4 | Font 6b/F6b+ |
| V5 | Font 6c/6c+ |
| V6 | Font 7a |
| V7 | Font 7a+ |
| V8 | Font 7b |
| V8+ | Font 7b+ |
| V9 | Font 7c |
| V10 | Font 7c+ |
| V11 | Font 8a |
| V12 | Font 8a+ |
| V13 | Font 8b |
| V14 | Font 8b+ |
| V15 | Font 8c |

**Source:** *North Wales Bouldering*, Simon Panton

climbing itself. A *three star route* (the top rating) should be a brilliant climb and most of the famous or classic climbs achieve three stars. This does not mean that climbs with only one or no stars are not worthwhile, in fact the star system can contribute to overcrowding on particular routes.

# 6.3 Understanding forces

An understanding of the forces generated in climbing falls is useful in order to use gear and techniques appropriately. It also helps when trying to make sense of safety standards and manufacturers' technical information. Force is measured in Newtons. Larger forces, such as those generated in climbing, are measured in kilonewtons (kN).

A climber with a mass of 100kg (about 15 stone) hanging on a rope exerts 1kN of force on the rope and anchors just through gravitational pull, whilst an abseiler bouncing down the rope or a climber ascending the rope might double this force. 2kN is a low force as far as climbing gear is concerned and the greatest damage caused by a bouncing abseiler or someone ascending a rope would be abrasion to the rope on rock edges. Remember loaded moving ropes are easily damaged. A climber who is seconding and falls with a small amount of slack could generate 2–3kN.

The force of most interest is that generated in leader falls and there are different ways to measure this.

## 6.3.1 Fall factor

The *fall factor* (FF) determines the peak impact force generated in the rope by a leader fall. The fall factor, which lies between 0 and 2 in normal climbing conditions, can be determined by dividing the length of the fall by the length of rope out. In other words it is a relationship between the length of a fall and the rope available to absorb that energy.

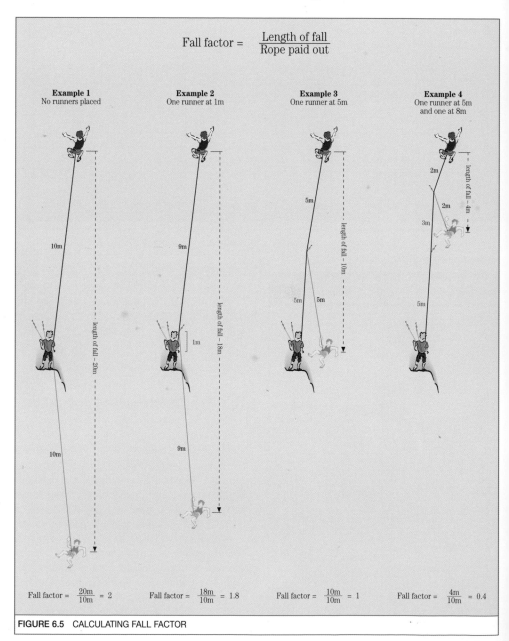

$$\text{Fall factor} = \frac{\text{Length of fall}}{\text{Rope paid out}}$$

**Example 1**
No runners placed

**Example 2**
One runner at 1m

**Example 3**
One runner at 5m

**Example 4**
One runner at 5m and one at 8m

Fall factor = $\frac{20m}{10m}$ = 2     Fall factor = $\frac{18m}{10m}$ = 1.8     Fall factor = $\frac{10m}{10m}$ = 1     Fall factor = $\frac{4m}{10m}$ = 0.4

FIGURE 6.5   CALCULATING FALL FACTOR

For example, a fall from 10m above the belay with no runners results in a 20m fall generating a fall factor of 2 (*Figure 6.5 Example 1*). This a severe fall and the leader falls below the belay, loading both the belayer and the anchors in a way that may not have been anticipated. The fall factor is reduced by placing runners so it is essential for the leader to place one as soon as possible when leaving the stance, even on easy ground, to avoid a Factor 2 fall (*Figure 6.5 Example 2*).

A leader fall with a fall factor above 1 puts high forces on all aspects of the system and could result in gear failure, so the leader should continue to look for opportunities to place runners with this in mind (*Figure 6.5 Examples 3 and 4*).

The fall factor is not the whole story as it does not take into account friction in the system, such as the rope rubbing against the rock or even the rope rubbing on karabiner bars. Also it does not take into account the effects of dynamic belaying, which tends to limit the maximum force.

### 6.3.2 Peak impact force

This is the highest force experienced at the moment a fall is arrested; the force is transmitted by the rope to the belay, the climber and the runners. The maximum possible force experienced by the falling climber and at the stance is limited by the design and standards for ropes and will not exceed 12kN. This force is possible in theory with a FF2 fall and non-dynamic belaying or the rope jamming in a crack or similar.

Force is concentrated on the top runner where it is double that experienced at the belay or by the falling climber due to the *pulley effect* of the rope exerting force on both sides of the karabiner. The maximum force exerted on the top runner would therefore be 24kN but this is reduced by friction at the karabiner to 20kN (again this is a worst case scenario using non-dynamic belaying and is very unlikely).

Dynamic belaying reduces these forces significantly and in typical falls (FF less than 1) using a dynamic belay system the force on the top runner rarely exceeds 7kN (see *Figure 6.6*). This force is increased by heavy climbers and big falls (FF above 1) to a maximum possible force on the top runner of 12kN. Leader falls without any runners clipped (FF2) may also generate forces of this magnitude. It has also been measured that

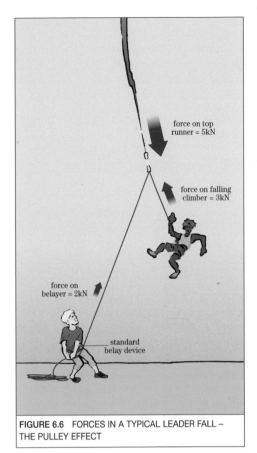

force on top runner = 5kN

force on falling climber = 3kN

force on belayer = 2kN

standard belay device

**FIGURE 6.6** FORCES IN A TYPICAL LEADER FALL – THE PULLEY EFFECT

## Forces summary

Maximum possible force at the belay = 12kN but typically between 2–4kN when using a standard dynamic belay device

Maximum possible force at the top runner (with dynamic belaying) = 12kN but typically between 3–7kN

the lowest possible force on the top runner in a leader fall is 3kN.

### 6.3.3 How does climbing equipment measure up?

So how does climbing equipment measure up to the forces required of it? EN and UIAA standards set maximum forces that can be transmitted to the climber: 12kN for a single rope. They also set minimum strengths for equipment which vary from 2kN for chocks and 5kN for frictional anchors (camming devices) at one end of the scale to 20kN for sewn tape slings. A comparison of strengths indicates where any weaknesses in the system may lie (see *Table 6.3*).

# 6.4 Equipment failures

With the exception of micronuts and very small camming devices the strengths of all equipment exceed the forces generated in typical short climbing falls (7kN maximum) in most cases with a reasonable safety margin. However, in a high impact fall (12kN maximum) it is possible for some gear, micronuts, micro camming devices and lightweight karabiners in particular, to fail purely due to overload.

The Equipment Investigation Panel (EIP) of the BMC sees a few such failures every year where the forces in a fall exceed the strength of the equipment used. Far more common however, are failures due to inappropriate use or misuse of equipment. For example, a few karabiners break every year because the gate is open when it is loaded (see *6.6.8 Karabiners* on page 55). Karabiners with a higher gate-open strength therefore give an increased margin of safety; in 1998 the standard for gate-open strength was raised from 6kN to 7kN reducing but not eliminating this type of failure. It is worth checking old karabiners to avoid using those not meeting the standard as crucial runners or in the belay. (Oval shape karabiners, designed for aid climbing where smooth handling is important, are inherently weaker and may have a gate-open strength as low as 5kN). For more technical information on the forces arising in falls, see *How strong does your Equipment need to be?* a presentation by Neville McMillan at the BMC Technical Conference 2003, available from the BMC as a Technical Committee Note.

# 6.5 Falling softly

Low impact force falls, in other words softer gentler falls, are better all round; the climber is less

| TABLE 6.3   TYPICAL EQUIPMENT STRENGTHS | |
| --- | --- |
| **Equipment** | **Strength** (kilonewtons) |
| ***Dyneema®* sling** | 22kN |
| **Typical 'D'-shaped karabiner** | *Loaded lengthways –* gate closed: 24kN gate open: 7kN *Loaded sideways:* 7kN |
| **Micronut** | 2–4kN |
| **No. 1 nut** | 7kN |
| **No. 9 nut** | 10kN |
| **Camming device** | 10–14kN |
| **Micro camming device** | 3–6kN |
| **Harness** | must withstand 15kN for 3 minutes |

likely to get injured, the belayer will hold the fall more easily and the gear is less likely to fail. Softer falls are achieved as follows:

**Minimising the fall factor**
See above.

**Using a low impact force rope**
After holding repeated falls ropes lose some of their energy absorption capacity. Some manufactures therefore recommend ropes with a low initial impact force to counteract this.

**Dynamic belaying**
Arresting a fall gradually is softer but longer. However, if a fall is too long there is an increased risk of the climber hitting a ledge or the ground. Waist belaying is the most dynamic method possible but inappropriate for holding big climbing falls. Grabbing belay devices and in particular those that are auto-locking are the least dynamic as they stop the fall abruptly. The slicker devices allow a little slippage before locking so are slightly more dynamic but require vigilance and quick reactions to hold unexpected falls. Most climbers opt for a fairly grabbing device, so there is less chance of dropping the leader (or being dropped!) but ensure the system is dynamic in other ways, such as:

- Ensure the belayer is attached to the anchors using rope not just slings
- Belay from the central rope loop not the harness belay loop
- Allow a little slack in the system before a fall

- Allow the rope to slip through in a severe fall (gloves essential)
- Avoid auto-locking devices on routes with natural protection

# 6.6 Equipment

## 6.6.1 Standards

The Safety Commission of the *Union Internationale des Associations d'Alpinisme* (UIAA) has been setting standards for climbing equipment for many years. Meeting these standards and gaining the UIAA label (see *Figure 6.7*) has always been voluntary but these benchmark approvals are widely acknowledged. Since 1995 European manufacturers have been required by law to meet standards for Personal Protective Equipment (PPE). This applies to all equipment to protect a person against falls from height (harnesses, ropes, nuts, karabiners, slings) or to protect against slippage (crampons and ice axes) or head protection (helmets). To gain the required CE (Communauté européenne) mark (see *Figure 6.8*), equipment must meet EN (European Norm) standards, which are based closely on the UIAA standards.

EN standards are a minimum and there is considerable variety within a category so those looking for high performance from a particular piece of gear, particularly ropes, helmets and nuts, should read the quoted test results carefully.

An immense pile of expensive gear is not needed before going climbing for the first time. It is far better to borrow or hire initially in order to gain an idea of what to buy later as there is much choice and a number of considerations.

## 6.6.2 Rock boots

Up until the mid 1950s climbing took place in nailed boots, plimsolls or stockinged feet. In Cornwall, soldiers experimented with a moulded rubber 'commando' sole which gave significantly improved friction and lightness before *kletterschue* in Germany and 'PAs' in France paved the way for the 'EB' which became the boot to wear throughout the 1970s. This was only superseded when the Spanish company Boreal launched *Fires* in the early 1980s, introducing sticky rubber for the first time. Today there is a baffling selection of boots, shoes and slippers to choose from.

A first pair of rock boots should be comfortable enough to wear all day but sufficiently well fitting to avoid heel lift or excess bagginess. Wearing thin socks with this type of boot does not affect their performance and will improve comfort on colder days. An all-round, mid-priced boot rather than a specialised performance model is a good choice. Models and styles vary considerably in width fitting and last shape; good shops that stock a wide selection will allow lengthy pacing around and may also have a section of test wall to try them out on. Good fit should override considerations of brand, colour and price.

## 6.6.3 Harness

The days of tying the rope directly around the waist are well behind us, thank goodness, and all climbing harnesses are manufactured to a high level of safety (minimum strength 15kN) with comfort in mind.

Fit is the most important factor when selecting a harness for rock climbing. The crutch to waist distance must be long enough to allow the waist belt to sit above the hips; this is where men's and women's harnesses often vary. A padded harness will be most comfortable; it should have at least four gear loops and preferably a central belay loop. The waist belt must adjust sufficiently for a range of clothing options to give a snug but not crushing fit that leaves at least 10cm of belt tail once the buckle is doubled back. Adjustable leg loops are useful but not essential to give a relaxed fit around the thigh. Alpine-style harnesses have less padding and are

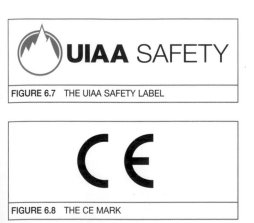

FIGURE 6.7   THE UIAA SAFETY LABEL

FIGURE 6.8   THE CE MARK

When selecting a harness for group use, some instructors prefer to use one without gear loops or rope keeper/retaining ribbons. This can help minimise tying-on and attachment errors.

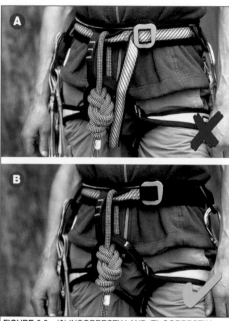

FIGURE 6.9 (**A**) INCORRECTLY AND (**B**) CORRECTLY BUCKLED HARNESS

lighter but less comfortable; they are designed to be put on 'nappy' style without having to step through the leg loops when wearing big boots or crampons.

A full body harness or sit harness combined with a chest harness should be considered for anyone without a waistline, such as children or those with more generous proportions around their waist. The higher attachment point ensures a hanging position just off vertical and eliminates the possibility of tipping upside down or, worse still, falling out of a poorly fitting sit harness. Belaying and abseiling from this higher attachment point requires some getting used to.

### 6.6.4 Helmet

The traditional style of helmets have a hard penetration-resistant shell made from fibreglass/resin composite or plastic with an internal cradle

to absorb the impact. They were originally designed with stonefall in mind and still offer the best protection from impacts to the top of the head, thus offering optimum protection for mountaineering, ice climbing or alpine climbing.

The modern styles of helmets combine either a hard or soft shell with an expanded polystyrene foam lining, which absorbs energy as it is compressed. Light and close-fitting, these helmets give good all-round impact protection, especially in a leader fall when a blow to the side or front of the head is possible. Their construction makes them less durable and penetration resistant and weaker in top impacts but they are a good rock climbing helmet.

Many modern helmets should be treated as 'one-hit wonders'; in other words they should be replaced if they've been dented, pierced or compressed at all. Some plastic helmets show no visible signs of damage but a hard blow should not be ignored. Plastics also deteriorate significantly over time so it essential that the manufacturer's recommended life expectancy is not exceeded.

Comfort, weight and fit are very important when choosing a helmet, otherwise it won't get worn or may come off in a fall. Different models suit different head shapes; some are sized and others are one size with an adjustable cradle. A well fitting helmet should feel reasonably secure even before the chinstrap is tightened. Once fully adjusted there should be no movement when the head is shaken and it should not obstruct peripheral vision or catch on a rucksack if the head is tilted upwards.

Helmets for group use should be hard-wearing, easy to adjust and, once damaged, show visible signs of this. It is important that the helmet is fitted to each individual group member properly, avoiding the common problems of twisted straps and broken buckles.

### 6.6.5 Rope
#### Construction
The first climbing ropes were made from hemp and manila, which had a tendency to break, so the introduction of nylon brought a significant improvement in safety. The traditional hawser laid construction, where braids of nylon were

# Rope types and their uses

 **Single**
9.4mm–11mm
57–82 grams per metre

Best choice for sport climbing and indoor walls as well as top-ropes and bottom-ropes. Also used on classic alpine routes, scrambles and single pitch traditional routes that take a direct line.

**Advantages**
- Ease of handling and fewer rope tangles

**Disadvantages**
- Limited to multiple abseils of half the rope's length
- Rope drag can be a problem

 **Half**
8mm–9mm
42–55 grams per metre

Double-rope technique requires two half ropes that may be clipped into runners separately. Best choice for traditional and multi-pitch routes, winter climbs and harder alpine routes.

**Advantages**
- Less rope drag
- Better protection for leaders as they clip protection and easier to protect seconds on traverses
- Allows full rope length abseils.

**Disadvantages**
- Trickier belaying
- Rope management can be awkward on small stances
- Greater overall weight.

 **Twin**
7.5mm–8.5mm
38–45 grams per metre

Both ropes are clipped into every runner. Not often used in the UK but popular on ice climbs, multi-pitch sport routes and alpine climbs.

**Advantages**
- Offer better protection against rope damage than a single rope and provide double the abseiling distance

**Disadvantages**
- Limited application in the UK

 **Confidence**
7mm–8mm

Ropes sold purely as a safety rope for walkers, light to carry but feel quite thin to hold.

**Should NEVER be used for lead-climbing**

**Low Stretch**
8mm–10.5mm
Also called static ropes. Designed for situations where rope stretch is a disadvantage. Ideal for rigging bottom-ropes, tyrolean traverses and as abseil ropes. Used as fixed ropes in big wall/ aid climbing, caving and canyoning.

**Should NEVER be used for lead-climbing**

---

twisted together was replaced in the 1950s by the invention of *Kernmantel* ropes. These didn't twist and their smoothness allowed the development of a whole range of belay, abseil and ascending devices. Kernmantel ropes are constructed from nylon filaments which are first spun together to make a strong yarn. Between four and six yarns are combined to form braids which are twisted to create the core. This twist-

ing, plus a coating and shrinking process, gives the rope much of its elasticity. At the final stage the core is covered with a braided, coloured sheath which may incorporate a middle marking or pattern change at the half-way point.

### Classifications
Ropes are classified and tested according to whether they are to be used singly or as a pair. In

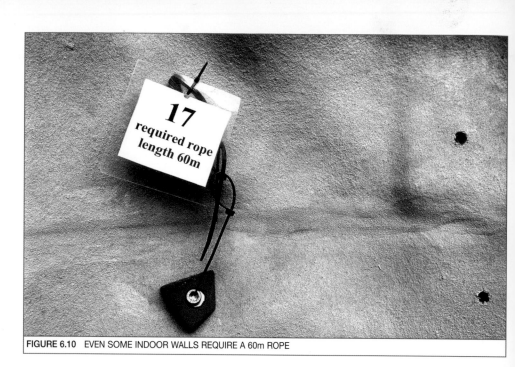

FIGURE 6.10   EVEN SOME INDOOR WALLS REQUIRE A 60m ROPE

the past, single ropes were 11mm diameter; half ropes were 9mm diameter, and twin ropes were slightly less than 9mm. However, ropes have continued to get thinner and lighter within their categories as technology has advanced. This means the choice is rather more complex than in the early days.

**Choosing a rope**

Eventually many climbers have a selection of ropes to suit the activity, but when buying a first rope it is important to consider what it will predominantly be used for. As suggested in *Rope types and their uses* above, a single rope offers simplicity yet sufficient adaptability to make it a good initial choice for novice climbers. When deciding on length it is worth noting that there has been a trend towards longer ropes over the years. Although 50 metres is adequate for traditional routes in the UK, many bolted venues, particularly on the continent, and even some indoor walls, call for 60 metres or longer.

When selecting a brand and model of rope it is important to read the small print, especially for climbers seeking high performance or particular handling characteristics. These are described by the figures quoted by manufacturers from the tests and measurements that are carried out. For example, the thinnest ropes are designed for high performance climbing where weight is at a premium, but this comes at the expense of durability. The mid-weight ropes in their category offer a good balance between weight and safety. Ropes with a higher sheath proportion, though heavier, are useful in situations where abrasion resistance is important, such as on indoor walls and when bottom-roping. Dry treated ropes are worth the investment in the UK because one way or another they'll probably end up getting wet. Wet ropes are heavier and more difficult to handle. The most effective treatments seal both the sheath and the individual filaments of the rope with a coating of Teflon or a fluoride solution that is then heat-treated.

**Rope care**

A rope bag and sheet protect the rope from grit and dirt, which can be ground into the rope by standing on it. All ropes should be washed regularly with water or a mild soap and dried uncoiled in a cool, dark place. Most damage occurs through abrasion whilst bottom-roping and abseiling. This can be minimised by careful positioning of the rope around edges, padding and use of rope protectors.

Old and slightly damaged ropes may not be suitable for holding big falls over edges but still have life in them for less demanding climbing. It

## Rope lifespan

| Frequency of Use | Approximate Life Span |
| --- | --- |
| **Never used** | 10 years maximum |
| **Rarely used** (twice a year) | up to 7 years |
| **Occasionally used** (once a month) | up to 5 years |
| **Regularly used** (several times per month) | up to 3 years |
| **Frequently used** (each week) | up to 1 year |
| **Constantly used** (almost daily) | less than 1 year |

In addition to frequency of use climbers should consider retiring a rope in the following cases:

- After a fall that is longer than 10m, results in a Fall Factor over 1 and has not been braked gently
- Rope has been in contact with chemicals, particularly acids

- Sheath is damaged and the core visible
- Sheath extremely worn and fuzzy or has slipped noticeably
- Strong deformities present (stiffness, nicks and sponginess)
- Rope is coated with grease, oil or tar
- Rope damaged by heat, abrasion or friction

**Source:** Mammut Ropes

is quite usual to down-grade ropes from leading to top-roping or wall use before retiring them.

### 6.6.6 Belay devices

The original way to hold a fall was to wrap the rope around either a spike of rock or the belayer's body. Early friction devices, including the karabiner brake and the friction or Italian hitch, made use of simply the rope and karabiners. The first dedicated belay device (the **Sticht plate**) consisted of a flat metal disc with a hole to feed the rope through and a spring to stop it jamming against the karabiner. The rope was then clipped to a karabiner on the harness, which bent the rope into a U shape. For maximum friction, the rope is pulled behind the plate to create a sideways S shape. All standard belay devices make use of this principle but nowadays there is also a number of various other devices designed for slightly different jobs. For ease of comparison they can be categorised as in the *Belay devices* sidebar on page 54.

Belay devices can also be compared according to how effectively they bite the rope using friction, pinching or a combination of both. **'Slick'** devices rely on friction and allow slack to be paid out smoothly and easily but this consequently makes holding a fall harder, whilst **'grabbing'** devices use a pinching action that stops falls more quickly but may be jerky when belaying and abseiling.

A good all-round **intermediate** device allows the rope to be paid out smoothly yet permits a fall to be held more easily and uses a combination of friction and pinching. It should be smooth when abseiling but with sufficient friction to allow the speed to be controlled.

Most **auto-locking** devices can only be used with a single rope, while standard devices can be used with one or two ropes and the majority of standard devices are designed for use with ropes of any diameter. In practise, however, some are very slick when used with 'skinny' half-ropes. If this is the case it is more secure to select a device designed specifically for use with half-ropes. Any new device should be used cautiously until familiarity with its function has been gained.

# Belay devices

### 1 Standard or Passive
**How they work**
Put a bend in the rope that creates enough friction for a belayer to hold a fall
**Good for...**
- All climbing and abseiling situations
- Light

**Disadvantages**
- Can be very 'slick' for novices
- Not easy to operate correctly in direct belays

**Group use**
- Simple to use but need careful instruction and close supervision initially

**Example**
- DMM Bug, Wild Country Variable Rope Controller, Black Diamond ATC-xp

### 2 Auto-locking
**How they work**
In theory they lock automatically under the force of a fall
**Good for...**
- Sport climbing when repeated falls are being held and on big walls

**Disadvantages**
- Belaying and abseiling are possible on a single rope only
- Lowering tricky to master
- Relatively expensive

**Group use**
- Sometimes used with groups but should not be considered as hands free, fail safe or ideal novice devices

**Example**
- Petzl Grigri, Wild Country Single Rope Controller

### 3 Auto-blocking
**How they work**
Can be clipped directly to the anchor allowing a belayer to bring up two climbers at the same time in a guiding situation.
Some can also be used as a passive belay device and for abseiling
**Good for...**
- Guiding situations

**Disadvantages**
- Very difficult to introduce slack or lower a climber who has fallen off when used in guiding mode

**Group use**
- Not normally applicable

**Example**
- Petzl Reverso, Trango B-52

FIGURE 6.11 STANDARD BELAY DEVICE

FIGURE 6.12 AUTO-LOCKING BELAY DEVICE

FIGURE 6.13 AUTO-BLOCKING BELAY DEVICE

Selecting belay devices suitable for use with and by groups involves some additional considerations such as: level of experience of group, instructor/climber ratio, aim of session and state and thickness of ropes used. For a one-off taster session with a large group the priorities are simplicity and safety so an Italian hitch and HMS karabiner may be the simplest option. If the session is an introduction to climbing, a standard belay device, though trickier to master is probably a better choice. Auto-locking devices are not necessarily simple to operate and need careful supervision.

### 6.6.7 Nut key

A nut key is inexpensive and indispensable for removing runners and anchors, especially if they have been loaded or poorly placed. It can be carried on a lightweight 'cosmetic' karabiner but better on an old snap-link that could be left behind in a retreat.

### 6.6.8 Karabiners

***Karabiners*** (which are essentially metal hooks with a sprung gate) were the first item of climbing hardware to be widely used. Those without a locking gate are also known as ***snap-links*** or ***snap-gates*** and are used for attaching the rope to runners (normally via a ***quickdraw***) and for carrying gear on the harness. They vary in size, shape, gate type, weight and strength; in particular it is worth checking the ***gate-open strength*** and the width of the gate opening. There has been a trend towards smaller and lighter karabiners but this can compromise both handling and safety. Many of the early karabiners were oval in shape and although these are still popular in aid climbing, they have been largely superseded by the stronger 'D' and offset 'D' shaped ones.

Karabiners are much weaker when loaded widthways or with the gate open. Even a momentary, or very slight, opening of the gate can lead to failure if it happens to coincide with the moment of loading. This can happen for a split second as the weight comes onto the karabiner or by it pressing against an edge, which forces the gate open. The wire of a nut or an edge of tape sling is enough to wedge the gate open and there have been cases of karabiner failure as a result (see *Figure 6.14*).

***Snap-links*** with a ***bent*** gate shape are designed for ease of clipping the rope in, as this design guides the rope into the karabiner.

***Wire gate snap-links*** are designed with lightness in mind but care must be taken to ensure there is nothing impeding the gate closure. Small karabiners can be fiddly to handle (especially with gloves on) unless they have a wide gate opening.

***Locking karabiners*** are used where it is crucial that the gate remains shut, such as at attachments to anchors, all points in bottom-rope systems, with a belay or abseil device and even on crucial runners. Manual locking screwgate karabiners are the most popular type but care must be taken to avoid over-tightening, which

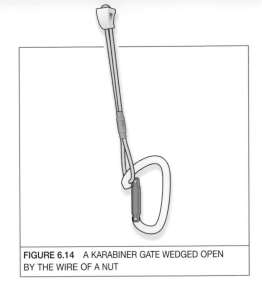

FIGURE 6.14  A KARABINER GATE WEDGED OPEN BY THE WIRE OF A NUT

makes them hard to undo. It is easy to forget to screw the gate up and climbers should get in the habit of checking them with a gentle squeeze.

***Auto-locking karabiners*** click shut as the gate is released, but some have been known to open accidentally with disastrous consequences. As a result many climbers avoid using them in key places, such as with a belay device or in bottom-rope systems, where a twisting load could be experienced.

***HMS*** (often called pear-shaped) karabiners are designed for use with an Italian hitch and have one wide oval end to accommodate the knot. Specialised karabiners (called connectors for the purposes of the EN standards) are identified by their 'connector name' on the back bar of the karabiner; 'H' for HMS, 'K' for *Kletterstieg* (*via ferrata*) and 'X' for oval karabiners (see *Figure 6.15*).

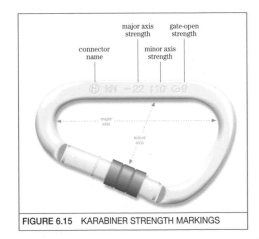

FIGURE 6.15  KARABINER STRENGTH MARKINGS

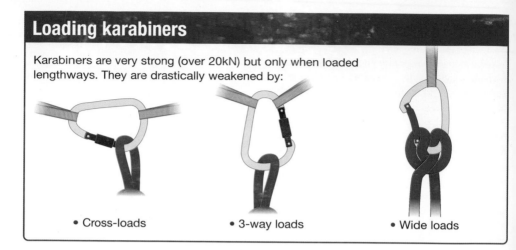

# Loading karabiners

Karabiners are very strong (over 20kN) but only when loaded lengthways. They are drastically weakened by:

• Cross-loads          • 3-way loads          • Wide loads

---

**Note:** In this book screwgates are referred to but in many cases any locking karabiner would be appropriate. If an HMS is specifically required this is stated.

### 6.6.9 Quickdraws

*Quickdraws* consist of two snap-links connected by a tape sling. There is normally a straight gate top karabiner (for attaching to the protection) and a bent gate bottom karabiner (for clipping the rope into). The sling may have a sewn pocket to hold the bottom karabiner captive, this prevents it from rotating. The sling may be between 10cm and 30cm long depending on the nature of the climbing. Short quickdraws minimise the length of a fall but may create rope drag.

### 6.6.10 Slings

*Slings*, known in the USA as webbing, are carried to make use of natural placements (spikes, threads, trees and so on) as runners or anchors. They are also useful for extending runners that are off to one side and for equalising two or more anchors to a central point. Most climbers opt for sewn slings made from nylon or *Dyneema®* (see *Dyneema® slings* opposite). Climbers still refer to 'short' 4ft slings worn singly around the chest and 'long' 8ft slings worn doubled. Manufacturers refer to the length of the closed loop so their metric equivalents are in fact short, 60cm and long, 120cm. There are also extra long, 240cm slings useful for attaching to big blocks and equalising anchors that are a long way apart.

*Daisy chains* are slings with a number of sewn sections along their length that are basically

designed for big wall climbing but are often used to facilitate clipping to anchors. It should be noted that in most models the stitching is designed to hold body weight only. Shock loading them should be avoided and they must never be clipped around the stitching only (see *Figure 6.16*).

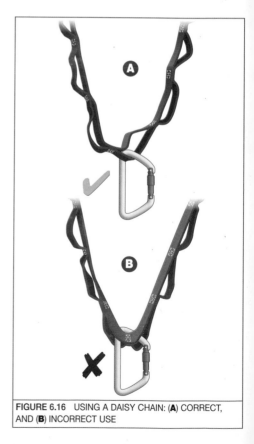

FIGURE 6.16   USING A DAISY CHAIN: (**A**) CORRECT, AND (**B**) INCORRECT USE

## Dyneema® slings

Dyneema® slings (also called *Spectra*® in the USA) are made from a mix of polyethylene (the white fibres) and nylon (the coloured fibres). It is, weight-for-weight, stronger than steel, abrasion resistant and doesn't stretch. It has a lower melting point than nylon, 110°C compared with 245°C, so a Dyneema® sling is more susceptible than nylon to melting from rope friction caused by pressure and fast movement. The polyethylene is resistant to chemical degradation but the nylon fibres and the nylon thread used to sew it are not.

### 6.6.11 Chocks

A collective name for the wedges used in cracks as runners or anchors. Runners are the basic protection points that a climber uses to safeguard against a fall when leading up a climb (see *10 Leading climbs* on page 111). Anchors are used to create a solid attachment point, normally at the top of the climb (see *6.8 Anchor selection* on page 58).

### Nuts

The most commonly used chocks are referred to as **nuts**. They originated as pebbles, which were jammed into a crack like a chock stone and threaded with a rope sling. These were soon replaced by hexagonal metal machine nuts, which could be carried on slings ready to use. The first modern nuts, which appeared in the 1970s, were straight-sided tapering wedges. Most now have two asymmetrical curved faces, one convex and one concave, creating a stable three points of contact design. Modern nuts also have tapered sides for use sideways. Modern nuts are made from aluminium alloy that are either mounted on swaged wire loops or slings of rope or *Dyneema*®. They can be used in cracks from about 7mm–30mm wide.

### Hexagonal nuts

The original hexagonal nuts had six symmetrical sides but later became asymmetric or **eccentric**

to give two width options plus a third, sideways, dimension. This offset design also enabled them to be cammed or twisted slightly in the crack. Modern designs use curved-faced models, which combine the classic hex shape with the benefits of concave and convex faces that allow the three points of contact stability. They are available on *Dyneema*® slings or wire (older models are probably still mounted on rope) and fit cracks between about 25mm and 140mm wide.

### Micronuts

Micronuts are straight-sided tapering wedges often constructed from copper or brass to fit the skinniest of cracks and seams from about 3mm wide. In the smaller sizes the breaking strength is low (2–4kN) so they should be backed up when used as crucial runners and avoided in belays.

### 6.6.12 Camming devices

Tri-cams were the first piece of gear designed to rotate and thus tighten in a crack using a basic mechanical principle. They are simple and effective but have been largely superseded by active **spring-loaded camming devices** (SLCDs).

Soaring Yosemite cracks inspired the development of such camming devices in the 1970s but it took seven years of persistence by Ray Jardine to produce the first camming devices with a trigger bar which allowed them to be placed and removed. These original SLCDs, known as *Friends*, revolutionised crack climbing when they were introduced in 1978 and now most manufacturers of hardware produce their own version. Camming devices can have a rigid or flexible stem with the latter performing more reliably in horizontal placements. Most SLCDs have four cams for maximum stability, but three cam models with a narrower width allow for placements in shallower cracks. Of more specialist use are **offset** cams for use in flared cracks and **mini-cams** for aid climbing. The smallest mini-cams are not designed for holding falls and do not reach the required EN standard of 5kN.

## 6.7 Choosing gear

There are several climbing gear manufacturers that produce similar products with subtle differences. When selecting a particular make and model it is important to compare strengths (remembering that EN standards are a minimum) but also to consider ease of handling, weight and price. Most climbers eventually settle on a favourite make or type of product, as familiarity with how the gear performs and handles is as important as anything else. Manufacturers regularly produce new models or make minor refinements to existing ones, making a state of the art gear list out of date virtually as soon as it's written. Up-to-date advice is available from shop staff and gear reviews in the climbing press and on climbing websites.

## 6.8 Anchor selection

An **anchor** is something secure to attach the rope and climber to. It might be a tree or boulder; a piece of gear placed in a crack or an **in-situ anchor** such as a **thread**, **stake**, **peg** or **bolt**. An anchor may be a single point or made up of many pieces. Anchors should be simple, solid and in the right place.

Boulders, blocks, spikes, flakes, threads and chockstones are often referred to as **natural anchors** and are the simplest types of anchor to find, check and set up. Trees also fall into this category but there may be an environmental price to pay for over-using them so climbers should be discerning.

Climbers often refer to **bombproof anchors** or ones that are undoubtedly solid; these can be easy to spot, as are the really poor ones. It is often the ones in between that cause most concern making it difficult to decide which are good enough. This judgement should get easier with experience but in the first instance, a fail-safe system of testing anchors will help avoid uncertainty and inadvertently using an insecure one (see *Testing an* in-situ *anchor* opposite).

### 6.8.1 *In-situ* anchors

These are quick and easy to use but often of indeterminable quality. An adapted version of the natural anchor check can be used to judge them (see *Testing an* in-situ *anchor* opposite).

Metal equipment is susceptible to **corrosion**, particularly at sea cliffs due to the aqueous chloride ions in salt. Cracks and thinning or eating

---

## Testing a natural rock anchor

### Look
Look for fracture lines around a spike of rock; see what is holding a block in place.

### Test
Test by thumping with the heel of a hand to detect vibration. Apply body weight from a safe position in all directions but particularly in the direction of loading, watching and feeling for movement.

### Feel
Feel for sharp edges that may damage a sling or the rope.

### Understand
Understand that different rock types are intrinsically more or less stable and learn the differences.

---

away of the metal can take place out of sight in the rock so visual inspection does not always reveal damage (see *Figure 6.17*). *In-situ* gear is also affected by any deterioration in the rock or soil quality surrounding it. **Stakes** in particular are vulnerable once erosion around them occurs (see *Figure 6.18*). The equipment may also have been poorly placed in the first instance and this is not always obvious. Tape and rope slings can be damaged visibly by chafing against rough rock and by ropes being pulled through them (see *Figure 6.19*). Always try to back up *in-situ* gear with natural or self-placed anchors.

"**UV radiation** degrades textiles at an approximate rate of loss of four per cent of its strength in three hundred hours of British summer sun but as much as seventy percent after eighteen months exposure to sunlight in desert regions." BMC *Care and Maintenance*, 2001.

FIGURE 6.17 THIS SNAPPED BOLT, WITH A SHINY HANGER, WAS LESS THAN TWO YEARS OLD

## Testing an *in-situ* anchor

### Look
Look at the rock or ground, is it solid or eroded? Check thoroughly for signs of damage or corrosion to the equipment.

### Test
Test by pulling and twisting.

### Feel
Feel for sharp burrs in metal and flat spots, nicks or fraying in slings.

### Understand
Understand the way force and leverage apply to each type of anchor.

FIGURE 6.18 EROSION AROUND A STAKE

FIGURE 6.19 *IN-SITU* ABSEIL SLINGS

## 6.9 Placing gear

### 6.9.1 Chocks

The best **placements** are those that provide maximum surface area contact between metal and rock in natural constrictions. Vertical and horizontal cracks as well as some pockets can all be utilised. A good placement will not wobble or move around in the crack and will resist a firm tug from the direction it is to be loaded. The most frequently used chocks are **nuts** with curved faces, which can provide a very stable placement if three points of contact are ensured (see *Figure 6.20*). Nuts can also be placed sideways in tapering cracks (see *Figure 6.21*), but such placements tend to be less stable and there is a risk of them turning through ninety degrees and dropping out of the crack. Care is also needed to avoid placing gear where there is a widening in the crack just below or behind the placement (see *Figure 6.22*).

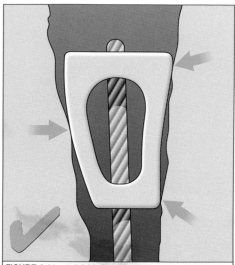

FIGURE 6.20   A GOOD PLACEMENT WITH 3 POINTS OF CONTACT IN A TAPERING CRACK

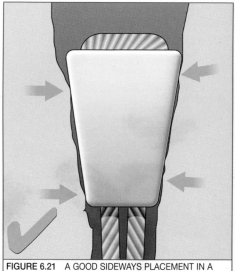

FIGURE 6.21   A GOOD SIDEWAYS PLACEMENT IN A GENTLY TAPERING CRACK

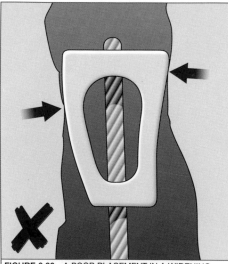

FIGURE 6.22   A POOR PLACEMENT IN A WIDENING CRACK

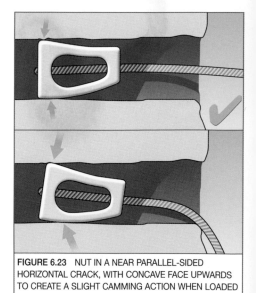

FIGURE 6.23   NUT IN A NEAR PARALLEL-SIDED HORIZONTAL CRACK, WITH CONCAVE FACE UPWARDS TO CREATE A SLIGHT CAMMING ACTION WHEN LOADED

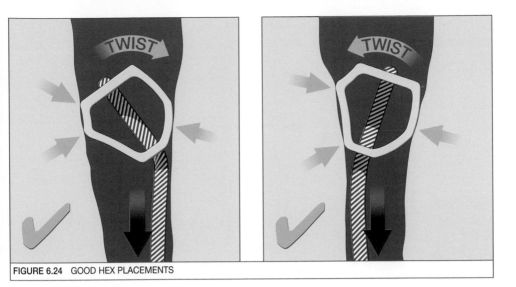

FIGURE 6.24   GOOD HEX PLACEMENTS

Horizontal cracks are more difficult to utilise especially when a downward load is anticipated; in this situation placing the nut concave face uppermost is the most secure since it encourages the nut to grip the crack as it tilts when loaded (see *Figure 6.23*). Placements that are deep in the crack are often more secure than those at the surface but can be awkward to place and difficult to retrieve.

Placements in parallel-sided, flared and open bottomed cracks are all difficult to arrange without a device that has a camming action. *Hexes* can be placed with some success in such situations but care is needed to avoid placements that merely sit loosely in the crack with very little surface area contact. It often takes two or three attempts to seat a hex effectively (see *Figure 6.24*).

Many climbers find it difficult to have confidence in micronut placements, which require careful positioning to maximise surface area contact. It is important to assess the quality of the rock as the smaller pieces of gear concentrate the force on a tiny area making the rock more susceptible to splintering. Given their inherent low strength (2–4kN) and the complexities of judging a good placement, they are often bunched in twos or threes to create a more reliable placement.

### 6.9.2  Spring-loaded camming devices

*SLCDs* work by applying load via the stem, which forces the cams out against the rock. It is easy to place a camming device badly and yet think the placement is secure because it stays in the crack. It takes considerable practise to place camming devices well and become confident in their use so they should be treated with caution initially. All the cams must make contact with the sides of the crack, preferably in the middle half of their expansion range, in other words the cams should be between ¼ and ¾ open (see *Figure 6.25*). The cams should be positioned symmetrically about the stem otherwise rotation will occur. In vertical cracks the camming device is placed with the stem in line with the anticipated direction of loading (see *Figure 6.26*). If it is not possible to align the stem in the direction of anticipated load (such as in a shallow, vertical bottoming pocket) the strength of the cam is seriously compromised.

In horizontal cracks or pockets the stem should be in contact with the lower edge of the rock (see *Figure 6.27*). Camming devices with rigid stems should be clipped at a tie-off point close to the cams to reduce leverage (see *Figure 6.28*). Those with flexible stems are the best choice in horizontal placements as long as the flexible section is in contact with the edge (see *Figure 6.29*).

Some models are designed to be used passively, in the 'umbrella' position like a chock and have reinforced *cam stops* so they can hold a fall with the cams fully open (see *Figure 6.30*). It is important to know whether the model being used is designed in this way.

# Placement of camming devices

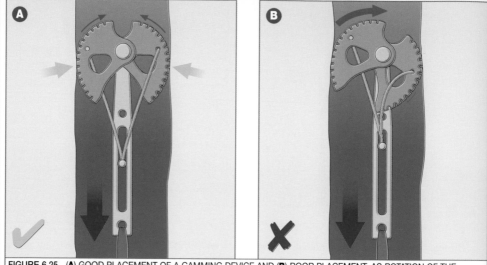

FIGURE 6.25 (**A**) GOOD PLACEMENT OF A CAMMING DEVICE AND (**B**) POOR PLACEMENT, AS ROTATION OF THE CAMMING DEVICE MAY OCCUR

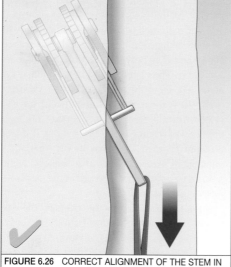

FIGURE 6.26 CORRECT ALIGNMENT OF THE STEM IN A VERTICAL CRACK

Gaining confidence in gear placements comes with practise. A popular way of experimenting with the gear is by placing them near the ground at the base of a crag and loading them with body weight. This must be done cautiously and without the possibility of a bad landing if the gear placement fails.

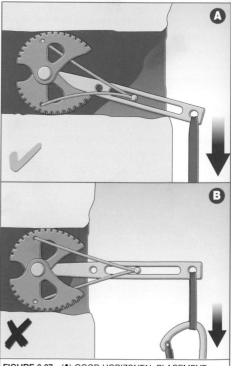

FIGURE 6.27 (**A**) GOOD HORIZONTAL PLACEMENT. DEVICE DEEP IN CRACK AND STEM IN CONTACT WITH LOWER EDGE OF ROCK AND (**B**) POOR PLACEMENT DUE TO TOO MUCH LEVERAGE ON THE STEM

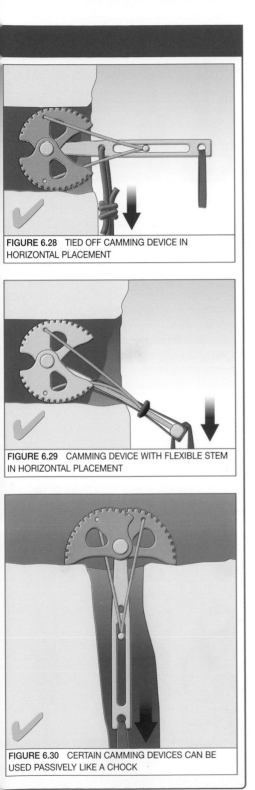

FIGURE 6.28  TIED OFF CAMMING DEVICE IN HORIZONTAL PLACEMENT

FIGURE 6.29  CAMMING DEVICE WITH FLEXIBLE STEM IN HORIZONTAL PLACEMENT

FIGURE 6.30  CERTAIN CAMMING DEVICES CAN BE USED PASSIVELY LIKE A CHOCK

# 6.10  Belay systems

There are several ways to arrange a belay according to the equipment and anchors available and the nature of any possible falls. They vary in the amount of force that is taken by the anchors and the belayer.

## 6.10.1  Direct belay

A belay system where the load goes directly onto the anchor. This may be the rope running behind a spike of rock and relying on the friction of the rope against rock to hold a fall. A slightly more flexible system is to place a sling on a spike and use an Italian hitch for friction; both these techniques are frequently used on scrambles. Particular care is needed when selecting anchors for direct belays as they must be suitable to take both the direction and force of a load. Ground anchors that resist an upward pull can be used in a direct belay to safeguard climbers on bottom-ropes. When a direct belay is used on a climb it will normally require more than one anchor. In this case it is normal to equalise the anchors with slings or the rope to create a secure central point to belay from.

It is not recommended to use a standard belay device in a direct belay, either from above or from a ground anchor, as it difficult to ensure the belayer will be in a position to brake effectively.

## 6.10.2  Indirect belay

A belay system where the belayer takes a part of the load in a fall. This is most commonly a waist belay which might be used because the anchors are poor and need cushioning or because minimal technical gear is carried. This system is used on scrambles but most frequently in the winter in conjunction with snow belays.

## 6.10.3  Semi-direct belay

This is the normal climbing set-up when the belayer is using the central rope loop as the focal point for transferring the load to solid anchors. A belayer who is well positioned should not feel much of the climber's weight in a fall.

## 6.11 Knots and hitches

Most climbers know how to tie several knots but find they only use two on the majority of climbs; a knot to tie on to the rope (figure of eight or bowline) and a knot to attach themselves to anchors (clove hitch or figure of eight). The ten knots and hitches (plus variations) listed here include all the useful ones a climber will ever need so it should not be an excessive challenge to learn them all. (Knots stay in the rope when tied but hitches need to be tied around something).

Learning knots is just a matter of practise; they should be repeated *ad nauseam* so the climber is in no doubt they have been tied correctly. Keep a short length of rope handy to practise with, while the kettle is boiling or when sitting in front of the TV. It also helps always to tie a knot the same way every time so the pattern becomes ingrained, being able to tie a knot with eyes closed is a good test.

### Overhand knot

The *overhand knot* is the simplest and quickest knot to tie. It can be tied in a single rope or it can be tied in a bight or fold of rope to create a loop. It is often used to join two ropes (see *Overhand to join two ropes* on page 69).

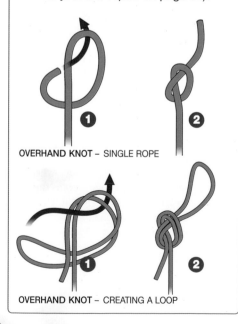

OVERHAND KNOT – SINGLE ROPE

OVERHAND KNOT – CREATING A LOOP

### Figure of 8

The *figure of eight* is one of the most popular knots because it is versatile and simple to learn. It is easy to see if it's been tied correctly as it looks like an 8 and is safe because making an error results in an overhand knot or a figure of nine, both safe knots in their own right.

A figure of eight has many variations, it can be tied in a single strand of rope or in a bight of rope to create a loop (*Figure of eight on a bight*). A loop can also be formed by re-tracing a single figure of eight (*Re-threaded figure of eight*). Two loops can be created by tying a *Double figure of eight on a bight*.

### Figure of 8 on a bight

When tied in a bight of rope, a figure of eight creates a closed loop, which can be used to attach the end of the rope to an anchor for example. It is normal to finish the knot by adding a stopper knot next to it or leaving a tail at least 25cm long.

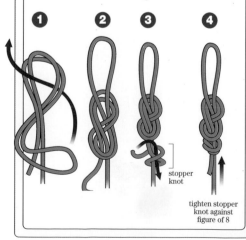

stopper knot

tighten stopper knot against figure of 8

## Re-threaded figure of 8

The most popular choice for tying on to the end of the rope. A single figure of eight is tied first, which is then re-traced with the end of the rope after it has been passed through the harness (*opposite*) or around an anchor (*overleaf*). A stopper knot is then added (see *Figure of 8 on a bight*).

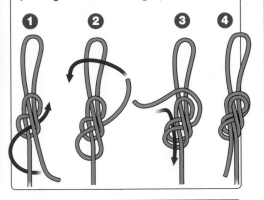

## Double figure of 8 on a bight

This variation creates two loops instead of one, which can be adjusted to different lengths. Useful in rigging top and bottom-ropes.

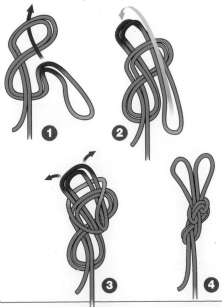

## Re-threaded figure of 8 on a harness

When tying on to the harness with a re-threaded figure of eight the single figure of eight is tied about one metre from the end of the rope. This end is then fed through the leg loops and waist belt of the harness until the knot is close to the harness.

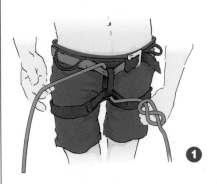

The single figure of eight is re-threaded with the end to create a fist sized loop, which is then pulled tight so that it looks neat and compact with the stopper sitting up against the knot. A loose, sloppy knot will get in the way when climbing and generates unnecessary additional slack in the event of a fall when it tightens up. *Always refer to the manufacturer's instructions to check the correct tying in point on the harness.*

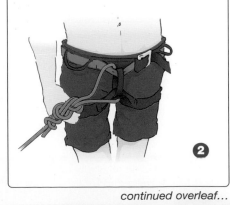

*continued overleaf...*

## Figure of 8 at an anchor

A figure of eight can also be used for tying to anchors that are out of reach without using an extra karabiner. Pull an arm's length bight of rope through the central rope loop. Tie the eight around the two strands of rope that are the continuation of the bight and pull opposing strands to tighten.

**1** **2** **3**

harness

**4** **5**

# Bowline

The traditional knot for tying on to the rope, trickier to learn than the figure of eight and not always obvious if it has been tied wrongly. It has a tendency to work loose during the course of a day so a stopper knot is essential, as is periodic re-tightening.

Some climbers still prefer it for speed of tying, its low bulk and the fact that it will untie relatively easily after it has been loaded.

**1** **2** **3** **4**

stopper knot

## Stopper knot

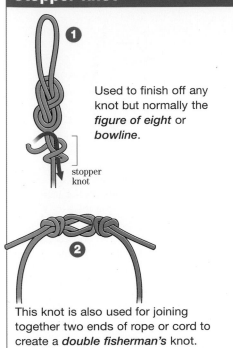

Used to finish off any knot but normally the *figure of eight* or *bowline*.

stopper knot

This knot is also used for joining together two ends of rope or cord to create a *double fisherman's* knot.

## Italian hitch

Also called the *Munter hitch*. A friction hitch used in belaying and abseiling. Very simple and effective but does tend to put kinks in the rope.

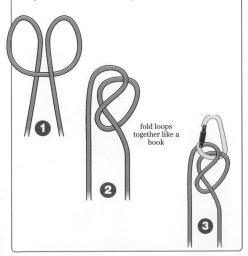

fold loops together like a book

## Clove hitch

Useful for tying on to anchors due to its simplicity and adjustability (**1** & **2**).

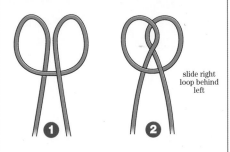

slide right loop behind left

The load rope should be positioned next to the back bar of the karabiner (**3**). When tying a clove hitch on a stake, the cross should rest at the back of the stake so it will tighten up when loaded (**4** & **5**).

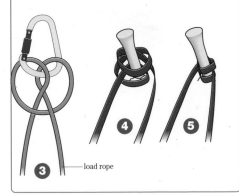

load rope

## Karabiner brake

A method of threading karabiners to create friction, used in abseiling.

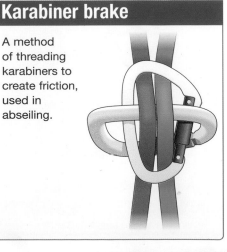

## Ordinary prusik

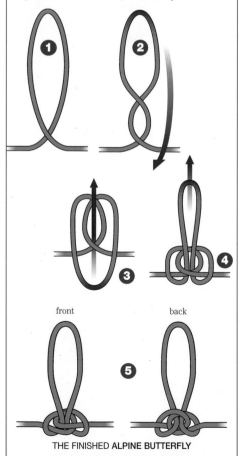

The best biting prusik but has a tendency to jam. Useful as the top prusik when ascending a rope (as there is little chance of inadvertently releasing it) and as the pulling prusik in hoisting systems.

THE FINISHED **PRUSIK**

## Alpine butterfly

A knot that creates a loop and takes a three way load which is useful, but not essential, for rigging anchors or attaching a person to the middle of a rope.

front        back

THE FINISHED **ALPINE BUTTERFLY**

## French prusik

A versatile prusik that can be released under load so can therefore be used as an autobloc in situations where it is loaded and then subsequently needs to be slackened, as with protecting an abseil or escaping the system.

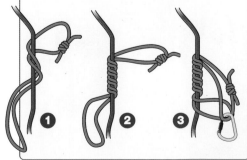

## Klemheist

This is a variation on a *French prusik* and works in a similar way. A *Klemheist* tied with a tape sling works well if no prusiks are to hand. See also *Dyneema® slings* on page 57.

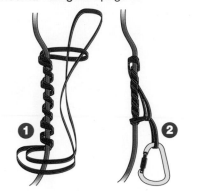

## Overhand to join two ropes

The quickest way to join two ropes and very effective as long as the knot is pulled tight and has tails at least 60cm long. It is slightly less prone to jamming in cracks when being retrieved from an abseil.

tails must be at least 60cm long

## Reef knot and Double Fisherman's to join two ropes

The traditional rope-joining knot uses a *reef knot* between the *double fisherman's* to make undoing the knot easier after loading.

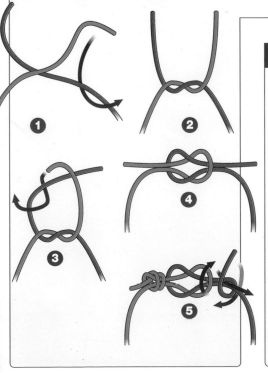

## Alpine clutch

A simple one-way clutch using just the rope and two similar shaped karabiners.

It is used in a 'hip hoist' with great effect.

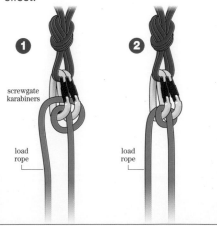

screwgate karabiners

load rope

load rope

## Lark's foot

Also called a *girth hitch*. A quick way to attach a sling to something such as a harness to make a cow's tail for clipping to anchors.

Can also be used to attach a sling to a stake or tree but it should be noted that the sling is weakened when used like this. It is not a good method of attaching a sling to a rock spike as it has a tendency to slide off.

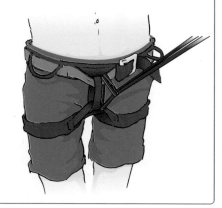

## Tape knot

For joining two ends of tape, to make a sling, for example. It is vital to tighten up as much as possible and leave long tails (at least 10cm) as this knot can creep along the tape over time.

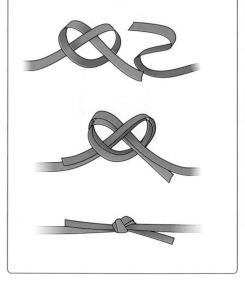

JUDE SPANCKEN ON A V4, **FISHERMAN'S STEPS NORTH**, ST BEES, CUMBRIA

Part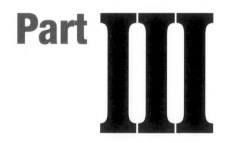

# Bouldering and single pitch climbing

# Bouldering

TIM CLIFFORD ON **CHERRY FALLS** V12, THE VIRGIN BOULDER, ALMSCLIFF, YORKSHIRE

*"Bouldering is the poetry of climbing."*

**Pat Ament**

Bouldering is loosely defined as unroped climbing up to a height above the ground where there is little risk of injury from a fall. However, to say it is risk free would be misleading. High problems and bad landings can add spice to the challenge. The essence of bouldering is climbing distilled to pure movement without the paraphernalia of ropes and gear, allowing a remarkable sense of freedom. It is creative play through problem solving, often with an emphasis on moves of great difficulty. Being able to try hard moves repeatedly is a convenient way to push limits and for some it is the purest form of climbing.

Bouldering can be very sociable, with plenty of banter or it can be pursued in solitude. It can also be a great way of getting a feel for the rock before climbing routes, whether as a first time novice or an experienced climber getting used to a new rock type. Movement skills can be learned and coached effectively when close to the ground. Bouldering was once considered by many as training for the 'real thing' but nowadays it is a distinct branch of climbing with a grading system, guidebooks and ethos of its own; it can take place at indoor walls, the base of a crag or at a specific bouldering venue.

# 7.1 Venues

### 7.1.1 Indoor walls
Large modern walls have bouldering sections distinct from the roped climbing areas. These sections vary from 3m–5m in height and may consist of moulded artificial 'rock' with changeable bolt-on holds or simply wooden panels where the position of bolt-ons can easily be varied to suit. The combination of both realistic features along with holds that can be moved around to change the selection of problems offers the most scope. Many walls set graded problems enabling a progressive approach.

### 7.1.2 Outdoors
Most crags offer some bouldering even if it is just along the base of the crag or on the first few moves of a route. In such situations attention should be paid to potential stonefall from above. Distinct bouldering areas away from the crag are preferable; these may consist of a mini section of crag or individual boulders. Venues that encourage upward moves rather than simply traversing are more versatile. There is not always an easy way off from the top of a boulder and climbers who have omitted to check out the descent may find themselves embarrassingly stranded. Bouldering guides are now available to many areas of the UK either in book form or as downloadable files from the internet.

# 7.2 Equipment

Bouldering has minimal gear requirements. *Rock boots*, although not absolutely essential, are the most obvious piece of equipment required for enjoyable and productive bouldering. A *chalk bag*, a rag for cleaning boots and a toothbrush for brushing off excess chalk or cleaning dirty holds can be added for little extra expense. A *crash pad* is a more costly but advisable addition for regular bouldering sessions, since they have made the sport safer and contributed to its popularity. These pads are essentially portable slabs of two different densities of foam in a nylon cover that greatly increase the pleasure of bouldering by reducing the shock on hip and knee joints from landings; something climbers will be grateful for in later years. Since they also lessen the likelihood of injury they can encourage a 'go for it' mentality. Clothing should allow freedom of movement and an item such as a duvet jacket is a good idea to keep muscles warm while resting between attempts.

# 7.3 Falling off

Falling off without injury requires spatial awareness and a cat-like instinct for landing. It is safer to jump before a fall, aiming for a landing zone free of such hazards as people and embedded rocks. Indoor walls usually have matting under the bouldering area but care is still needed to avoid awkward landings that may result in a twisted ankle or stumbling backwards and colliding with other climbers. Head injuries are not unknown when climbers rebound off matting into the wall itself. (See also *9.1 Using walls*, page 106.)

FIGURE 7.1   INDOOR BOULDERS AT RATHO

Crash pads are commonly used outdoors, but they need to be carefully positioned to protect where a fall is most likely to occur or cushion the nastiest ground. Landing on a pad covering a boulder or hiding even a small pointed rock can still result in a bruised heel or awkward tumble.

Falling off without a pad requires a cautious approach and careful assessment of the ground to avoid landing amongst rocks or uneven ground. Climbing back down as far as possible to shorten the jump or fall will reduce the chance of injury.

## 7.4  Spotting

With or without a mat, someone to *spot* the landing is desirable on many problems. Effective spotting requires 100% concentration and a good spotter will give a climber the confidence to make tricky moves above an awkward landing. A spotter does not literally catch the falling climber, but rather breaks the fall and guides the climber onto the landing site feet first, safeguarding the head and spine. The best way to deal with falls from vertical problems is to support just above the waist and steer the climber to a safe landing. If the climber falls from an overhanging problem the spotter should support the climber under the shoulders above the centre of gravity to allow the feet to swing down to the ground first. A spotter can also push a falling climber away from a danger such as a large boulder. High problems are best protected by a team of spotters. Although the spotter should be in close to safeguard the climber, there should be no interference with the ascent by touching the climber and inadvertently giving support. The spotter certainly won't get any thanks for that!

FIGURE 7.2   GOOD SPOTTING ON A STEEP PROBLEM

FIGURE 7.3   GOOD SPOTTING ON AN OVERHANG

FIGURE 7.4   VIGILANT SPOTTING ON A HIGHBALL PROBLEM

## 7.5  Highball problems

There is no clear distinction between **boulder problems** and **micro-routes**. Problems finishing a long way off the ground are referred to as **highball** but every climber must make a personal assessment of what to attempt without a rope; it's an entirely personal process and climbers should resist peer pressure and only attempt what feels right. Recognising when it's time to walk away from a problem is vital. The recent practise of **padding-out** the ground below short but bold routes has certainly reduced their seriousness but raised some ethical arguments.

## 7.6  Grades

Boulder problems are graded according to the cumulative difficulty and overall physical 'feel'. They do not take into account the height of the problem or the landing. The two grading systems that are predominantly used worldwide are the **Fontainebleau** (Font) and **V** grades. The latter is an open-ended number system introduced by John Sherman to rate problems at Hueco Tanks in Texas during the late 1980s. It is the one most widely used in Britain and currently ranges from V0 to V15. Font grades are popular with climbers who have climbed extensively in France's bouldering Mecca Fontainebleau (see *Table 6.2 Bouldering grades* on page 45 for comparison). Although it is difficult to compare V grades with British climbing grades, as a rough guide V0 equates to British 5a/5b. (Climbing grades are explained on page 44). It is important not to become obsessed with grades and remember that the beauty of the line and style of ascent are at least as important. Climbers also vary widely in size and strength and this will affect how they perceive the difficulty of a problem.

## 7.7  Environmental considerations

In addition to 'treading lightly' to reduce the environmental impact of climbing (*1.7 Minimising*

Many instructors and coaches find bouldering sites provide the perfect venue for introducing movement skills, demonstrating and practising technical topics or running fun sessions with children. Activities may range from trying a few problems repeatedly in order to hone technique to roaming over a wide area scrambling over, under and through a rocky obstacle course. Relatively large groups can be managed reasonably safely whilst all are actively involved but this does require careful structuring including setting height limits, working as pairs or threes and defining how to descend.

If group members are expected to spot each other effectively, the techniques need covering thoroughly; in particular where to be positioned, how to prevent a slip, soften a fall, guide a landing and safeguard the head and back. Boulderers do not normally wear helmets, but it is often appropriate for groups under instruction to do so, especially children, as it is quite possible to roll backward hitting the head. Additionally it also allows novices to get used to wearing them before climbing routes. Ideas for imaginative use of boulders for training or play are covered in *Chapter 5: Training & improving technique* on page 35.

*impact*, page 9), there are considerations with particular relevance to bouldering. These include not chipping holds or wire brushing; removing excess chalk and tick marks (chalk lines indicating holds) after a session; not using resin (pof) and using a crash pad to protect the ground below popular problems from erosion.

climbers elect to use a 'back-rope' system, which involves trailing an anchored rope, placing runners and relying on a self-locking belay device to hold a fall. If a multi-pitch route is being climbed in this way, once the pitch has been successfully lead, the climber must then abseil down and 'clean' the pitch (in other words remove the runners) before re-ascending the abseil rope back to the belay.

# 7.8 Soloing

Climbing without a rope at all is a pure form of climbing, allowing freedom of movement without the interruptions of runners to place, ropes to arrange or partners to wait for. Routes can be *soloed* in a fraction of the time it takes to lead them and a successful solo can be a rewarding experience. However, the seriousness of soloing even a very easy climb or route familiar to the climber should never be underestimated.

Being unable to make a move or to downclimb would leave the climber stranded in a precarious position and the consequences of a hold breaking, a foot slipping or being hit by an object from above could spell disaster. Many climbers carry some means of protection with them while they solo; possibly a rope and small rack or a sling and a few runners to clip into a point of protection for a particular move. On harder pitches some

# 7.9 Deep water soloing

*Deep water soloing* (DWS), as the name suggests, involves climbing routes or boulder problems without a rope above a watery landing, normally the sea. It is a branch of soloing that became popular on the south coast of England in the 1980s. Connor Cove is regarded as the birthplace of DWS, which then became popular at Lulworth Cove and Berry Head.

The attraction of DWS lies in its simplicity. As with any form of soloing, the fluidity of movement unhindered by rope-work has a great appeal to many climbers. But unlike ordinary soloing where the consequences of a fall would be disastrous, climbing above deep water provides a more amenable landing. Many climbers feel sufficiently confident to be able to try hard routes and even 'push their grade'.

FIGURE 7.5  PETE ROBINS ON THE CRUX OF THE BOLD **TSUNAMI** (E4 6a), CONNER COVE, DORSET

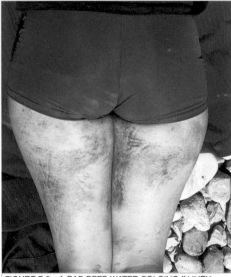

FIGURE 7.6  A BAD DEEP WATER SOLOING INJURY

(or worse) (see *Figure 7.6*) and possibly winding that may leave the fallen climber unconscious. It is a wise precaution to climb as a group, or at least to have one 'buddy', so there is always someone standing by ready to assist an injured climber. Indeed at DWS meets there is normally a rescue boat on stand-by.

Falls onto the back or stomach are the worst and although some climbers have the spatial awareness to twist their bodies into a feet first position in mid-air, it is normally best to jump off rather than fall. This also enables the climber to push off from the rock to ensure a clear landing.

Very calm inland lakewater has a great deal of surface tension making the landing much harder than one into churned up water. Throwing something in or a swimmer kicking about in it first can break surface tension. Soft, churned up water, though better for the landing, may present its own hazards in the form of swell or waves that may throw the swimmer against the rock or make getting out the water difficult.

Many DWSs take place on existing climbs and so take their grade from the original line. New solos are graded using the British trad grades or the French (bolted route) system.

That is not to say that falling off routes into the sea is without hazards. Misjudging water depth or failing to notice submerged rocks could spell disaster and even falls into deep water, if taken awkwardly, can result in severe bruising

# Single pitch climbing

MARIE BAMBURY ON **INTERMEDIATE ROUTE** V Diff, SENNEN COVE, CORNWALL          Photo: Mike Robertson

Many climbers 'cut their teeth' at single pitch venues, getting to grips with the intricacies and technicalities of climbing without the additional commitment required by longer routes.

# 8.1  Single pitch venues

Single pitch venues are those where routes are climbed predominantly in one rope length from the base to the top. In reality there may be considerable overlap of single and multi-pitch routes at the same venue; indeed many two pitch climbs can be climbed in one pitch and vice versa. The classification is useful for introducing the techniques of climbing as a progression; the reason being it is common, though by no means essential, to get to grips with single pitch climbs before moving on to multi-pitch routes. The rope-work is more straightforward, the routes often escapable and the hazards fewer. This does not mean, however, that single pitch climbing is non-serious.

## 8.1.1  Overview of single pitch crags

This section encompasses all single pitch venues found in the UK and Ireland, not just those that fall into the remit of the ***Single Pitch Award*** (SPA), see opposite. The selection of such crags is vast and they differ widely in character and style, even between neighbouring ones. Those found in the south of England are a good example, where the limestone headland of Portland has safe, bolted routes with easy access yet a few miles down the road Swanage has a far more serious feel requiring abseil approaches and an awareness of loose rock. A stone's throw inland and the unique sandstone crags of Bowles and Harrison's Rocks offer yet another dimension.

Much of the sea cliff climbing in Devon, Cornwall, Gower and Pembroke is single pitch, whether on granite, limestone or shale, but the visiting climber must distinguish between those that are friendly and those with tidal bases and eroded, crumbling tops which provide a more thought-provoking experience.

Derbyshire and Yorkshire undoubtedly host the greatest concentration of single pitch venues in the UK; everything from the 5km gritstone edge of Stanage with its ten minute walk in and choice of over 1,200 routes from Moderate to E8, to quietly tucked away quarries with two or three worthwhile climbs.

Snowdonia and the Lake District are better known for their bigger cliffs but both areas have a sprinkling of smaller crags. In North Wales the atmospheric Llanberis slate quarries and bolted limestone cliffs of Pen Trwyn stand out as unique

locations whilst one of the Lake District's most popular climbing areas is the predominantly single pitch Shepherd's Crag in Borrowdale.

The granite slabs and walls of Dalkey Quarry just outside Dublin are probably Ireland's most popular single pitch venue with over 250 routes from Diff to E6. West coast sea cliffs offer the other main opportunities with steep compact limestone at Aillaide (the Burren), County Clare; horizontally bedded and overhanging juggy sandstone at Muckross Head and amenable quartzite slabs and walls at Malinbeg, both in Donegal.

Despite the dominance of its mountain cliffs, Scotland boasts many single pitch venues and a number that are yet to be developed. The Whangie and Auchinstarry Quarry are popular Central Lowland venues easily accessible for the areas of densest population. By contrast many of the crags in the North West Highlands such as the Reiff sea cliffs remain relatively quiet. Bolted routes are found on the compact rock of Weem.

## 8.1.2  Hazards

Single pitch crags are not completely free from objective danger, though there are certainly fewer hazards than on bigger cliffs. It is important to be aware of loose holds on routes and stonefall from above, especially if the cliff top is eroded or if other climbers are moving around.

Tidal sea-cliff venues are the most serious single pitch climbing areas. An understanding of tides including both daily and monthly variations and an appreciation of local influences on the speed at which a cliff base can become engulfed is vital. Choosing to fit in a route just before an incoming tide can put pressure on the leader to rush and so make mistakes. The tide can also preclude the simple option of lowering back off a route if it proves too hard or if a problem is encountered. A far safer approach is to get on the route as soon as a dropping tide allows access; this is particularly important at venues with large tidal variations such as Gower in South Wales. Unexpected freak waves or wash from fast sea vessels do occasionally catch climbers out.

# 8.2 Top-roping

In this system the belayer is anchored at the top of the route in order to give the climber a secure rope from above. **Top-roping** has long been used to practise harder routes prior to leading, even though this approach provokes debate and/or criticism. Some climbers would go as far as to call it a form of cheating. As a group activity, top-roping enables a succession of climbers to attempt the same climb and is often how novices experience their first climbs.

**Note:** Operating the rope from below is also a type of top-roping, sometimes referred to as 'bottom top-roping'. For clarity this particular system is referred to as **bottom-roping** and is covered in more detail in **8.4 Bottom-roping** on page 90.

### 8.2.1 Setting up a top-rope

Having chosen a route from the guidebook, the top of the climb must be located. This can be surprisingly difficult especially at complex or tree covered venues; identifying a landmark or leaving a rucksack below and out from the start of the route will help.

The belayer decides on the best position to operate the rope from; this is normally close to the edge, directly above the line of the climb and with a view down the route. Anchors are then selected to secure the belayer in this position.

The anchors should give support to the belayer and ideally be in line with the anticipated load. *Anchor—Belayer—Climber* all in line is a simple

FIGURE 8.1   TOP-ROPING

way to remember this. The belayer can determine this by standing with their back to the climb or abseil and looking straight ahead. Ideally the anchors will be directly ahead or just a little off to the side. Anchors a long way off to one side are difficult to use as they may not provide the anchor-belayer-climber line or they may create wide angles between the anchors (see *Figure 8.2*). Sometimes the belayer must decide between security and being perfectly in line.

### Always take care moving unroped at the top of cliffs

**5 NOTES FOR INSTRUCTORS   Personal safety**

Instructors often find themselves working under time constraints and at familiar venues where there can be a pressure and temptation to cut corners for the sake of speed. It is therefore particularly important for instructors to pay good regard to their *own* personal safety.

## 8.2.2 Attaching to anchors

There are many systems for *attaching to anchors*. A safe system will include, as a minimum, the basic *3 anchor essentials*:

- Anchors equally loaded
- Anchors independently tied off
- Angles between anchors 60° or less

In other words the load should be *shared evenly* between all anchors by ensuring *equal tension* in each strand of rope from the belayer to the anchor. There should be a *separate tied off link to each anchor* so one is not reliant on the other and there is no risk of a shock load on the remaining anchor if one should fail. Care should be taken to avoid wide angles between anchors due to the resulting additional load this generates (see *Figure 8.2*).

In addition, a system that is simple and quick to adjust is highly desirable. The one described below requires the belayer to first tie into an end of the rope and is identical to the system lead climbers would use on reaching the top of a pitch.

When more than two anchors are needed the stages already explained above are simply repeated. If there are anchors that are both in and out of reach combine the two systems attaching to the furthest away anchor first.

Clove hitches have been used in this example because they are delightfully easy and quick to adjust. A system using a figure of eight tied with a bight of rope through the central rope loop also works well, uses fewer screwgate karabiners and therefore creates fewer links in the system. This method is also slightly more dynamic but it is trickier to get the tension right and difficult to adjust once the knot is tied, however it is worth practising for those occasions when the screwgates have run out! (See *Figure of 8 at an anchor* on page 66.)

## 8.2.3 Equalising anchors with slings

To minimise the amount of rope used at the belay and to simplify attaching to multiple anchors it is possible to *link and equalise the anchors with slings*, thus creating a single attachment point. This can be done in a number of ways depending on the spacing of the anchors. For example, two anchors about an arm span apart can be linked with a long (120cm) sling on each. Overhand knots can be tied to adjust the slings to the correct

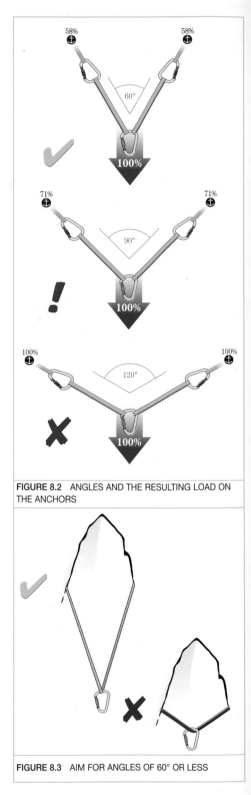

FIGURE 8.2   ANGLES AND THE RESULTING LOAD ON THE ANCHORS

FIGURE 8.3   AIM FOR ANGLES OF 60° OR LESS

### Single anchor within reach

Tie a clove hitch to a screwgate karabiner at the anchor.

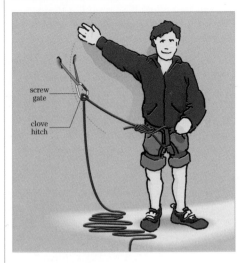

screw gate

clove hitch

### Single anchor out of reach

Any adjustment is best done at the belayer to avoid moving back and forth to the anchor to get the correct tension. Clip the rope through a screwgate karabiner at the anchor before moving close to the desired position, tie a loose clove hitch to a screwgate karabiner attached to the central rope loop, tighten the screwgate, then move to final position and adjust tension. This way the belayer is attached before moving to a precarious position at the cliff top.

clove hitch on screwgate on central rope loop

### Two anchors within reach

Clove hitch to the first anchor, leave some slack then clove hitch to the second anchor, bring the rope back to a clove hitch on a screwgate karabiner on the central rope loop. Adjust any of the clove hitches to ensure equal tension.

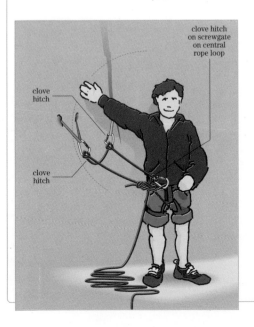

clove hitch on screwgate on central rope loop

clove hitch

clove hitch

## 3 anchor essentials

- **Anchors equally loaded**

- **Anchors independently tied off**

- **Angles between anchors 60° or less**

### Two anchors out of reach

Clip both anchors and move towards desired position holding the middle bit of rope between the anchors and the slack rope. Clove hitch the middle bit of rope from the first anchor, get into position and adjust tension before adding a clove hitch from the second anchor. A large HMS karabiner may be sufficient to seat two clove hitches but if there is any concern of creating a load too wide for the karabiner two separate screwgate karabiners should be used instead.

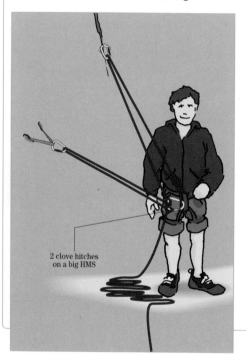

2 clove hitches on a big HMS

2 'D' shape karabiners

length. If the anchors are closer together, one long (120cm) sling may be sufficient to link both but care must be taken to avoid wide angles. To ensure the anchors are equalised and independent an overhand knot can be tied at the balance point and the karabiner clipped through both halves of the sling (see *Figure 8.4*). Alternatively an overhand knot is tied in a bight of sling creating a loop to clip into (see *Figure 8.5*). Three anchors may be linked with this method but an extra long (240cm) sling would be needed (see *Figure 8.6*).

*Self-equalising methods* of linking anchors are popular where bolt belays are the norm and when it may be necessary to alter the belay position mid-way through the climb. The karabiner is clipped through a cross in the sling so it can

move freely back and forth to the correct point of equal tension. The risk is that if one anchor fails there will be shock loading of the other anchor as the karabiner slides along the sling (see *Figure 8.7*). An overhand knot tied part way down the sling can minimise this shockload (see *Figure 8.8*). This system is not recommended with natural or hand-placed anchors.

### 8.2.4 Position of belayer

The belayer may decide to sit or stand depending on a number of factors, such as the size of ledge and height of anchors. A sitting stance with feet well braced is the most secure for inexperienced belayers to adopt and is also appropriate when the anchors are below waist level to avoid unnecessary strain on the belayer's back and legs when

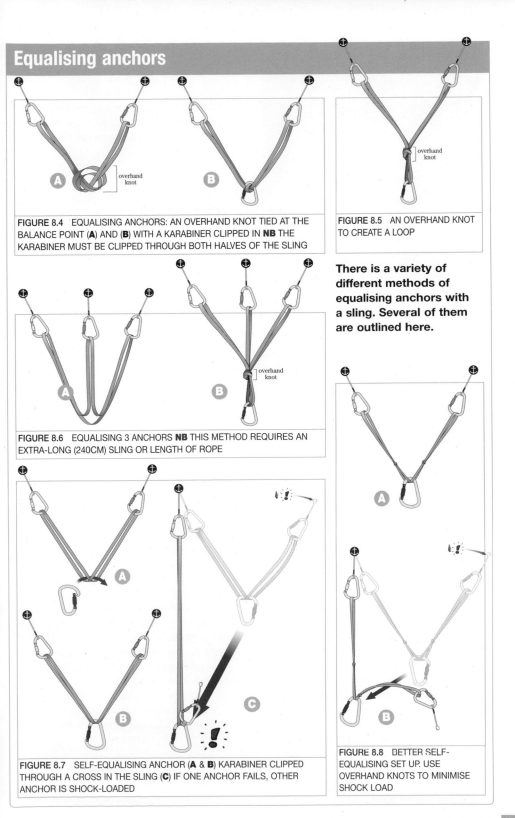

FIGURE 8.4 EQUALISING ANCHORS: AN OVERHAND KNOT TIED AT THE BALANCE POINT (**A**) AND (**B**) WITH A KARABINER CLIPPED IN **NB** THE KARABINER MUST BE CLIPPED THROUGH BOTH HALVES OF THE SLING

FIGURE 8.5 AN OVERHAND KNOT TO CREATE A LOOP

FIGURE 8.6 EQUALISING 3 ANCHORS **NB** THIS METHOD REQUIRES AN EXTRA-LONG (240CM) SLING OR LENGTH OF ROPE

There is a variety of different methods of equalising anchors with a sling. Several of them are outlined here.

FIGURE 8.7 SELF-EQUALISING ANCHOR (**A** & **B**) KARABINER CLIPPED THROUGH A CROSS IN THE SLING (**C**) IF ONE ANCHOR FAILS, OTHER ANCHOR IS SHOCK-LOADED

FIGURE 8.8 BETTER SELF-EQUALISING SET UP. USE OVERHAND KNOTS TO MINIMISE SHOCK LOAD

FIGURE 8.9   A SECURE STANDING STANCE WITH HIGH ANCHORS

Belaying is a tricky skill to learn requiring practise and experience in order to become safe. Novices require careful instruction and close supervision while learning to belay, hold falls and lower. This is best done with the instructor alongside watching closely, correcting mistakes and holding the dead rope in readiness to act as an additional brake if required.

holding a fall. The 'live' rope should not run over the belayer's legs, as there is a risk of them being trapped by the rope in a fall with painful consequences. Standing feels secure if the anchors are high and close by; this position has the advantage of allowing a better view down the route (see *Figure 8.9*).

# 8.3 Belaying

Once the *belayer* is securely attached and in a well-braced position, the climber at the foot of the route ties to the end of the rope and the belayer pulls up any remaining slack rope. The belayer feeds a bight of rope through an appropriate belay device and clips it to a screwgate karabiner on the central rope loop ensuring the gate is locked and the rope is free of twists. The rope leading from the belay device to the climber is called the *live rope* and the inactive, slack rope on the other side is known as the *dead rope*.

Consideration must be given to which should be the *brake* or *control hand* to provide optimum braking as this is not simply a case of using

the preferred hand. Whether sitting or standing, a semi-sideways stance is adopted due to the attachment point being at the front of the harness and the anchors behind. The brake hand is the one furthest away from the climber (the *uphill hand*); this means that if the belayer is facing towards the right this is the right hand and facing towards the left this is the left hand. It is important to be ambidextrous with this skill. This belaying position should allow the dead rope to be pulled right back creating a tight S-bend through the *belay device* giving maximum friction. If the orientation of the device is incorrect the belayer's body can block this optimum braking position (see *Figure 8.10*).

The belayer has one final check of the anchors, knots and karabiners before telling the climber when to set off. To ease communication and avoid misunderstandings it is normal to use the recognised *climbing calls*, even when toproping; these are explained on page 118.

As the climber moves up slack is generated; this is *taken-in* using a secure sequence of hand movements (see *Taking in* overleaf). The climber won't always give any warning of a slip so there needs to be a fail-safe system of taking in that enables the belayer to react in a split second to sudden movement. Effective belaying requires teamwork. The belayer feels and watches for upward movement that indicates the need to take in slack, but the climber should be patient if the belayer is slow, waiting or if necessary asking for the rope to be taken in.

## 8.3.1 Holding falls and lowering

If the belayer is correctly positioned with tension in the anchor ropes and belaying with minimum

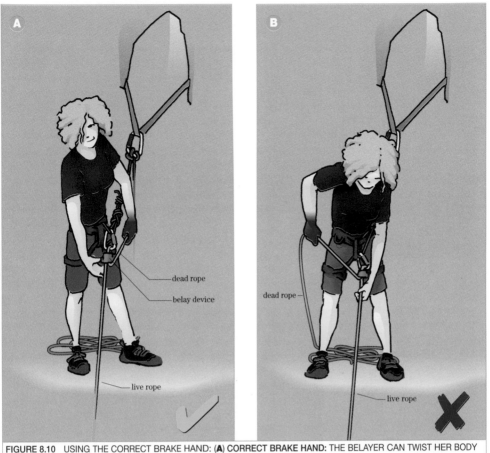

FIGURE 8.10 USING THE CORRECT BRAKE HAND: (**A**) CORRECT BRAKE HAND: THE BELAYER CAN TWIST HER BODY AWAY FROM THE PULL AND BRAKE EFFECTIVELY, AND (**B**) INCORRECT BRAKE HAND: THE BELAYER CANNOT TWIST HER BODY AWAY FROM THE PULL AND THEREFORE CANNOT BRAKE EFFECTIVELY

slack, ***holding*** a falling second should not be dramatic. There will be a certain amount of tightening up of knots and rope stretch that helps absorb the energy of a fall. Correct belay technique should ensure there is minimal slippage and there is certainly no excuse for dropping a second! The worst potential fall for a second is from a traverse that may result in a pendulum, but the belayer should easily hold even this type of fall.

In most situations it should be possible for the belayer to ***lower*** the climber back to the ground if necessary. The belayer takes firm hold of the dead rope, normally with two hands and feeds out rope slowly and smoothly. The climber meanwhile leans back and walks down the rock (see *Figure 8.11*). If there are sharp edges lowering may not be possible without the risk of damage to the rope.

### 8.3.2 Other systems

If there are several climbers to complete the same route it may be beneficial to opt for a belay system that can be set up, left in place and clipped in to and out of easily. Such systems have the additional benefit of being easy to escape from if a problem needs sorting; two examples are described here.

Two or more bombproof anchors are linked with one end of the climbing rope or a separate rigging rope to create a V. It is best to start with a figure of eight on the bight tied in the end of the rope attached to the first anchor and a clove hitch at the second anchor for ease of adjustment. At the apex of the V, a figure of eight on a bight is tied to create a loop to clip onto and belay from (see *Figure 8.12B*). A double figure of eight on a bight can also be used here to create

**1** The right hand reaches down the *live rope* while the brake hand holds the *dead rope* back in the braking position;

**2** the *brake hand* comes forward bringing both ropes parallel so the slack can be fed through the device with a 'pull/push' action;

**3** the brake hand comes back to the braking position;

**4** the right hand is transferred to the dead rope next to the brake hand;

**5** the brake hand jumps along the rope close to but not touching the belay device;

**6** the left right goes back to the live rope ready to start again.

two loops, one for the belayer to clip onto and one to attach the belay device but it is crucial to position the belay device at waist level (see *Figure 8.12*).

An alternative system is to link the anchors as previously described but then to belay directly from the anchors using an Italian hitch (see *Figure 8.13*).

### 8.3.3 Italian hitch
This is a versatile *friction hitch* that can be used in place of a belay device for belaying, lowering and abseiling. It is often used on scrambling or

mountaineering routes where speed is important and minimum gear is carried, as it only requires an HMS screwgate. It is simple to operate, so is often a good choice for novices to use but it can kink the rope.

When using an Italian hitch as a direct belay with a top-rope the belayer attaches to the anchors for safety with a cow's tail (see *Lark's foot* on page 70) but can move around on the ledge and get into the optimum position to operate the Italian hitch. The belayer should be in front and slightly to one side of the belay (see *Figure 8.14*).

FIGURE 8.11   LOWERING A CLIMBER SECURELY TO THE GROUND

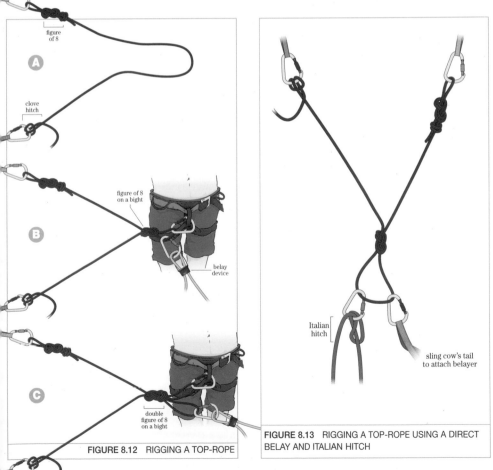

figure of 8

**A**

clove hitch

**B**

figure of 8 on a bight

belay device

**C**

double figure of 8 on a bight

FIGURE 8.12   RIGGING A TOP-ROPE

Italian hitch

sling cow's tail to attach belayer

FIGURE 8.13   RIGGING A TOP-ROPE USING A DIRECT BELAY AND ITALIAN HITCH

# Operating an Italian hitch

= left-hand movements  = right-hand movements

brake hand

live rope
to climber

**1** Feed slack through the HMS with a hand on each rope

**2** Move the non-brake hand onto the dead rope below the brake hand

**3** Slide the brake hand back up the rope

**4** Move the non-brake hand back to the live rope

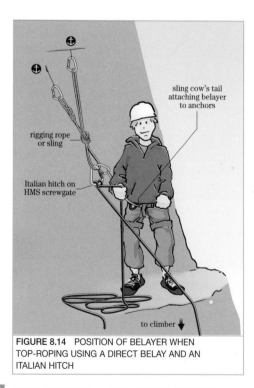

sling cow's tail attaching belayer to anchors

rigging rope or sling

Italian hitch on HMS screwgate

to climber ↓

**FIGURE 8.14** POSITION OF BELAYER WHEN TOP-ROPING USING A DIRECT BELAY AND AN ITALIAN HITCH

### 8.3.4 Operating an Italian hitch

Slack is taken in through the Italian hitch ensuring a firm grip on the dead rope at all times. This can be done by sliding the brake hand back up the rope after taking slack in as shown above. Alternatively the brake hand can be jumped back up the dead rope as with taking in using a belay device (see *Taking In* on page 88). To pay out slack or lower with an Italian hitch keep a hand on each rope and feed the slack through slowly and smoothly.

## 8.4 Bottom-roping

This term describes a system in which the belayer is positioned on the ground and the climber moves up to a *lower-off* point just below the crag top and is lowered back down. It is an effective and convenient way to manage and supervise larger groups of novice climbers but it can create a concentrated environmental impact. A further disadvantage is that novices miss out on

**90** **ROCK CLIMBING** – SINGLE PITCH CLIMBING

the special feeling of 'topping-out' and fail to get a true picture of what *real* climbing is like. It is, however, a popular and widely used system (see *Figure 8.15*).

## 8.4.1 Anchor selection

There are a few additional considerations when selecting anchors for a bottom-rope system, as the anchors will be repeatedly loaded and out of sight once climbing starts. The best choice of anchors are those that can take a multi-directional load, such as threads and deep-seated nuts that are not likely to move in the crack with the risk of loosening or jamming. Camming devices are best avoided if possible, as they are prone to 'walking' into cracks when movement occurs. Slings on blocks or spikes can be used if there is no risk of them lifting off. *In-situ* gear is sometimes found at venues popular with groups and should be used with the normal caution. Very occasionally one anchor may suffice, if it is undoubtedly bombproof, but normally two or more will be required. It should be noted that it is not just the anchor itself that is a potential weak link but also the connecting equipment (slings, karabiners, and so on).

## 8.4.2 Rigging a bottom-rope

A separate rope is used for rigging at the top; this should ideally be a low-stretch rope to minimise abrasion. This links the anchors in a series of V shapes that takes the apex of the V to the top of the climb so it rests just over the edge. There are many ways to achieve this but all should incorporate the *3 Anchor Essentials* (see page 83, *Attaching to anchors*). The system illustrated in *Figure 8.13* for top-roping works well if the V is extended over the edge.

Another simple system is to clip the end of the rope to the first anchor with a figure of eight, then zigzag the rope to the edge and back to the next anchors until all are incorporated. Grab the bundle of V apexes, adjusting the tension between them before tying a chunky overhand knot in the whole lot (see *Figure 8.16*).

The *climbing rope* is suspended from the rigging rope using a screwgate karabiner. If there is a concern about the gate undoing, two screwgates can be placed side by side with the gates facing opposite ways. This will tend to reduce friction as the arc through which the rope is forced is made wider and will also tend to make the screwgates stand at 90° to the rock thus further reducing

FIGURE 8.15 BOTTOM-ROPE CLIMBING WITH A LARGE GROUP OF YOUNGSTERS

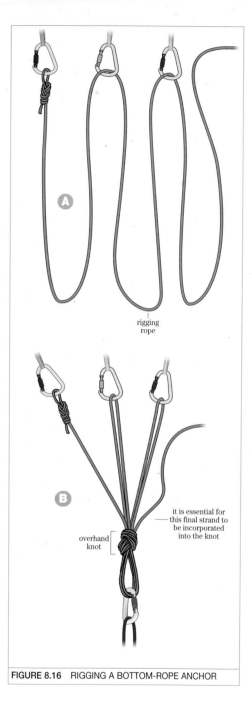

**A**

rigging
rope

**B**

overhand
knot

it is essential for
this final strand to
be incorporated
into the knot

FIGURE 8.16   RIGGING A BOTTOM-ROPE ANCHOR

the ground from erosion. Carpet squares work well and can be held in place by attaching them to the rope or anchors with a length of cord or rope.

### 8.4.3  Belaying from below

The climber ties on to one end of the rope and the belayer chooses from a range of options. If weights are even the belayer will stand close to the base of the crag and use a belay device attached to the harness belay loop. The belayer should be attached to a *ground anchor* if there is a possibility of being lifted off the ground or if it is impossible to stand in close to the base of the crag. This can be done with the rope or a sling (see *Figure 8.20*).

### 8.4.4  Lowering back down

Once the climber reaches the lower-off point, the belayer takes in any slack, holds the climber's weight and gets comfortable with both hands on the dead rope. The climber looks down to check the belayer is ready before leaning back away from the rock. The belayer feeds the rope through the device slowly and smoothly by letting it slide through the fingers or by jumping the hands down the rope, keeping them well away from the device to avoid getting pinched (see *Figure 8.21*). Most climbers feel vulnerable when being lowered as control is with someone else; novices also find it extremely intimidating and need a gentle introduction.

Novices should have a practise session of lowering and being lowered close to the ground to help avoid problems later on. The person controlling the lower needs supervising and back-up in the same way as when belaying. Lowering with an Italian hitch requires the knot to invert around the karabiner, which can be alarming to watch the first time.

friction and wear. If the karabiners are arranged gate downward then rope vibration unscrewing the gate is kept in check by gravity.

*Rope protectors* and padding or matting should be placed under the rigging rope at any wear points to protect the rope from abrasion and

Novices often gain their first experience of belaying while bottom-roping and require clear instructions in the sequence of hand movements and careful supervision. A second novice should also hold the dead rope as a back-up with the instructor in very close attendance (see *Figure 8.17*).

Simpler alternatives to a standard belay device may be considered for use with novices and groups that are quicker to master and easier to monitor. For example an Italian hitch can be attached to the harness, or directly to a ground anchor (see *Figure 8.18*).

The latter is a good system providing the anchor is bombproof and it is often used if the belayer is light. The method of operating the Italian hitch can be adapted to involve a group of belayers by introducing the *bell-ringing* technique where one person pulls down on the live rope and two or more pull out on the dead rope (see *Figure 8.19*).

FIGURE 8.17 TWO BELAYERS

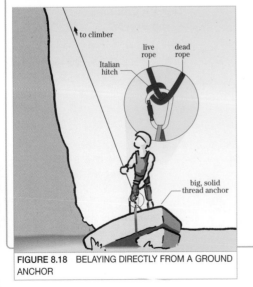

FIGURE 8.18 BELAYING DIRECTLY FROM A GROUND ANCHOR

FIGURE 8.19 "BELL-RINGING" WITH AN ITALIAN HITCH

## 8.4.5 Avoiding and solving problems

Bottom-rope climbing is a controlled activity and problems encountered are rare if sessions are carefully planned, well managed and adequately supervised. The most common situation that may arise during bottom-rope climbing is that of the climber becoming 'stuck' through fear and losing the confidence to lower back down the route. Suitable route choice and a progressive approach to harder climbs minimises the chances of this but in most cases it is easily solved by a tight rope and gentle coaxing. Far less common is the

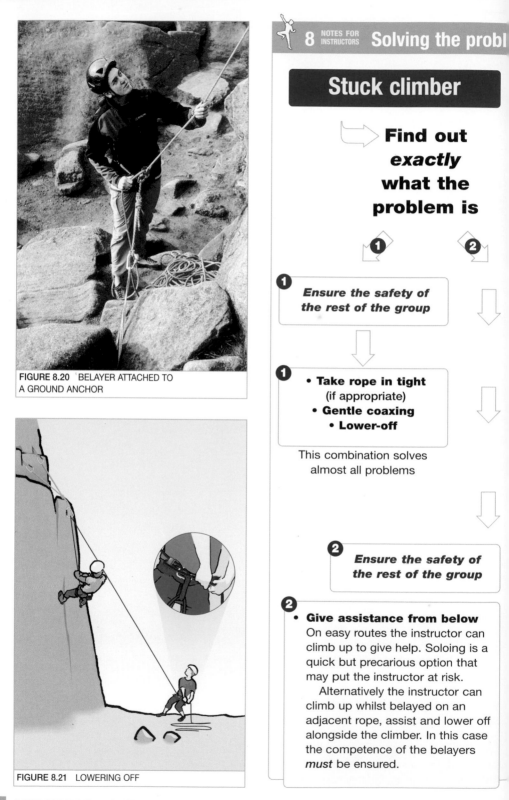

FIGURE 8.20 BELAYER ATTACHED TO A GROUND ANCHOR

FIGURE 8.21 LOWERING OFF

## Stuck climber

➡ **Find out *exactly* what the problem is**

**①** **②**

**①** *Ensure the safety of the rest of the group*

**①**
- **Take rope in tight** (if appropriate)
- **Gentle coaxing**
- **Lower-off**

This combination solves almost all problems

**②** *Ensure the safety of the rest of the group*

**②**
- **Give assistance from below**
  On easy routes the instructor can climb up to give help. Soloing is a quick but precarious option that may put the instructor at risk.
  Alternatively the instructor can climb up whilst belayed on an adjacent rope, assist and lower off alongside the climber. In this case the competence of the belayers *must* be ensured.

**③** | Ensure the safety of the rest of the group

## ③

- **Give assistance from above**

**Abseil**

On steep routes or if there is no safe way for the instructor to reach the stuck climber from below, assistance can be arranged from above. The instructor rigs an abseil rope and descends to a position alongside the climber.

The instructor can sort out the problem, descend to the ground and then oversee lowering.

Alternatively the instructor can abseil while the climber is lowered. If there is any doubt about the reliability of the belayer, the instructor and climber can be attached with a short sling. This acts as a safeguard for the climber (see *Figure 8.20*).

**Top-rope**

If the second climbs off-route and is faced with a pendulum or climbs past the lower-off, a top-rope may be needed.

The instructor arranges the top-rope and drops an end with a figure of eight knot and screwgate attached for the climber to clip into, ensuring that this is clipped to the correct point on the harness.

The original belayer on the ground pays out slack or removes the rope completely as the climber continues up to safety, protected by the new rope.

## Group safety

**The instructor must ensure the safety of the remainder of the group before attending to the incident.**

This may be as simple as asking everyone to come down to the ground safely but quickly. If there is only one instructor with sole responsibility for the group it is preferable for him or her to solve the problem without leaving the group unattended.

If novice belayers are involved it is essential they are well-briefed and have a suitable back-up; tying a knot in the dead rope behind the belay device is one quick and simple safeguard.

To avoid anxiety in the rest of the group, particularly if there is an injury, they will need reassurance that everything is OK.

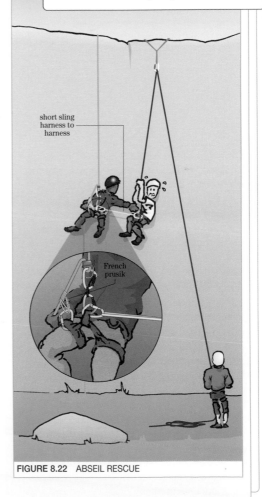

short sling harness to harness

French prusik

**FIGURE 8.22** ABSEIL RESCUE

## Clipping or tying onto rope

Tying onto the rope is undoubtedly the safest system to use, providing the knot is tied correctly through the appropriate part of the harness.

Clipping onto the rope with a figure of eight on a bight and screwgate karabiner is faster and simpler. However, there is a number of potential problems with this system and the manufacturer's instructions should be checked first. The karabiner could be left unlocked creating the possibility of it opening inadvertently and there is also the possibility that the karabiner may rotate to become cross-loaded (see *Loading karabiners* on page 56) or it may be clipped incorrectly to the harness.

Careful checking before climbing is essential.

problem of a climber becoming physically stuck, by wedging a knee or a finger in a crack for example, but once again this is normally remedied by talking the climber through the problem and minimising panic by giving calm reassurance. Other possible awkward situations include climbers traversing off-route so they are faced with a nasty pendulum or climbing above the lower-off where they risk a leader fall. These situations are unlikely to occur with careful route selection, arrangement of the ropes and adequate supervision but would require a rapid response from the instructor if they did.

Problems can arise through belayer error and inexperience such as the climber being dropped or being lowered too quickly, incorrect tying on or incorrect attachment and use of belay devices. In most cases these potential problems can be eliminated by careful supervision and routine safety checks. However, if problems or awkward situations do arise, a logical approach to solving them ensures the simplest and safest solution is reached. Mostly such 'rescues' can be carried out without any time pressure.

## 8.5 Abseiling in a single pitch environment

*Abseiling* involves the descent of a rope using a friction device to control speed. For novices it may be a thrilling experience yet many climbers feel uneasy with its potential seriousness. There are many reasons why climbers choose to abseil. It may be necessary to reach the base of the route, retrieve a piece of stuck gear, give assistance to another climber or inspect a climb. However, at single pitch venues abseiling is seldom the only or best means of descent to reach the base unless it is a sea cliff (see *Figure 8.23*).

Abseiling is extremely popular as a fun activity with groups. In deciding whether to abseil, in particular as an activity in its own right, careful thought should be given to the environmental impact. Wear and tear caused by abseiling is considerable when large numbers descend repeatedly at the same spot. Trampling in the take-off and landing zones leads to loss of vegetation and subsequent soil erosion. Ropes rubbing consistently in the same spot results in deep grooves at the top of the crag and the passage of boots and shoes slithering down the same line of rock quickly leads to polishing. Heavily used abseil sites are often characterised by their dirty appearance; this is due to the fact that the area at the top is often muddy and because abseiling routinely takes place in the wet. Abseiling is best avoided at particularly sensitive sites (see *Figure 8.24*).

### 8.5.1 Equipment for abseiling

It is possible to abseil on either two half-ropes or one single rope. For group use it is preferable to use low-stretch ropes to minimise the abrasion

There are many alternatives to abseiling at a crag with groups, which should be considered in areas where the environmental impact is great. A dedicated *abseil tower* may be a better alternative for example.
To minimise impact at the crag rotate the sites used and choose areas away from recognised climbs that do not have a fragile top. Use mats or rucksacks to pad out under ropes at wear points.

FIGURE 8.23    SEA CLIFF CLIMBS OFTEN REQUIRE AN ABSEIL APPROACH

Please do not abseil or
lower off on any part of
the main wall area.

This is a geologically
sensitive site.

Thank you
Trevbarrow Management Advisory Group
Lancaster City Council

FIGURE 8.24    ABSEILING IS OFTEN DISCOURAGED AT SENSITIVE SITES

caused by dynamic ropes rubbing on edges. The sheath of a loaded dynamic rope rubbing back and forth across an edge, even a rounded one will quickly become damaged. The sheath may look worn or furry and it may be possible to see flecks of nylon on the rock. If this abrasion goes unnoticed the sheath may wear right through exposing the core, which is then also susceptible to damage.

The thickness and finish of the rope will affect the amount of friction experienced whilst abseiling and should be taken into account when selecting an appropriate abseil device, along with the steepness of the terrain and the experience and weight of the abseiler.

In a climbing situation it is normal to *abseil with the belay device* rather than carry an additional abseil device. Most belay devices also work effectively in descent though the amount of friction they afford varies. A slick device coupled with a shiny, thin rope can lead to an alarmingly rapid descent, whilst a grabby device used with a furry thick rope will feel jerky and slow to operate. Dedicated abseil devices tend to run more smoothly and are easier to operate, especially for novices. The most popular is a figure of eight descender, which is simple, effective and has a large surface area to dissipate heat.

The Italian hitch is effective for abseiling; there is sufficient friction, the ride is quite smooth and it works with one or two ropes. An HMS screwgate should be used and it is important to have the dead (brake) rope running over the back bar rather than the gate side of the karabiner to avoid inadvertently unscrewing the gate (see *Figure 8.25*).

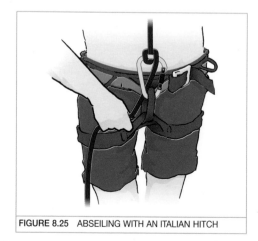

FIGURE 8.25   ABSEILING WITH AN ITALIAN HITCH

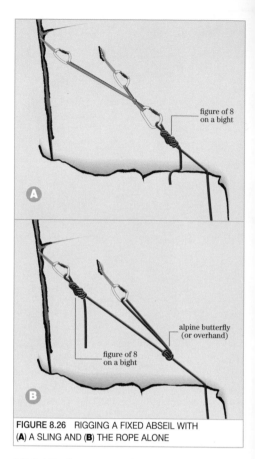

FIGURE 8.26   RIGGING A FIXED ABSEIL WITH
(**A**) A SLING AND (**B**) THE ROPE ALONE

## 8.5.2 Rigging an abseil

*Anchors* should be solid and appropriately located; they are selected by applying the same criteria as for belay anchors. This should take into account the direction of load and in addition it is best if anchors are high and back from the edge to facilitate the take-off. At a single pitch venue it is unlikely the anchors will need to be abandoned so there is no reason to cut corners; in other words, use more rather than fewer anchors.

The rope can be either fixed or retrievable. A fixed abseil rope is attached securely at the top to allow for repeated descents using any method that incorporates the *3 Anchor Essentials* (see page 83, *Attaching to anchors*). This may use the rope or slings to link and equalise the anchors (see *Figure 8.26* above, and *Equalising anchors* on page 85).

## 8.5.3 Arranging a retrievable abseil

If the only means of reaching a climb is by abseil and an additional abseil rope is not carried, a

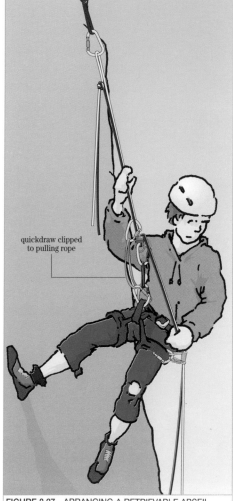

quickdraw clipped to pulling rope

**FIGURE 8.27** ARRANGING A RETRIEVABLE ABSEIL

*retrievable abseil* (where the ropes are pulled down after descent) is called for. The anchors must first be centralised to a common point with slings or a separate length of *rigging rope*. The final attachment point should rest close to the edge but not over it. To ensure minimum friction and least damage to slings or rope when the rope is pulled down, it is best to use a screwgate karabiner to attach the rope. A *single rope* is attached at its middle marker, but if the rope has no middle mark run the rope through from the two ends to find the mid-point.

When abseiling on *two ropes*, they are joined together using either an overhand knot or a double fisherman's knot separated by a reef knot (see *Knots and hitches* on page 69). The overhand knot has the advantages of being quick to tie and slightly less prone to jam in cracks because the knot will tend to 'roll away' from the rock when one end is pulled, but it must be tightened well after tying to avoid slippage. The rope with the knot is the one that is pulled to retrieve the rope. To avoid forgetting which this is, a long quickdraw or short sling can be clipped from the harness belay loop to the rope to be pulled (see *Figure 8.27*). For tips on avoiding getting the ropes jammed see *Figure 14.3 Arranging a multiple abseil* on page 151 and **14.5 Jammed ropes** on page 152.

### 8.5.4 Throwing the rope

Before *throwing the rope*, the abseiler should be attached either to the rope or an anchor to enable a good look over the edge to check for climbers or anything the rope may catch on. If there is any doubt that the ropes may not reach the ground, a figure of eight knot should be tied in each end (to avoid abseiling off the end of the rope). For a tangle-free throw, first feed the rope into a pile next to the edge so the end on top of the pile is the free end. Coil or lap several neat handfuls from this end, look one last time, shout "rope below" and throw the coils out and down, the rest of the rope should follow. Check the rope has reached the ground, if not pull it up and throw again. In windy conditions the rope may be blown sideways, so either lower the ends slowly with a weight attached or descend with the ends. This can be done with the rope coiled around the

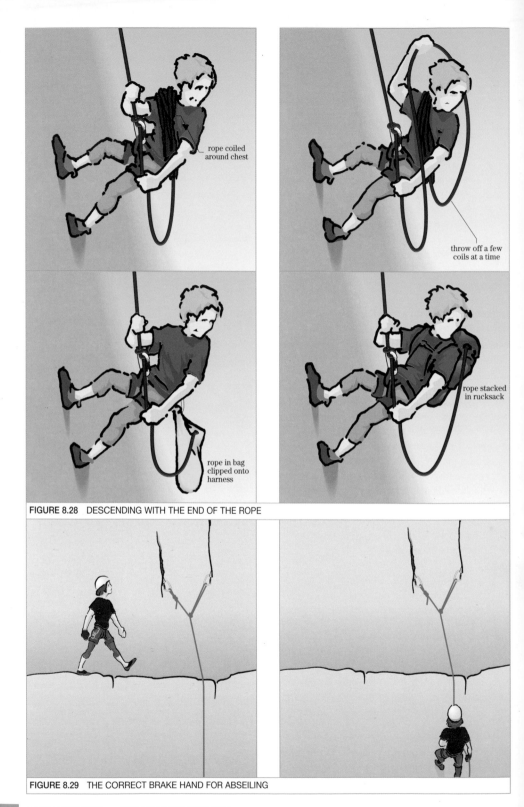

rope coiled around chest

throw off a few coils at a time

rope in bag clipped onto harness

rope stacked in rucksack

FIGURE 8.28   DESCENDING WITH THE END OF THE ROPE

FIGURE 8.29   THE CORRECT BRAKE HAND FOR ABSEILING

body so a few coils are dropped at a time or with the rope feeding from a rucksack or a bag clipped to the waist (see *Figure 8.28*).

### 8.5.5 Attaching to the rope

The abseil or belay device is threaded with the abseil rope and attached to the harness belay loop with a screwgate karabiner. It is best to avoid clipping the karabiner through the waist belt and leg loops, as it is possible to create a cross-loading in which the karabiner is inherently weak (see *Figure 8.30*). Harnesses without a central loop can be modified using a *Maillon* (a very strong metal connector) or sling to create a central attachment point (see *Figure 8.31*).

To decide which hand is the brake hand the abseiler should start by standing parallel to the abseil rope and then the downhill hand is the brake hand. In other words, if the abseiler prefers to use the right hand to do the braking this should be the downhill hand when standing parallel to the rope (see *Figure 8.29*). For novice abseilers it is often a good idea to extend the abseil device as shown in Figure 8.32C to enable both hands to do the braking. This system is also useful on steep abseils where friction may be limited due to a slick device/thin rope combination.

### 8.5.6 Safety back-up

The commonly used abseil devices do not lock automatically; in other words, if control of the rope is lost, it is possible to slide very quickly and disastrously to the ground. A *safety back-up system* is a very good idea for all abseilers; there are several methods to choose from according to the experience of the abseiler and nature of the terrain.

Many climbers use an *autobloc*, which is very simply a clutch to grab the rope when control is lost. It takes minimum extra equipment and no time at all to add so why be without it? A popular method is to *add a French prusik* to the rope below the abseil device; this is attached to either the leg loop or belay loop of the harness. (see *Figure 8.32A*). Care must be taken to ensure the prusik cannot touch, or become entangled with the abseil device, otherwise it may fail to grip the rope when needed (see *Figure 8.32B*). To avoid this problem many climbers prefer to extend the abseil device (as described above) by attaching it to the harness with a quickdraw (see *Figure 8.32C*). However, if the prusik is clipped to the harness loop it is possible (on vertical abseils especially) for the quickdraw to rub against the prusik and knock it open with alarming results.

The prusik can also be attached above the abseil device but if loaded the prusik can be hard to release especially if it is at full arms stretch. This system is used when it is necessary to pass a knot on an abseil. (see page 158, *Abseiling past a knot*). It is a mistake to treat any prusik autobloc method as foolproof. If the abseiler needs to let go of the rope with both hands, to remove a runner or give assistance to another

FIGURE 8.30   CROSS-LOADED KARABINER

FIGURE 8.31   USING A MAILLON TO CREATE A CENTRAL ATTACHMENT POINT

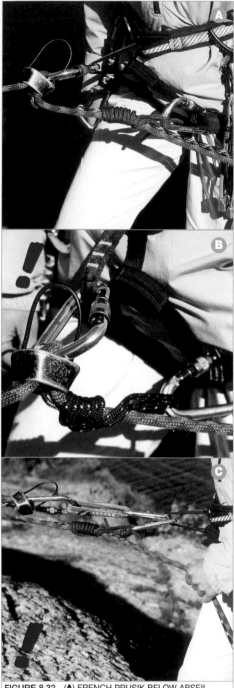

The best safety back-up system for novices is an additional *safety rope* operated from the top, coupled with a *releasable abseil* rope. This protects for loss of control as well as other potential problems such as hair or clothing jamming in the device.

The abseil rope is secured with a system that is easy to release even whilst it is loaded, such as an Italian hitch tied off as shown in *Figures 8.33*. This rope should just touch the ground so it does not get trodden on and any twists can spin out, the remainder of the rope is stacked neatly next to the anchor.

The safety rope, which is tied to the abseiler's harness as in a climbing situation, can be operated from a direct or indirect belay. A direct system is preferable as it allows the operator to move around freely and sort problems easily. An Italian hitch is a good choice and should be set up alongside the abseil rope. One set of good anchors is sufficient for both but it should be organised so it is not cluttered. The operator can be secured using a cow's tail. If a problem arises such as the abseiler getting hair or clothing caught in the abseil device it can be solved quickly and effectively as follows:

1 Take in tight and tie off safety rope.
2 Untie and slacken the abseil rope so the hair or clothing can be taken out.
3 Either re-tie the abseil rope and continue the abseil or lower the abseiler to the ground on the safety rope (*Figure 8.35*).

For tying off a belay device, see page 129.

FIGURE 8.32 (**A**) FRENCH PRUSIK BELOW ABSEIL DEVICE CLIPPED TO LEG LOOP (**B**) WATCH OUT FOR THE PRUSIK TOUCHING THE ABSEIL DEVICE AND BEING KNOCKED OPEN (**C**) ABSEIL DEVICE EXTENDED AND PRUSIK TO BELAY LOOP, BUT WATCH OUT FOR QUICKDRAW KNOCKING PRUSIK OPEN ON VERTICAL ABSEILS

climber for example, an additional back-up should be used. This can be arranged by tying a knot in the rope below and clipping it to the harness or by wrapping the rope several times around the thigh.

A quick additional back-up is for the first person down to stand just to one side, out of the 'line of fire' of any falling rocks or objects, loosely holding the rope. By pulling hard on the rope it is possible to stop an out of control descent.

# releasable abseil

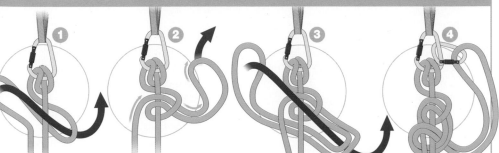

FIGURE 8.33 TYING OFF AN ITALIAN HITCH: (**1**) CREATE A LOOP BEHIND THE LOAD ROPE AND FEED A BIGHT OF ROPE THROUGH THIS LOOP. IT HELPS IF THIS IS DONE AS CLOSE TO THE ITALIAN HITCH AS POSSIBLE (**2**) PULL MORE SLACK THROUGH (**3**) TIE A HALF-HITCH TO SECURE (**4**) CLIP THE TAIL BACK TO THE ANCHOR FOR ADDITIONAL SECURITY

FIGURE 8.34   ABSEIL AND SAFETY ROPE SETUP

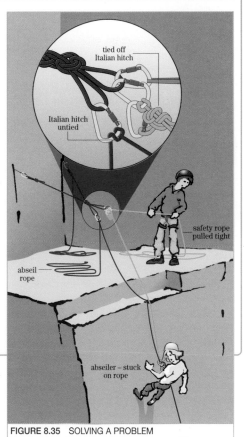

FIGURE 8.35   SOLVING A PROBLEM

For those responsible for taking groups abseiling, whether as part of a climbing day or as a one-off experience, there are a number of additional considerations. Issues of group size, crag etiquette and other crag users have already been discussed in the environment section, but specific considerations include choice of site, managing the group, an awareness of, and avoidance of potential conflicts.

An ideal site for a first time abseil is a short slab with easy access to a flat and spacious top and base to allow for the group to wait their turn in safety and comfort. This should be away from popular climbs and ideally not on an existing climb at all. The rock should be solid without ledges or overhangs.

To avoid potential problems the instructor should be able to move around at the top and see the abseilers reach the ground; the direct safety rope system recommended allows for this movement. Abseilers should be well briefed and 'tidied-up' to minimise things such as long hair or loose clothing that could become caught in the abseil device.

A common problem facing instructors running abseiling sessions is that of nervous abseilers refusing to commit their weight to the rope or freezing part way down; leaning backwards over a drop is a very unnatural thing to do! Previous experience of climbing and being lowered off a climb helps novices gain trust in the system. High anchors that are back from the edge encourage abseilers to put their weight on the rope before the edge is reached. Gentle coaxing and a snug safety rope to start with will boost confidence, whilst a wide stance with a 'tipped-back' body position increases stability.

**FIGURE 8.36** A WELL-ORGANISED GROUP ABSEIL

LEADING ON AN INDOOR CLIMBING WALL

# Indoor climbing walls

It has been estimated that over 80% of climbers use indoor climbing walls and one in five new climbers start out indoors.

*BMC survey*

9

Walls are an accepted part of the climbing scene and have had a significant influence on climbing standards and styles. There are over 250 indoor climbing walls in the UK coming in all shapes and sizes from one or two panels at the end of a sports hall to converted factories, churches and purpose built complexes. The original climbing walls that appeared in the late 1960s were vertical brickwork with holds chipped out of the pointing or with lumps of real rock inset. The majority were suitable for traversing only rather than upward movement and their main benefit was for climbers to improve finger strength during the winter months.

The first purpose built wall was created by climbers at Leeds University and is credited with contributing to a notable rise in climbing standards in Yorkshire at that time. The early walls were neither inspiring nor suitable for novices, groups or youngsters, but all that changed when the first modern wall opened in 1991. Climbers drove for hundreds of miles to visit The Foundry in Sheffield, which became a model for the new breed of wall, catering for a wide spectrum of users from the casual first timer to the dedicated high performance trainer. Youngsters became a growing user group and competitions became regular events.

Wall designers today must take into account all these various user groups and even small walls encompass a variety of angles from slabs to dramatic overhangs. Most medium to large walls have distinct bouldering and roped sections with the roped parts further separated into top-roping or leading areas. 'Trad' climbing sections are sometimes incorporated to allow for practising gear placements and some walls even have routes with stances where it is possible to learn the basics of multi-pitch climbing and abseiling.

More recently still, indoor walls have expanded to incorporate ice climbing, high ropes courses (see *A.4 High Ropes Courses* on page 216), caving and even skiing all under one roof. This phenomenon of the outdoors going indoors is a bizarre but growing trend, with climbing being hyped as the latest adrenaline and gym addict's sport. It is therefore no surprise that about 15% of wall users never climb outside at all.

Walls are listed in climbing magazines and the Mountaineering Councils produce directories to help interested parties locate their nearest facility.

# 9.1 Using walls

For smooth running and to prevent accidents climbing walls have to be managed effectively and each wall has its own set of rules or code of conduct. Many of the larger walls are members of the *Association of British Climbing Walls* (ABC) which promotes safe practise and quality management through agreed codes and standards.

It is normal practise that experienced climbers must take responsibility for their own safety by signing to acknowledge they are competent in putting on a harness, tying on and belaying. Novices must undergo an induction or period of training or be accompanied by an experienced adult who agrees to look after them. There are various policies about under-18s, with some walls insisting that all minors are accompanied by an adult, whilst others are happy to allow entry to those over 14 years who have been vetted or trained by the wall staff and have parental consent.

### 9.1.2 Safety
Most accidents at walls take place on the bouldering sections, normally due to bad landings resulting in shoulder dislocations, arm and ankle injuries. Climbers often assume the matting gives a greater protection from injury than is the case and take uncontrolled falls rather than climb or jump down. Such falls onto thick matting occasionally result in head injuries when the climber rebounds against the wall. Climbers wearing a harness are at risk of injury by landing on top of their own belay device so it is best to remove the harness altogether while bouldering. Extra gear taken into the building should be neatly stowed to prevent cluttering the climbing areas with objects that could be landed on or tripped over.

Many bouldering areas are overhanging or have caves and when busy there is a real danger of falling climbers landing on someone below. Awareness of who is above and below as well as resisting the temptation to lounge on the matting are crucial to minimise such collisions.

In the roped areas most accidents and near misses are due to belayer error, often caused by inexperience, poor communication or a moment of distraction. Lowering too fast and sloppy belaying of leaders result in climbers being dropped. When top-roping, many belayers fail to appreciate that it is important to keep the rope tight as the climber sets off in order to prevent them hitting the floor on rope stretch.

Experienced climbers too are occasionally caught off guard due to the relaxed atmosphere in walls. It is not uncommon, for example, for harness buckles to be left half threaded and knots improperly tied. Busy walls are noisy and there are often distractions, such as someone to talk to or watch, and it is also difficult to look up at the climber on steep routes without causing neck strain. These all reduce the vigilance of the belayer which, when coupled with low friction in the system, can result in difficulty in holding unexpected falls. Injuries sustained in a fall from height are obviously likely to be serious, though miraculously many climbers survive long falls due to the cushioned matting that many walls have, even in the roped areas.

In addition to damage sustained in falls many climbers find themselves with injuries due to over-use or pushing their bodies too hard. Strained tendons and pulled muscles are far too common and the biggest single contributory factor is not warming up properly (see **Chapter 3: Warming up** on page 21).

### 9.1.3 Techniques

Climbing on an indoor wall is really a simplified version of climbing outside on rock. The basic techniques of tying on and belaying are identical. In most walls there are options for top-roping and leading. Top-roping areas are set up ready for use and the climber simply ties to one end of the rope while the belayer attaches an appropriate belay device to the other. It is normal to clip the belay device to the harness belay loop ensuring the manufacturer's instructions are followed. Many climbing centres use specialised wall ropes designed to cope with the heavy demands of this environment; these have a higher proportion of sheath to core and the handling is stiff, particularly when new. Care is required when using a new, shiny rope in conjunction with a slick belay device.

Leading areas are normally equipped with quickdraws, but ropes are not provided for leading. Some walls insist on the use of single ropes but if half-ropes are used they must both be clipped into every runner and the anchor. Leaders should take particular care when clipping the second bolt, just as when outside, as it may be possible to hit the floor in a fall from alongside the second runner, if slack has been pulled up to clip. On reaching the top the leader will find either a specially shaped snap-link karabiner, a screwgate fixing or possibly both linked into two bolts. The snap-link may be adequate for the leader to lower off but for top-roping a screwgate is required.

The belayer should stand close to the base of the wall to avoid being pulled in when holding a fall (see *Figure 9.1*). Many belayers fail to do this because it makes viewing the leader awkward on steep routes. However, if the belayer stands sideways and turns to face outwards as the leader gets higher the belayer can watch without getting neck strain. A light belayer may consider attaching to a ground anchor if the leader is heavier; many walls have bolts in the floor or sandbags as

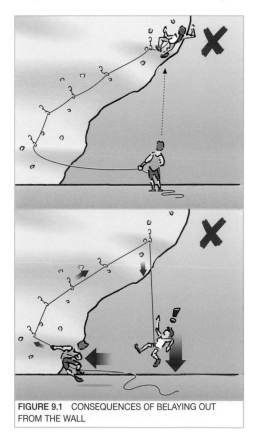

**FIGURE 9.1**  CONSEQUENCES OF BELAYING OUT FROM THE WALL

FIGURE 9.2 PRACTISING TECHNIQUE ON AN INDOOR CLIMBING WALL

**ROCK CLIMBING** – INDOOR CLIMBING WALLS

FIGURE 9.3 DANGER OF TOP-ROPING STEEP ROUTES WITHOUT THE QUICKDRAWS CLIPPED

weights for this purpose. In some cases it may be appropriate to belay directly from a ground anchor but climbers should check that the anchors are suitable to be used in this way.

When climbers are top-roping on overhanging routes it is important they re-clip the quickdraws as they lower off to avoid a subsequent climber taking a big swing in a fall. Though this may be fun for the climber, it is rarely amusing for the innocent bystander who receives the blow to the back of the head! (See *Figure 9.3*). Re-clipping on very steep walls is strenuous and awkward; it requires the belayer to lower and hold the climber alternately. The climber can either swing back and forth to grab the quickdraw or reach down to the next quickdraw as soon as possible. Then holding the quickdraw in both hands the climber continues being lowered until just below it, swinging the body in towards the wall and getting the feet on as the clip is made.

## 9.2 Transferring from indoors to outdoors

Making the transition from using indoor walls to climbing outside is a big step. Many competent wall-users who have gained considerable climbing fitness indoors find it frustrating going 'back to basics' for a while, but the process of gaining experience on rock is difficult to short cut without taking unnecessary risks.

There are several ways to smooth the transition. For example, many climbing walls, outdoor centres and qualified individuals offer specialist instruction in taking the next step safely. Alternatively, when joining a climbing club, the more experienced members are normally willing to show the way.

Many wall climbers start off outside by bouldering or on sport routes for simplicity and find this enables them to continue climbing at a technical grade close to that normally achieved indoors. However, new climbers should make themselves aware of the additional complexities involved. In particular how to move on different rock types, 'read' the moves, judge landings and assess the quality of bolts and lower-offs. (For bouldering see *7 Bouldering* on page 73 and for sport climbing see *11 Sport Climbing* on page 119).

Making the transition to leading 'trad' routes is undoubtedly the most complex. Whether under instruction or not this normally involves climbing routes that are technically much easier than normally climbed indoors, at least for a while. This ensures that the principles of placing protection, rope management and setting up belays can all be practised without 'testing the system' (or falling off) too often. Moving up through the grades (if this is an aim) will follow as experience and confidence grow.

The number of organised groups using climbing walls has steadily increased, in many cases providing walls with their greatest proportion of visitors. Some walls are designed to cope with such demand, whilst in others it creates conflicts of space just as on a crag and ways to avoid problems are similar to those used outside. Additionally there are several issues that are unique to the indoor environment.

## Other users

Some wall managers discourage groups during peak times to minimise conflict with other users and for the group to get the most out of a session. Novices may feel overwhelmed by the atmosphere in a busy room and find it difficult to concentrate on learning new skills. Operating on a quiet wall also makes the job of the instructor a great deal easier.

## Equipment

Most of the equipment used on a wall is identical to that used outside. Few climbers use helmets on a wall but most instructors prefer their group, especially children and novices who are less aware of the hazards, to wear them. Striking the head in an awkward fall is a possibility. Helmets make keeping an eye on the group easier and imparts an important safety message to novices who may go on to climb outside later. Some walls have policies about appropriate belay devices and techniques.

## Working at a busy wall

Effective group management and teaching is difficult in a noisy environment full of distractions. If it is impossible to find a quiet corner for initial briefings these may be better done beforehand or outside. For teaching and supervising it is normally best to keep the group close together but this becomes impossible at busy times. If the group is going to spread out it is essential that adequate supervision is not compromised.

Keeping the group in control without becoming a drill sergeant is at times difficult and instructors may opt to simplify the intended session to make life easier, bearing in mind the importance of safety above all else.

## Personal safety

Instructors should not neglect their own safety. For example when leading routes to set up additional top-ropes they should ensure the belayer is sufficiently competent and experienced to hold a fall and lower. Wall staff are also often available and willing to help out.

(For leading on walls see *10 Leading climbs* opposite and *11 Sport climbing* on page 119)

PATCH HAMMOND LEADING **THE BUTCHER** E3 5c, ST GOVANS, PEMBROKE

Everyone decides that they are ready for their first lead at a different point; for some it may follow a lengthy apprenticeship as a second whilst others may transfer from indoor to outdoor leading in a short space of time. Some try it and decide it's not for them.

# Leading climbs

**10**

# 10.1 Leading climbs

New leaders should have an appreciation of the risks involved and a grasp of the basic principles of placing runners and the forces involved in a fall, as well as the ability to construct a sound belay.

Evaluating the risks involved is difficult without previous experience. However, with eyes wide open and a common sense approach, many of the obvious dangers can be identified. Hazards during the approach include stonefall, a serious abseil or a tidal approach. On the route itself it is important to consider the spacing and quality of protection, loose holds and the nature of the belay at the top. It is also worth checking out the descent route. The experience of the belayer is of great importance, as the leader must have 100% confidence in the belayer to hold a fall.

Selecting an appropriate route for a first lead can make all the difference; a good choice is one that follows a well-protected obvious line at a grade easily within the leader's ability. It may even be a route previously seconded to give the psychological advantage of knowing the moves.

Finding the route and interpreting guidebook information coupled with the ability to read the rock is a crucial part of learning to lead that takes time and mileage. It is often helpful to match the crag and picture from a distance, locating key features, landmarks and routes. Once on the route signs of wear like polished holds and worn runner placements are good indicators that the right line is being followed, especially if it is a classic 'three star' route (for an explanation of the star system see *6.2 Climbing grades* on page 44). Some of this information is found in guidebooks, the rest is gained by inspecting the crag carefully and by talking to other climbers.

## 10.1.1 Lead rack

How much and what gear to carry is a balance between weight and covering every eventuality. A basic lead rack weighs in at between 3–4kg (6–8lb), but it is tweaked according to the nature of the route. Leaving behind the biggest runners when there are obviously no wide cracks can save up to a quarter of the total rack weight, whilst a crack of continuous width will require doubling or even tripling of a particular size. The likely nature of gear required for the top anchors must also be borne in mind.

The suggested lead rack below would be appropriate for most single pitch routes up to Very Severe grade (see *6.2 Climbing grades* on page 44). Longer pitches require more quickdraws and harder routes may call for specific items of gear such as micronuts or larger or smaller camming devices for example.

## 10.1.2 Organising the gear

To save time and avoid fumbling when placing runners, the gear should be racked in the same way every time. The exact order is a matter of personal preference but clipping gear in size order, being consistent with the way the karabiners face and clipping the belay device and screwgates

## Basic lead rack

| Wired nuts | Quickdraws |
|---|---|
| sizes 1–10 × 2 sets | 4 × short (10–15cm) and |
| (sizes 7–10 could be carried on rope) | 4 × long (25–30cm) carried doubled |

| Hexagonal nuts | Slings |
|---|---|
| sizes 5–8 | 2 × short (60cm) plus 2 snap-links on each |
| or | 2 × long (120cm) plus screwgate on each |

| Camming devices | Belay device |
|---|---|
| 2–3½ | with a screwgate, plus one or two spare screwgates for the belay |

out of the way at the back of the harness can all help. If the harness feels heavy and gear loops overcrowded, some gear can be carried over a shoulder on a bandolier. Slings can be carried diagonally across the chest with long slings clipped end to end with a karabiner for ease of removal.

## 10.2 Belaying

An optimum position for belaying a leader is standing side on to the rock with the brake hand furthest away from the rock. This reduces the possibility of letting go of the rope in self-preservation if pulled towards the rock when holding a fall. Just as important is a stable stance on even ground; this may be impossible amongst boulders in which case sitting may be better. A position close in to the rock minimises the outward load on the runners and the distance the belayer may be pulled in a fall (see *Figure 10.1*). If there is loose rock on the route a position close in but off to one side, out of the line of fire, is safer.

### 10.2.1 Anchor for the belayer
A ground anchor should be considered for the belayer if the leader might take a big fall or is significantly heavier than the belayer. If the route starts from an exposed ledge or steep ground, an anchor is needed to avoid the leader pulling the belayer off in a fall before placing the first runner. If none of these situations arise the belayer need not be anchored and is thus better able to move slightly in order to get a better view of the leader or dodge stonefall for example.

### 10.2.2 Technique for belaying a leader
The belayer feeds out slack with a hand on either side of the belay device, then slides the hands back down the rope to feed out more. This is done at the pace the leader is moving keeping the rope slightly slack. An arm's length of slack is paid out quickly as the leader clips a runner, more if the runner is above head height. The leader calls for 'Slack' and the belayer should anticipate it by watching closely. The leader doesn't want the slack too early yet equally doesn't want to be pulling hard for it. Patience is useful here; the belayer has a difficult job to do and the leader may be feeling stressed!

FIGURE 10.1   BELAYING CLOSE IN TO THE ROCK

Once a high runner has been clipped and the leader moves up, the belayer can take in the slack that is generated with the normal bombproof taking in technique (see *Taking in* on page 88). A belayer who watches the leader all the time anticipating the need for tight or slack rope, avoids chatting, drinking coffee or reading the guide book is worth their weight in gold! The leader needs to know that the belayer is ready to react at any moment otherwise confidence will be eroded.

### 10.2.3 Holding a fall
The anticipation of *holding a leader fall* for the first time is nerve-racking. "What will it feel like?" and," how easy will it be to hold?" are sensible questions to ask. An attentive belayer who is vigilant with the technique has nothing to fear. The brake hand stays firmly below the device and the belayer sits back to counteract the upward pull. Longer falls may pull the belayer off the ground and a small amount of lift is perfectly normal, indeed adds to a dynamic system. However,

if the belayer is pulled high off the ground the leader falls further so there may be a greater risk of injury or even the possibility of a ground fall. The belayer is also at risk of being lifted against overhanging rock.

### 10.2.4 Runner placements and spacing

*Runners* must be able to hold the downward force of a falling climber but must also resist an outward pull to avoid being lifted out. Multi-directional runners such as threads, cams or deep-seated nuts do this best but are not always available. To test how well a nut is seated it is first tugged downwards then gently flicked upwards; if it lifts out it should be seated again with some sharp tugs (this should be done with one hand firmly on a good hold). A nut that refuses to seat firmly may lift out when the leader climbs past it or in a fall and should be treated as marginal.

Extending runners adequately is essential to minimise tiring rope drag for the leader and help prevent runners lifting out; this is particularly important at any change of direction. Excessive friction created by the rope rubbing against the rock inhibits the energy absorbing capacity of the rope along its whole length. In other words rope drag can result in a shorter fall and less force at the belay but a greater force on the falling climber. If the rope is running over rough or sharp rock it may even lead to abrasion damage in a fall. There is often a trade-off between rope drag and length of fall, in other words most of the time climbers try to minimise rope drag by extending runners but not if the consequences of falling further are bad.

It is possible, though luckily infrequent, for the rope to unclip itself from a karabiner during a fall. This is most likely with bent gate karabiners and when the quickdraw sling is stiff. This problem is minimised by correct clipping in the first place. Avoid the rope running across the gate side of the karabiner or clipping from front to back, which twists the quickdraw. Clip from behind the karabiner with the gate facing away from the direction of travel (see *Figure 10.2*).

The first few runners in a pitch are placed to prevent a ground fall and the spacing needs to be closer here than higher up. The actual distance fallen is not only the distance climbed above a runner but also depends on the amount of rope stretch and slippage at the belay device, as well as how much slack or friction is in the system. In

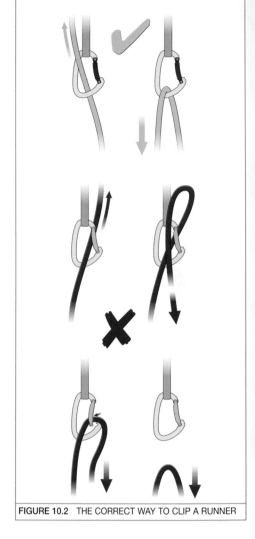

FIGURE 10.2  THE CORRECT WAY TO CLIP A RUNNER

other words the length of the fall is hard to predict but is usually further than imagined so the spacing of runners should reflect this. In reality though it is a case of placing runners as the opportunity arises.

*Bunching runners* before hard moves or unprotected sections is a sensible precaution, especially if their quality is marginal or uncertain. Getting comfortable and secure to place a runner with one hand whilst holding on with the other is a vital skill requiring good foot placements and subtle shifting of body position to take weight off the arms. Hanging off a straight arm helps make it less strenuous in some situations (see *Figure 10.3*).

FIGURE 10.3 HANGING OFF A STRAIGHT ARM WHILE PLACING A RUNNER TO MAKE IT LESS STRENUOUS

## 10.2.5 Traverses

Runners to protect the leader and second on *traverses* should be closely spaced to give both actual and psychological security (see *Figure 10.4*). Runners placed before hard moves protect the leader and after hard moves protect the second. Long quickdraws minimise rope drag and help prevent runners lifting out but at times this must be balanced against the length of the fall. If a traverse is poorly protected, the leader should attempt to belay back above the traverse so the second has a rope above them (see *Figure 10.5*). When moving onto a traverse having first climbed straight up an upward and outward pull is exerted on previous runners; this can be minimised by a multi-directional runners at the start of the traverse (see *Figure 10.6*). Routes with long traverse sections are easier to protect with double-ropes; this is covered in **Double-rope technique** on page 134.

*In-situ* runners such as pegs, threads and jammed gear are sometimes 'lifesavers', providing quick security but they should be assessed

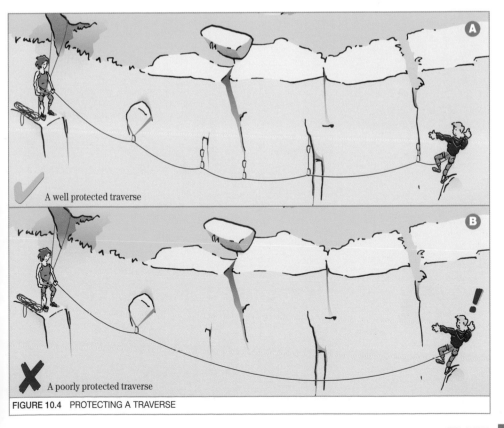
A well protected traverse

A poorly protected traverse

FIGURE 10.4 PROTECTING A TRAVERSE

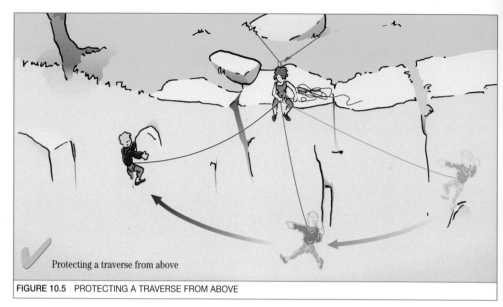

Protecting a traverse from above

**FIGURE 10.5**  PROTECTING A TRAVERSE FROM ABOVE

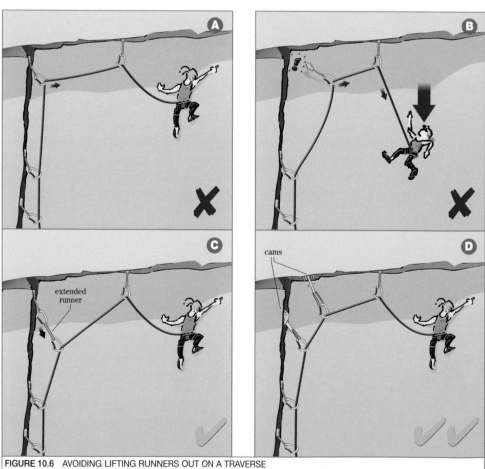

extended runner

cams

**FIGURE 10.6**  AVOIDING LIFTING RUNNERS OUT ON A TRAVERSE

FIGURE 10.7 *IN-SITU* RUNNERS ARE USED CAUTIOUSLY. HERE THE LEADER AVOIDS USING THE OLD TAPE ON A TIED-OFF PEG BY ADDING HIS OWN

FIGURE 10.8 A CLIMBER DEMONSTRATING GOOD 'IN-FLIGHT' TECHNIQUE WHEN FALLING

realistically as they may have been damaged by falls or natural ageing (see *6.8 Anchor selection* on page 58). Leaders often clip an *in-situ* runner as protection before a better runner is placed (see *Figure 10.7*).

### 10.2.6 Falling off

Taking falls into space on steep routes is preferable to falling on easy angled ground or above ledges. Extra runners should be placed to protect hard moves above bad landings. Anticipating the fall and pushing away from the rock can help avoid scrapes and knocking runners out (see *Figure 10.8*). Sprained ankles can be avoided by swinging into the rock with relaxed legs, absorbing the impact with bent knees. In a long fall it is often best to hold the rope to prevent it wrapping around a leg. Headfirst falls are often a result of the leader being flipped by the rope; a foot or leg behind the rope can cause this. The rope must be positioned carefully between the body and the rock to avoid this, using a toe or knee to flick the rope out of the way and stepping through. Avoid the rope running underneath the thigh (see *Figure 10.9A & B*).

### 10.2.7 Backing off

In some situations backing off or retreating back down the pitch is preferable to falling. In particular, on easy angled ground or if the runners are poor. The belayer can play a vital role by giving the encouragement and advice needed for the leader

> **Wearing a helmet undoubtedly makes leader falls safer.**

to down climb to the nearest runner, which can be checked, backed-up if required and then lowered off from. It is safest to leave all runners in place to back-up the top runner (as they can be retrieved later); lowering should be slow and smooth.

### 10.2.8 At the top

After topping-out, taking a moment to regain composure will let the adrenaline subside and enable the leader to focus clearly on setting up a belay. Once the first anchor has been placed this should be clipped like a runner as a safeguard whilst looking for others. The basic principles of belaying at the top are the same as when setting up a top-rope, covered on page 81.

## 10.3 Communication

Belaying in sight of the second eliminates most communication problems. Once out of sight, even on short routes, it can be difficult to hear shouts above wind, sea or road noise. *Climbing calls* are a universally recognised system that should minimise confusion when communication is difficult. It is much easier to interpret a snatch of a shout when it is expected. In other words, climbers anticipate the calls according to

FIGURE 10.9   ENSURE THE ROPE DOESN'T GO BEHIND THE LEG

how much rope has fed out, at what pace and how long it's taken.

When it is obvious that communication is going to be a problem it is wise to set a simple strategy in place beforehand; this normally involves a system of tugs. Individual tugs can be confused with the leader pulling up slack to clip a runner, so it is safer to use several sharp tugs to indicate "I'm safe". The second can remove the belay device and then wait. The leader takes in all the slack and then repeats the tugs to indicate

"Climb when you're ready". Experienced climbers also anticipate when the leader has stopped climbing, is belayed, is taking in and so on, by watching all the rope movements carefully.

Learning all the climbing calls at once may be information overload for new climbers. It may be best to stress just the key call, *"Climb when you're ready,"* so the second knows not to make a move until that signal is heard. The other calls are less crucial and can be introduced gradually.

## Climbing calls

| Leader: | *"Safe"* |
| | (I'm attached to the anchors or no longer need belaying) |
| Second: | *"You're off belay"* or *"Take in"*. (Pull up the slack rope) |
| Leader: | *"Taking in"* |
| | (I'm pulling up the slack rope) |
| Second: | *"That's me"* |
| | (There is no more slack) |
| Leader: | *"Climb when you're ready"* |
| | (I have you on belay) |
| Second: | *"Climbing"* (I'm setting off) |
| Leader: | *"OK"* (I'm watching you) |

In addition the second may use:
- *"Slack"* (I need some rope)
- *"Take in"* (Take the rope in)
- *"Tight rope"* (Take the rope in)
- *"Watch me here"* (I'm at a tricky move and might fall)
- *"I'm off"* or *"Take"* (I'm about to fall off)

Avoid climbing call hybrids such as "Take in slack", as they only result in confusion.

TIM EMMETT ON **ROAD RAGE** F7b+, CHENE CLIFF, PORTLAND, DORSET

Photo: Mike Robertson

# Sport climbing

**Sport climbing takes place on bolt-protected routes which, in the UK, are found predominantly on single pitch limestone crags and some quarries.**

The nature of the rock at sport climbing venues tends to be compact, with the majority of routes graded 5b or above (see *6.2 Climbing grades* on page 44). The French grading system, which has been adopted at most *sport climbing* venues, requires translating to make a comparison with UK trad grades; sport grades are roughly 1–2 grades higher, so an F6b would be a UK 5b/5c (see *Table 6.1 A comparative table of climbing grades* on page 45 for a comparison). Climbers often try pushing their grade when climbing on bolts, as there are fewer concerns about poor runners and falling. It should be noted though, that bolt quality varies from venue to venue and deteriorates with time, so they should always be inspected for signs of corrosion or damage.

It is often assumed that sport climbing is a non-serious facet of the sport and this is true up to a point. There are few objective hazards, the protection is reliable and the decision making simple. However, accidents still occur, often involving experienced climbers making silly mistakes or through poor communication. Sport route lengths vary and it is not unknown for climbers to lower off a route without noticing the rope is too short. The simple precaution of tying a knot in the end of the rope or always tying it to the rope bag can prevent this. Other examples of incidents include the climber leaning back at the anchors to lower without realising the belayer has removed the belay device and casual belaying resulting in longer falls than necessary. Vigilance and simple, effective systems are required in sport climbing as much as any other area.

# 11.1 Types of bolt

The two main types of bolt are *expansion bolts* and *cemented* or *glued bolts*. Expansion bolts normally have a 10mm or 12 mm diameter stem or sleeve, which expands to grip the drilled hole as the bolt is screwed in. A karabiner is clipped

## Equipment

Sport climbing requires very little specialist equipment that is not included in a normal equipment list (see page 112). However, the following items make life easier:

### Rope
A single rope is the best choice although two half-ropes will suffice as they can be clipped alternately as normal or both into each bolt as a twin system.

However, this is harder than clipping a single rope and can become messy. A 60 metre single rope allows lowering off from almost every sport route and two 50 metre half-ropes would allow the leader to abseil from the same point.

### 10–15 Quickdraws
Most of these should be short to minimise fall length with a couple of longer ones for reducing rope drag. It is best to have an ordinary gate karabiner

for clipping to the bolt and a bent gate for ease of clipping in the rope. Be wary of altering their role as the bolt karabiner can get nicks in the metal from the bolts themselves, which may then damage the rope.

### Belay device
Many climbers opt for an auto-locking device for holding repeated falls or a slick device for ease of paying out slack but the belayer must be confident in holding any fall.

### Screwgate
Often used on the first bolt for additional security.

Sling and screwgate used as a cow's tail for attaching to the lower-off.

Old karabiner for leaving behind.

### Clip stick
For pre-clipping the first bolt.

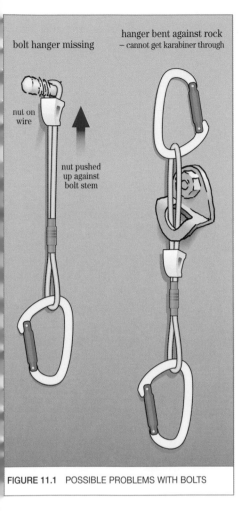

bolt hanger missing

hanger bent against rock
– cannot get karabiner through

nut on wire

nut pushed up against bolt stem

FIGURE 11.1 POSSIBLE PROBLEMS WITH BOLTS

FIGURE 11.2 REPLACING AN OLD EXPANSION BOLT WITH A GLUED BOLT

to an integral or additional hanger screwed onto the stem. The hanger can not be lowered from directly so at the lower-off two expansion bolts are normally linked to create a central lowering point, ideally with a chain and ring.

Glued bolts can be a single stem with a captive eye or a 'U' staple; these are normally fixed into the drilled hole with epoxy glue, which also helps to protect the steel from corrosion. The quickdraw is clipped straight to the eye or staple and they can be lowered off from directly.

Bolts should always be inspected for signs of damage. On expansion bolts the hanger can be damaged by repeated falls or it may unscrew or be missing altogether. A wired nut can be placed on a hangerless stem or slid through a bent hanger that is too tight a fit for a karabiner (see *Figure 11.1*). Less obvious damage is caused by corro-

sion, which can attack and weaken the stem. Corrosion is often most pronounced where the stem enters the rock and in severe cases can cause the bolt to snap.

## 11.2 Reaching the first bolt

If the moves off the ground to reach the first bolt are tricky, the belayer can act as a spotter. Alternatively, the first bolt can be pre-clipped by using a telescopic *clip stick* with a quickdraw and the rope attached. Alternatively it may be possible to clip the first bolt from an adjacent route whilst lowering off. This is done by reaching across and clipping a quickdraw to the bolt, then clipping the rope in and also clipping the rope above this bolt to a quickdraw attached to the harness belay loop. Having lowered off, the rope is pulled down from the anchors leaving the rope through the new bolt (see *Figure 11.3*).

## 11.3  Clipping bolts

In an ideal world the leader should clip each bolt from a comfortable position having climbed alongside it (see *Figure 11.6*). This minimises the amount of slack out and is much less strenuous than clipping from below. ***Clipping the bolt*** at full stretch is tempting, as it effectively gives the leader a runner above their head but is more likely to result in fumbles and longer falls if the climber falls before clipping the rope in. Care is needed in particular at the second bolt where it is often possible to hit the ground in a fall when attempting to clip it with an armful of slack.

### 11.3.1  At the lower-off

When the ***lower-off*** is reached it is normal to clip any part of it as a runner initially; the belayer takes the weight of the leader at this point if required. The leader should then take a moment to recompose while deciding how to arrange the lower-off. There are a few options according to whether the route is to be lead again, ***top-roped*** or ***stripped***. If the route is to be lead again, the leader need only clip at least two quickdraws to the anchor, ideally directly to the bolts and lower from these. If the route is to be top-roped, screwgates can be used to replace the quickdraws, or the anchors are threaded with the rope.

### 11.3.2  Threading the lower-off

The leader attaches to one or both of the anchors with a cow's tail or a quickdraw but remains belayed from below, asking for slack as necessary but without shouting "safe" to avoid any confusion. If the bolts are staple type or there is a ring or Maillon wide enough to take two strands of rope, a bight of rope is threaded through them. A figure of eight is tied in this bight and clipped to a screwgate on the harness belay loop. The original knot is untied and the loose end of the rope pulled through the lower-off (see *Figure 11.5*).

If it is not possible to feed a bight of rope through the lower-off, the leader has to untie from the rope and thread a single strand instead.

FIGURE 11.3  CLIPPING THE FIRST BOLT OF AN ADJACENT ROUTE AND USING A QUICKDRAW TO BRING DOWN A BIGHT OF ROPE. WHEN THE CLIMBER UNTIES AND PULLS THE ROPE THROUGH THE TOP ANCHOR, IT IS LEFT CLIPPED INTO THE FIRST BOLT OF THE OTHER ROUTE.

FIGURE 11.4  USING A QUICKDRAW TO STAY IN LINE WITH THE ROUTE WHILST STRIPPING IT

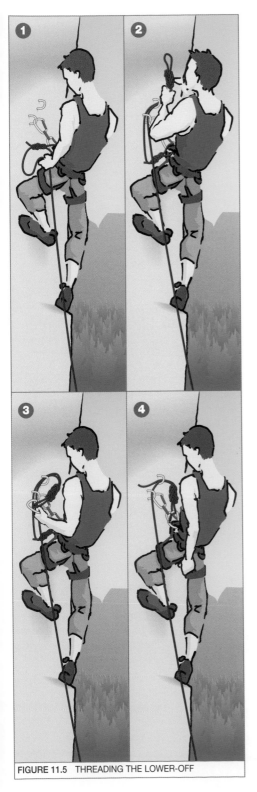

Before doing this the leader should tie a figure of eight in the rope and clip it to the harness belay loop; this serves as additional security and as a back up if the rope is dropped. The anchor is threaded with the end of the rope, which is then tied back though the harness and the figure of eight back-up untied.

Since leaders sometimes abseil from the lower-off, it is crucial to avoid confusion with the belayer. Before lowering off the leader should look down and communicate with the belayer who takes in any slack before holding the leader's weight. It is always worth the leader having one final check of the knot and anchor before unclipping the cow's tail and lowering off.

### 11.3.3 Stripping routes

The leader may need to strip the route if no one is seconding or to make life easier for the second. On traversing or steep lines it is better for the runners to be left in place to protect the second from pendulums or swinging away from the rock. To keep the leader in line with the route and in contact with the rock whilst lowering, a quick-draw is clipped from the harness belay loop to the rope (see *Figure 11.4*). The belayer stops the leader just above each bolt to remove the quick-draw from it.

On steep routes stripping the quickdraws can be very strenuous. The leader may need to pull in to the next bolt on the rope leading down to the belayer. The harness quickdraw is usually re-clipped below the bolt before unclipping the rope from the quickdraw and then removing it from the bolt. It may be necessary for the leader to unweight the rope by pulling onto the rock in order to do this.

At the lowest bolt on overhanging routes there is the potential for the leader to unclip and take a massive swing that could result in hitting the ground. To avoid this the leader pulls onto the rock, unclips the bolt but then climbs back up the route a bit before lowering off. If the climbing is hard above the lowest bolt the next to last bolt is left clipped while stripping the final bolt.

FIGURE 11.5  THREADING THE LOWER-OFF

FIGURE 11.6 CLIPPING FROM ALONGSIDE THE BOLT

# Problem avoidance & solving

BELAYER HAS A CLEAR VIEW OF HIS PARTNER ON **THE ASP** E3 6a, STANAGE

The best way to deal with
problems on the crag is to
avoid them in the first place.

When climbers and instructors are asked how often and what sort of problems they've encountered when rock climbing, the answers are usually "not many" and "quite mundane".

Epic tales involving major evacuations from the crag are thankfully few and far between. However, those same climbers and instructors also admit to feeling reassured by having a repertoire of rope tricks tucked in the corner of their memory 'just in case', much like knowing that the first aid kit is always packed in the rucksack.

Inexperienced climbers find that simple little things do go wrong or nearly wrong quite often, whilst experienced climbers are able to avoid those same mistakes.

Anticipating and avoiding problems in the first place is the best option; failing that most problems can be solved by *TLC*, in this case, *T*ight rope, *L*ooking for the easiest option and *C*oaxing to continue upwards or downwards (but a little tender loving care won't go amiss either). When even this doesn't work the application of common sense and a few simple rope techniques should do the rest.

Gaining insight from others' mistakes is a useful way to shortcut the learning process. The majority of simple problems are due to:
- poor route choice;
- inaccurate route finding;
- lack of communication between belayer and climber;
- belaying in an inappropriate place;
- lazy or sloppy belay technique;
- poor group management; and
- poor judgement of the ability of partners or groups.

All of these problems are avoidable! Some problems are unavoidable but even these, especially at single pitch venues, are normally simple to solve. Problems that are most likely to occur with groups under instruction whilst bottom-roping or abseiling are covered elsewhere (see *8.4 Bottom-roping* on page 90 and page 96 for *8.5 Abseiling in a single pitch environment*). Other situations that may arise in normal climbing situations are described below.

If a leader or second has fallen and is injured it is almost always possible to lower them directly to the ground and sort the problem out there. This is normally the quickest, simplest and safest option. A second who is frozen through fear will usually respond to gentle coaxing and reassurance combined with taking the rope in tight to persuade them either up or down. A frozen leader may need coaxing in order to back-off the route (see *10 Leading climbs* on page 111) or the help of a top-rope or abseil rope from a neighbouring team. Climbers who are in difficulty shouldn't be afraid to ask or shout for help; other climbers are almost always willing to assist knowing that one day it may be them needing the help.

On the rare occasion that a second or leader is well and truly crag-fast and there is no help at hand, the belayer may need to be inventive or try something a little more complicated. Every situation is different but will probably involve either a simple hoist (see page 163) to get a stuck second past a tricky move or escaping the system in order to abseil down or go for help. The following techniques are ones that are not overly complicated and useful in a number of situations.

Additional and more complex problem solving techniques are covered in *Chapter 15: Multi-pitch problem solving*, from page 155.

# 12.1  Prusiking

The ability to *ascend a fixed rope* may come in handy in a number of situations. Climbers who have abseiled in at the wrong location or discovered the intended route too difficult may need to escape up the abseil rope. This is most common at sea cliffs where the routes cannot always be viewed from the top. At venues where there is no easy escape it is wise to leave the abseil rope in place until the climb is completed. A second who has fallen off a traverse onto unclimbable ground or is simply unable to follow a pitch may also need to climb the rope they are hanging on.

- Tie an ordinary prusik to the abseil rope and attach this directly to the harness belay loop with a screwgate karabiner.
- Tie a French prusik below this and attach a long sling, either with a karabiner or directly using a lark's foot. Create a foot loop in the sling with an overhand knot or by clove hitching the sling around the foot, alternatively use a lark's foot to make a step in loop (see *Figure 12.1*).

FIGURE 12.1   PRUSIKING UP A ROPE

### Never rely on a prusik alone

Add a safety back-up by tying a clove hitch in the rope below the prusiks to a screwgate attached to the harness belay loop and feed slack through the clove hitch at regular intervals. This method can also be used to descend ropes. Other combinations of prusik knots can be used as long as they bite the rope effectively.

- Alternate weight between prusiks by standing in the foot loop whilst sliding the top prusik then hanging from this to move the foot prusik. Prusiks must be completely unweighted before sliding; the ordinary prusik is loosened with a thumb flick against the knot before sliding.

## 12.2  Accompanied abseil

There are occasions when it may be advantageous for an experienced climber to abseil alongside

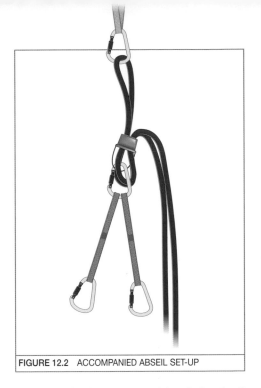

FIGURE 12.2   ACCOMPANIED ABSEIL SET-UP

someone who is nervous or injured. An abseil rope is arranged as normal, remembering that the anchors must be solid enough to hold the combined weight of two people. The basic set-up is simple: one abseil device with two slings attached (see *Figure 12.2*). The more experienced abseiler or 'rescuer' must ensure there is sufficient friction to make a controlled descent and should always use a safety back-up (see *8.5 Abseiling in a single pitch environment* on page 96). Adding a second friction device to the rope above the first and connecting the two together can increase friction. The sling lengths can be varied to put the climbers side by side if the injuries are minor or one below the other if the 'casualty' needs looking after. The casualty can dangle below and face the rescuer if the ground is steep or slightly above and across the rescuer's lap on easier angled rock. In this position the rescuer can pull the casualty clear of obstacles (see *Figure 12.3*).

### 12.2.1  Tying off a belay device

Tying off the **belay device** while it is loaded involves a little dexterity but should only take a few seconds. It is best done in a way that also allows it to be easily untied again whilst still under load. With the rope held tightly in the locked off position a small bight of rope is fed

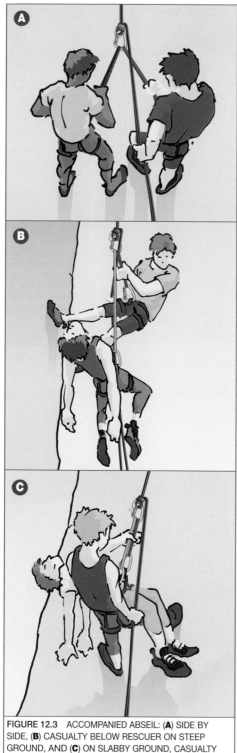

FIGURE 12.3   ACCOMPANIED ABSEIL: (**A**) SIDE BY SIDE, (**B**) CASUALTY BELOW RESCUER ON STEEP GROUND, AND (**C**) ON SLABBY GROUND, CASUALTY ABOVE RESCUER, ACROSS LAP

through the karabiner. A second bight of rope is passed through this first bight so it jams against the karabiner, ideally on the back bar. At this point the rope should no longer slip through the belay device and the rope is secured by tying one or two half hitches either around the back bar of the karabiner or on the loaded rope just in front of the belay device. Tying off an Italian hitch is done in the same way except it is tied in front of the knot (see *Figure 8.31* on page 103). The tail can be clipped back to the anchor as an additional back-up.

### 12.2.2  Escaping from the system

Very, very occasionally it may be necessary for the belayer to get out of the system in order to give assistance to a stuck or injured partner or to go and get additional help. Sometimes it may be necessary to escape in order to get a better view of what the problem is. It should be remembered that escaping the system is normally a last resort when all the simple and obvious measures have failed.

This basic procedure will vary according to how the belayer is attached to the anchors. If a direct belay is being used escaping is simple because there is no load on the belayer, the belay device (often an Italian hitch) is tied off and the belayer is free to 'escape'. When the belayer is tied to the anchors as in most normal climbing situations the process is slightly more complex, see Example 1 opposite. If the anchors are not centralised with slings or are out of arm's reach it is different again, see example two.

Yet another way to escape, and the simplest of all, is to tie off the belay device, unbuckle the harness and climb out of it. This is very quick but care must be taken if the belayer is in an exposed position and it can only work if the harness itself plays no part in the system.

## Personal safety

**Rescuers who have escaped the system MUST ENSURE THEIR OWN SAFETY by moving carefully away from the edge or by arranging another attachment to the anchors, with a sling and karabiner for example.**

# Escaping from the system

## Example 1

The belayer is tied on with the rope; anchors in reach and centralised.

**1** Tie off the belay device.

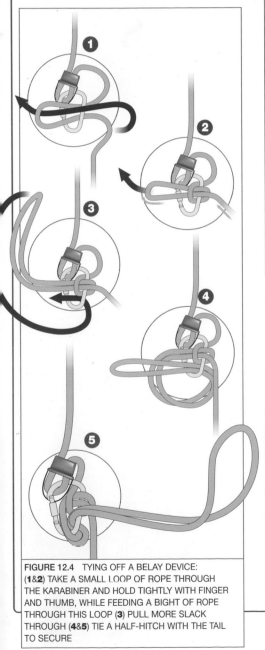

FIGURE 12.4 TYING OFF A BELAY DEVICE: (**1&2**) TAKE A SMALL LOOP OF ROPE THROUGH THE KARABINER AND HOLD TIGHTLY WITH FINGER AND THUMB, WHILE FEEDING A BIGHT OF ROPE THROUGH THIS LOOP (**3**) PULL MORE SLACK THROUGH (**4&5**) TIE A HALF-HITCH WITH THE TAIL TO SECURE

**2** Attach a French prusik to the loaded rope in front of the belay device. Connect this prusik with a sling to the main anchor point and tighten up.

French prusik

**3** Untie the belay device locking knot and feed through slack until the load is transferred via the prusik to the anchor; watch for slippage at the prusik.

# Escaping from the system *Example 1 continued*

**4** Tie the rope back to the anchor as a back-up with either a clove hitch or better, a tied off Italian Hitch

**5** The belayer is now able to remove the belay device and escape, the anchors are checked and backed up if necessary.

# Escaping from the system

## Example 2

The belayer is tied on with the rope but the anchors are either out of reach or not centralised.

Identical to Example 1 except at stage two rather than attach the French prusik to the main anchor point, it is connected to another prusik wrapped around the anchor ropes. A *Klemheist* tied with a long sling works well in this situation.

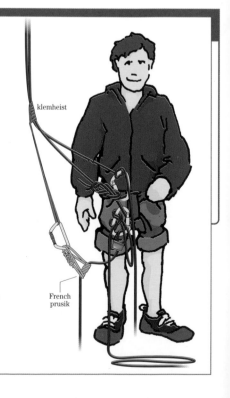

klemheist

French prusik

JAS HEPBURN ON **SPIDER** HVS 5a, EAST FACE OF AONACH DUBH, GLEN COE       Photo: Allen Fyffe

# Part IV

# Multi-pitch climbing

There are hundreds of multi-pitch crags across the length and breadth of the UK and Ireland with variety to match the quantity. At one end of the spectrum are roadside crags like Tremadog in North Wales with routes up to 70m that involve two and three pitch routes, whilst at the other extreme Ben Nevis has routes more than 400m high involving at least 11 pitches, from which a retreat would prove a lengthy procedure. To add to the variety, there are also sea stacks that require a boat ride, swim or tyrolean traverse just to get started and long mountaineering routes such as those on the Cuillin of Skye which combine pitched climbing with easier scrambling sections.

Techniques for moving efficiently on the scrambling sections of multi-pitch routes are considered in *Part V*, starting on page 171.

Scotland hosts the largest and remotest cliffs in the UK with some venues being visited by only a handful of climbers in a year. The 300m high sandstone headland at St John's Head on the Isle of Hoy is one such example, though the neighbouring sea stack known as the Old Man of Hoy is a relatively popular attraction. In the North West Highlands a three hour walk-in to reach the cliffs is not unusual; Carnmore crag tucked away in the midst of the wild Fisherfield mountains and the Triple Buttress on Beinne Eighe are two of Scotland's more remote mountain venues.

Climbing in Ireland is also a relatively solitary experience, especially on its multi-pitch crags. The best known and impressive of these is Fairhead on Antrim's north coast, where over two miles of columnar dolerite form endless vertical cracks and chimneys up to 90m in height. Granite mountain crags abound in Ireland, some with easy access and friendly open climbing such as Glendalough in the Wicklow Hills and Pigeon Rock in the Mourne Mountains. Others require one and a half-hours of walking to isolated loughside settings, as is the case at Lough Belshade in Donegal. One of the country's finest glacial corries hosts the unique Coumshingaun, with two and three pitch routes set amongst cliffs of knobbly conglomerate up to 350m high.

The mountains of England and Wales have more accessible crags with higher concentrations of both routes and climbers. Most of the Lake District's mountain crags are reached on good paths in one or two hours. Esk Buttress and the Central Buttress on Scafell, and Gimmer Crag in the Langdale Valley typify the idyllic settings and compact volcanic cliffs of good quality rock and routes.

Wales' speciality is variety and accessibility. A 20-minute walk from the road in the Ogwen Valley gives access to linked climbs totalling 300m from an introductory warm-up on the Idwal Slabs to a grand finale near the summit of Glyder Fawr. Next door in the Llanberis Pass, a three kilometre long stretch of road gives access to ten major cliffs and over twenty minor ones; it is little wonder there is a parking problem in the valley. Adventurous sea cliff excursions abound in Wales from the esoteric flavour of the Llyn Peninsula to the popular quartzite cliffs of Gogarth on Anglesey and the limestone of Pembroke. For a taste of more remote Welsh rock, Cadair Idris and the quiet cwms of mid-Wales hold the answer.

## Hazards

Multi-pitch venues, whether big or small, have a greater number of challenges than their single pitch neighbours. Ledges, breaks and lines of weakness conceal loose rock even if the routes themselves are sound. Adventurous sheep or goats as well as careless climbers are often to blame for stonefall sent down otherwise solid crags. Mountain cliffs in particular are exposed to forces of erosion; cycles of freeze/thaw action ensure an abundant supply of loosened rock waiting to be knocked off in the spring by the unwary. Certain rock types are inherently unstable with big rock falls occurring periodically with or without climbers; often the climber just happens to be the final straw.

Complex approaches and descents create their own hazards, sometimes taking climbers into the looser areas of the cliff, which can also be natural channels or funnels for stonefall. Climbing in the mountains calls for an appreciation of the environment and an awareness of additional skills that may be required to deal with extreme and changeable weather, navigation in poor visibility or darkness, route finding in complex terrain and river crossings. Minor incidents acquire an additional seriousness due to scale, remoteness and inaccessibility, whilst more serious accidents such as being struck by stonefall or sustaining an injury in a fall half-way up a mountain route with a two hour walk-out are a daunting prospect.

GEORGE SMITH USING EFFECTIVE ROPE WORK ON **FREEBIRD** E1 5b, CASTELL HELEN, GOGARTH

This chapter outlines appropriate gear and techniques for multi-pitch climbing, including methods of coaching, instructing and guiding.

**Rope work**

# 13

The rope work and techniques used on single pitch routes are basically similar to those required on longer climbs. The main differences involve route finding, communication and belaying on ledges where space and choice of anchors may be limited. For these reasons climbers new to multi-pitch routes often find them both intimidating and awkward, so it is wise to initially select routes that have short pitches and obvious, large stances. Many climbers choose routes a grade or two below their normal leading standard until they feel confident on longer climbs.

When deciding what to carry on a route first consider timing, being realistic about how long it could take to lead, find a belay and second each pitch. Thirty minutes per pitch is a fast time but an hour is not unusual if the grade is near the climber's limit. Add on a little extra time for going off-route, retrieving a piece of jammed gear or having a bite to eat and suddenly a five-pitch route with a two-hour approach and complicated descent is looking like a very long day! A few extra items in pockets, a jumper tied around the waist and shoes clipped onto the back of the harness may suffice in mid-summer otherwise a light rucksack can be carried by the second.

If it is not planned to return to the base of the route to collect gear after the climb, careful thought should be given to footwear and rucksack contents in the first place to avoid carrying excess gear on the climb. A climbing rucksack should be close-fitting, narrow and compact; those with a stiff internal frame tend to catch the back of the helmet when the head is tilted. The waist belt should sit above the harness or be clipped out of the way around the back so it does not block access to gear loops (see *Figure 13.1*).

An appropriate rack for a multi-pitch route should not only include the gear likely to be needed as runners, but also gear for a belay at either end of the pitch (a typical belay requires 2–3 pieces of gear plus karabiners). Select appropriate gear from *Additional gear for multi-pitch routes* (opposite) according to the route, location and conditions, remembering that it is important to get the right balance between being adequately prepared and over-burdened. An attempt to carry all the items listed would be epic!

**FIGURE 13.1** CLIMBING WITH A LIGHT RUCKSACK ON **MAIN WALL** HS 4b, CYRN LAS

# 13.1 Route finding

The key to successful *route finding* on long climbs is to have a mental map of the bigger picture. This is gained from viewing the crag at a distance, studying the guidebook picture and reading all relevant information, which may be contained in the introduction as well as the route description itself and perhaps even in the descriptions of neighbouring climbs. Time spent working this out beforehand is rarely wasted. Major features on the crag should be identified and their relationship to the selected route noted, as this will help 'navigation' when on the rock.

# 13.2 Double-rope technique

Most climbers choose *double-ropes* for multi-pitch routes as they help reduce rope drag and give greater scope for protection. For example runners that are off to one side can be clipped without zig-zagging the rope. Two ropes also make an abseil retreat more efficient.

# Additional gear for multi-pitch routes

- Extra long (120cm) slings with screwgates
- Extra quickdraws, especially longer ones. Short (60cm) slings tripled can be used as quickdraws or slings – *Figure 13.2* shows how
- Additional technical gear as required by the route, plus 4–6 extra karabiners, an extra set of nuts and some additional hexes or camming devices to equip the belays
- Prusik loops, old karabiner, abseil 'tat' and small penknife: for retreats and descents
- Guidebook or copy of route description and descent information

- Lightweight wind/waterproof and warm layer (clothing that fits in a stuff-sack that can be clipped to the harness is useful)
- One belay jacket that can be switched between belayers
- Food and drink
- Footwear for descent
- Rucksack or bumbag
- Map and compass
- Small first aid kit
- Head torch
- Whistle
- Lightweight survival blanket or small group shelter

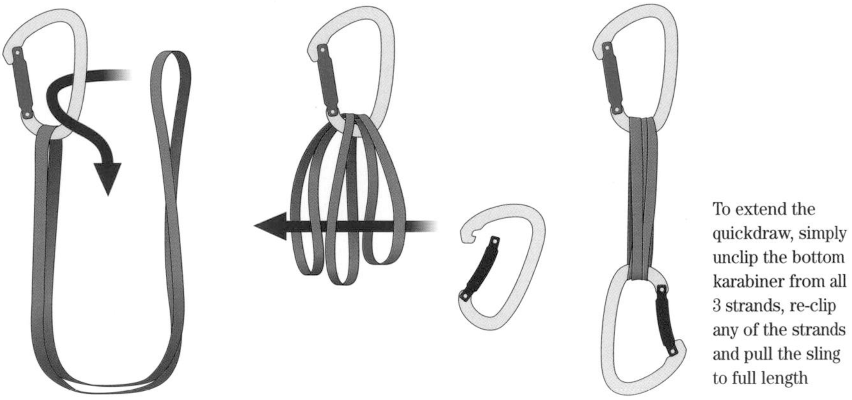

To extend the quickdraw, simply unclip the bottom karabiner from all 3 strands, re-clip any of the strands and pull the sling to full length

**FIGURE 13.2** SHORTENING A SLING

The climbers tie the two ropes through their harness as normal ensuring they both have the same left and right rope without twists in between. If the pitch is straight up, the leader clips runners alternately; otherwise they are clipped left or right side as appropriate (see *Figure 13.3*). **Traverses** can be protected to keep rope drag to a minimum by clipping runners alternately or one rope for the higher runners and one for the lower ones (see *Figure 13.4A*). Alternatively one rope can be clipped along the traverse and the other kept free so it protects the second from above (see *Figure 13.4B*).

***Attaching to the anchors*** with two ropes is straightforward; one rope can be clipped to each

anchor and the belay device is clipped to both central rope loops.

The technique of ***belaying double-ropes*** requires some practise; having firm control of both ropes whilst paying out or taking in slack on just one at a time is tricky to master. Many climbers find it helps to separate the two ropes on both the dead and live rope sides. On the dead rope the break hand splits the rope between the ring and middle fingers. The thumb and first two fingers curl around both ropes all the time while the last two fingers grip just one. This makes it easier to grip one rope while the other is paid out or taken in, yet still have a firm grip on both ropes at all times. On the live rope the hand can

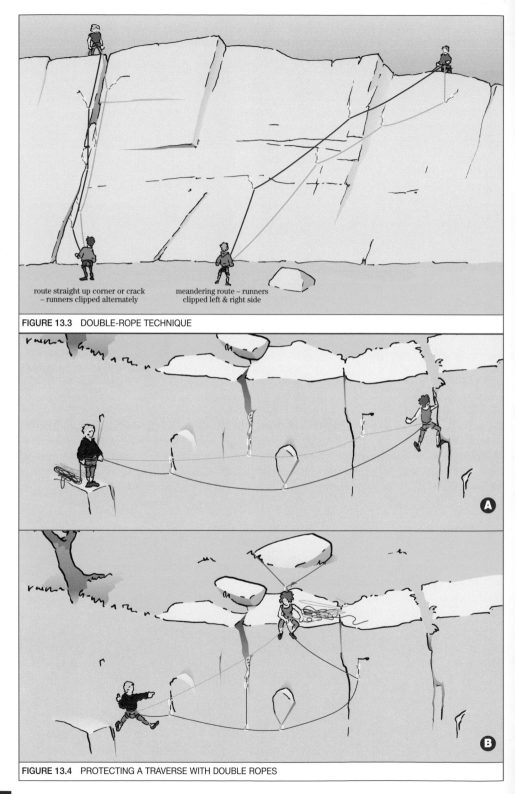

route straight up corner or crack
– runners clipped alternately

meandering route – runners
clipped left & right side

**FIGURE 13.3** DOUBLE-ROPE TECHNIQUE

**Ⓐ**

**Ⓑ**

**FIGURE 13.4** PROTECTING A TRAVERSE WITH DOUBLE ROPES

alternate between ropes, hold both together or split them between the fingers (see *Figure 13.5*).

## 13.3 Belaying and stance organisation

The **anchors** selected on intermediate stances need to withstand a downward load if the second slips off and must also resist an upward pull if the leader falls from the next pitch. The best choice of anchors are those that take a multi-directional load such as threads, deep-seated nuts and camming devices. Sometimes it is necessary to make a move or two up the next pitch to get a suitable placement. Anchors that are at the front of a ledge are awkward to make use of, unless for an upward pull. On loose rock or if the choice of anchors is poor many pieces may be needed to create a good belay (see *Figure 13.6*).

Small ledges often become **semi-hanging** stances which require the belayer to lean on the anchors in order to stay on the ledge. In this situation, the anchors selected and method of attaching must give good support to the belayer. The rope can be stowed by **lapping** it back and forth over the anchor ropes; this is best done neatly by gradually decreasing the length of the fold each time so it pays out smoothly later. Alternatively, it can be lapped over a foot and transferred to a sling clipped to an anchor.

On **constricted** stances it is important to ensure the brake hand is not blocked by the rock (see *Figure 13.7*). Ideally the same **belay position** is used for bringing up a second and belaying a leader, but occasionally some adjustments are needed. For example, the obvious position for the belayer to be in while bringing up the second may be sitting on the ledge whilst the best position to belay the leader on the next pitch may be standing or vice-versa.

Getting re-organised at the end of a pitch is straightforward if the climbers are alternating leads. The second arrives at the stance and finds the most comfortable position to stand; on constricted ledges it is often better for the second to stop at a convenient place just below the stance. On a large ledge the leader can safeguard the second temporarily by tying an overhand knot in the dead rope just behind the belay device but on

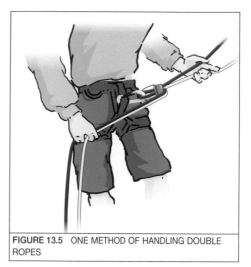

FIGURE 13.5   ONE METHOD OF HANDLING DOUBLE ROPES

FIGURE 13.6   IF THE ANCHORS ARE POOR, USE PLENTY OF THEM

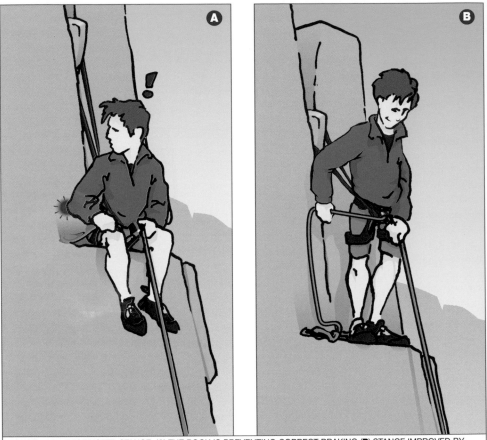

FIGURE 13.7 RESTRICTED STANCE: (**A**) THE ROCK IS PREVENTING CORRECT BRAKING (**B**) STANCE IMPROVED BY STANDING AND TWISTING SIDEWAYS

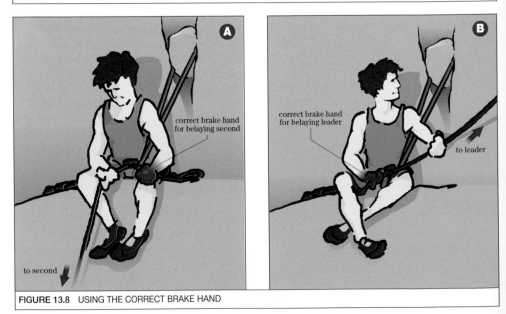

correct brake hand
for belaying second

to second

correct brake hand
for belaying leader

to leader

FIGURE 13.8 USING THE CORRECT BRAKE HAND

small stances the second should clip into one or more of the anchors with the rope or a sling. Both climbers now have free hands to get organised for the next pitch. This involves re-racking the gear, reading the guidebook and checking the orientation of the belay device. It may be necessary for the belayer to adjust the belay device to ensure the brake hand becomes the one furthest away from the leader, this may involve unclipping the belay device and turning it around (see *Figure 13.8*). It is important that the new leader is safely clipped in to the anchors at this point.

If one climber is leading all the pitches, there is a little more re-organising to do at each stance. The second must tie into the anchors and get comfortable, then run the ropes through so the leader's ends are back on the top of the pile and finally the second puts the leader on belay. The leader retrieves and re-racks any gear from the second, has a final check that everything looks OK and then unclips from the anchors and sets off.

## 13.4 Runners

The first runner when leaving the stance is crucial for avoiding severe falls by keeping the *fall factor* below two (fall factors are explained on page 46). If there is not a runner immediately obvious, one of the belay anchors can be clipped as a runner, providing it is really secure and will take an outward pull. This can be unclipped by the belayer once the leader has placed a few more runners if it causes rope drag. Subsequent runners are then placed as needed to protect hard sections and to avoid falls onto ledges (see also *10.2.4 Runner placements and spacing* on page 114).

## 13.5 Introducing novices to multi-pitch routes

It is difficult to predict how a novice will cope with the additional exposure of a longer route, so keeping the grade easier than previously climbed

is a sensible precaution. A good choice of route is one with large stances and good anchors to make organisation easier. Often it is at the stance that the feeling of exposure is noticed for the first time; this is because the climber is no longer focusing on the rock and has the opportunity to look around. For this reason semi-hanging stances should be avoided and opportunities sought to arrange belays well back from the edge whenever possible.

Simple belays, where the anchors have been equalised with slings to create a single attachment point, as illustrated in *Figure 8.4 Equalising anchors* on page 85, will speed up changeovers at the stances. This system also makes life easier when climbing as a team of three to avoid rope tangles and is one that instructors and guides regularly use.

Keeping pitches short and belaying in view of the second will ease communication. A friendly face looking down is a great confidence boost to a nervous second and allows the leader to spot and avert any potential mistakes. It is crucial that the climbing calls are understood, especially "climb when you're ready", to avoid the second unclipping prematurely.

Retrieving stuck runners or belay anchors on multi-pitch routes is a hassle. To ensure they are easy for a novice to remove, they should be placed from a comfortable ledge or good holds, without over-reaching, and should not be seated too vigorously. If the leader memorises how each runner is placed, tips on how best to retrieve them can be given. General helpful advice for taking out runners may be given at the outset including:

- remove the runner as soon as it comes into reach;
- leave the runner clipped to the rope while removing to avoid dropping it but avoid any outward rope tension on a camming device as this can make it impossible to remove;
- look carefully first how a runner has been placed;
- loosen it in the crack then lift to the widening with the nut key if necessary; and
- resist indiscriminate pulling on stubborn runners.

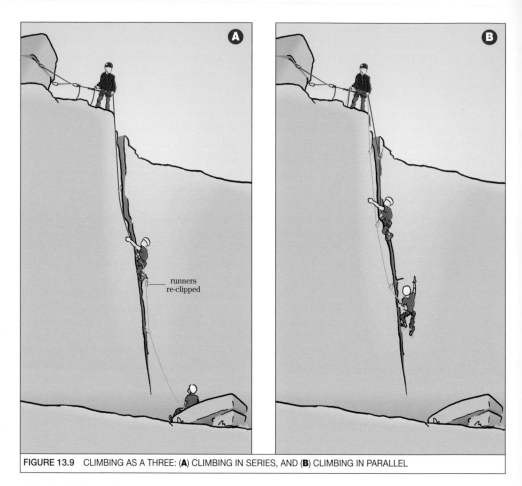

FIGURE 13.9   CLIMBING AS A THREE: (**A**) CLIMBING IN SERIES, AND (**B**) CLIMBING IN PARALLEL

## 13.6  Climbing as a three

Climbing as a team of three, whether as equals or a leader and two novices, requires particularly careful rope management, arrangement of runners and stance organisation. There are two options for organising the ropes, the first and simplest is to run the ropes *in series* or all in a line. The leader climbs on one rope, belays and brings up the first second who trails a rope for the other second (see *Figure 13.9A*).

The other option is to run the ropes *in parallel* so the leader climbs with two ropes, one to each second (see *Figure 13.9B*). The seconds can either follow the pitch one at a time or climb simultaneously a safe distance apart, if the leader is happy belaying two independent climbing ropes. For enjoyment this spacing should be sufficient to prevent competition over hand or foot holds. It also ensures that if the top second falls

the lower second is not affected. Climbing in parallel requires meticulous organisation by the leader and co-operation between the seconds to avoid creating twists in the ropes; different coloured ropes makes this easier. A team of equals may be happy to make the decision for the leader to climb on two half-ropes and for each second to follow on just one half-rope but it must be remembered that manufacturers may not recommend such use. It is not appropriate for novices or clients under instruction to climb on a half-rope, so the leader needs to trail two full-weight ropes. In this situation lighter and thinner single ropes are obviously an advantage.

### 13.6.1  Protecting two seconds
When climbing in series the leader places runners for one rope which will protect both seconds. The first second unclips the runners from the rope and re-clips them on the trailing rope. It

FIGURE 13.10   CLIPPING RUNNERS FOR 2 SECONDS

is normally a good idea for the least experienced second to climb first, leaving the more experienced second to strip the belay and remove the runners. If the seconds are of equal ability they can swap positions at the end of each pitch, so they both get the chance to remove runners and belay from above etc.

When climbing in parallel, the leader must protect both ropes; this can be done in two ways. The simplest system is to place runners alternately on one rope and then the other; this protects both seconds equally well if the pitch is reasonably direct. If there is a particular tricky move that needs protecting for both seconds, a strategic runner is clipped on the first second's

A fall when leading on two single ropes clipped into the same runner can create a high impact force; the amount of rope stretch is halved but the load on the runner doubled. In addition the load may be moved away from the spine of the karabiner, reducing its breaking strength and there's a possibility that with uneven amounts of slack, one rope could run over the other and cause severe melting or abrasion.

rope who makes the move then re-clips the runner onto the other rope to protect the last second.

The alternative is to clip both ropes into each runner but into different karabiners, ideally at separate distances from the runner to allow the ropes to run smoothly. This is done with two quickdraws of different lengths or a sling tied in the middle (see *Figure 13.10*).

### 13.6.2  Stance organisation with two seconds

Three people and two 50m ropes require careful positioning at the stances otherwise chaos quickly takes over. It is essential that the seconds clip to the anchor in an order that will not create tangles as they leave the stance. This is achieved if each new arrival at the ledge always clips underneath the last person's ropes and karabiner (see *Figure 13.11*). It is helpful for each climber to have not only a different colour rope but also an easily identified screwgate.

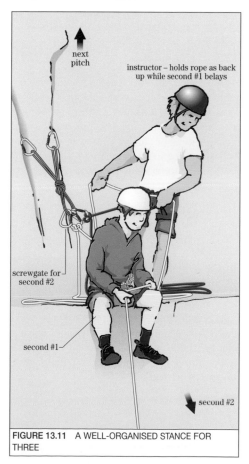

FIGURE 13.11   A WELL-ORGANISED STANCE FOR THREE

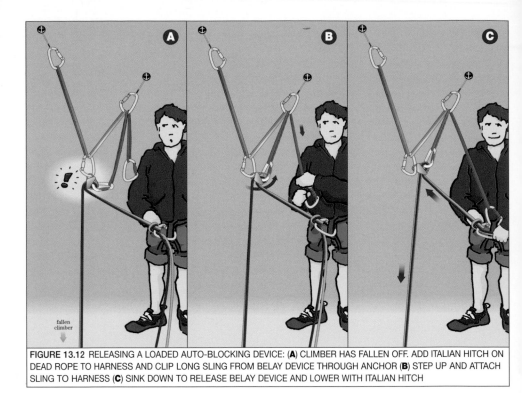

FIGURE 13.12 RELEASING A LOADED AUTO-BLOCKING DEVICE: (**A**) CLIMBER HAS FALLEN OFF. ADD ITALIAN HITCH ON DEAD ROPE TO HARNESS AND CLIP LONG SLING FROM BELAY DEVICE THROUGH ANCHOR (**B**) STEP UP AND ATTACH SLING TO HARNESS (**C**) SINK DOWN TO RELEASE BELAY DEVICE AND LOWER WITH ITALIAN HITCH

It is important to consider where everyone will stand or sit and where the ropes can be stacked. Lapping the ropes over the anchor ropes as described above often helps on small ledges. Before setting off the leader should ensure that both seconds are comfortable and will be able to leave the ledge without first having to sort out rope tangles.

### 13.6.3 Belaying two seconds
It is possible to belay two seconds who are climbing at the same time with a standard belay device in a normal semi-direct system. This requires nimble handling skills to enable slack to be taken in at different rates, whilst at the same time ensuring it is possible to hold a fall on either rope or indeed that both seconds could be held if they fell at the same time. It is wise for one second to pause for the other second to complete tricky moves so the belayer's attention can be alternated between the two.

Guides and instructors who regularly belay two seconds at the same time often opt for an auto-blocking device attached directly to the belay. Such devices are specifically designed for this job and allow both ropes to lock independently. In other words the operator can take in slack on one rope then the other separately. The main disadvantage of these devices is that it is very difficult to lower a fallen climber back down or feed out slack if the rope is under tension. To unlock a loaded device it normally needs to be released using body weight. This can be done by clipping a karabiner through the device and attaching a sling which runs through a high anchor then clips to the harness. The belayer sinks down and lifts the device into the unlocked position. The lower is controlled by adding an Italian hitch clipped to the harness (see *Figure 13.12*).

# 12 NOTES FOR INSTRUCTORS Teaching climbing

There are few hard and fast rules about instructing climbing other than ensuring safety but there are many ways an instructor ensures clients gain as much as possible from climbing sessions. Knowledge of the clients' previous experience, needs and level of confidence coupled with an understanding of how they learn and perform best is important background information. This is best built up over time but in reality is often gleaned in a brief chat before heading for the crag; in this case the instructor will need a plan with built-in flexibility. It is worth remembering that clients seek instruction because they lack experience in a particular area and it is vital to address this specific weakness.

For complete novices or those with very little previous experience the most valuable use of time is that spent actually climbing, yet it is easy for the instructor to get side-tracked into doing lots of static teaching first. In an ideal world novices will have had the opportunity to have learned and practised basic skills beforehand to avoid wasting valuable time at the crag. Failing that, essential new skills are best introduced briefly and progressively. The base of a climb is seldom a good teaching venue from a safety point of view and a novice may be too anxious, excited or impatient to concentrate.

## Venue and route choice

Certain venues lend themselves particularly well to teaching and learning about climbing. They are normally accessible and have minimum objective hazards. It is important that the routes climbed illustrate teaching points clearly; for novices this may be good runners and simple belays whilst for a more experienced climber it may be complex route finding and awkward stances. The grade of the route should be considered carefully; most successful instructing takes place on routes where the climber feels in control or gently pushed rather than being stretched to the limit of ability.

## Guiding, instructing and coaching

Guiding, instructing and coaching are distinct but closely related skills. Guiding involves leading an individual or party on a particular route or to a summit whilst instructing implies there is an emphasis on teaching. The term coaching is often used to specify improving movement skills. In reality there is considerable overlap between all three approaches as it is virtually impossible to complete a guiding day without some instructing, even if it just how to belay. Likewise, almost all instructional days involve an element of guiding and both guides and instructors often incorporate coaching skills into sessions. The terms are useful to describe the emphasis of what an instructor is offering or to determine what a client seeks.

Clients seeking instruction often want to learn techniques in order to go and climb by themselves, whilst those looking for guiding are probably more interested in the experience of climbing a particular route. Climbers may decide they need coaching to push their grade or improve at a particular style of climbing.

It is important that everyone is clear at the outset which approach is called for, even though this may change later. For example an instructional day may develop into a guided experience to speed things up if the weather deteriorates. Different approaches can be combined to give mileage on the rock with learning along the way and an experienced instructor will dip in and out of these approaches regularly according to the situation.

In guiding situations control is retained by the instructor who employs techniques with speed and efficiency in mind. This could involve running the ropes in parallel and making use of direct belays and centralised anchors for example. Instructional days are more varied and complex with the techniques used reflecting the nature of what is being taught. The following tips are tried and tested but instructors must also use their imagination, have a flexible approach and be adaptable to different situations.

- Get climbing as soon as possible rather than overload with information before touching the rock.
- Introduce skills progressively and spaced over the course of the route, day or week.
- Remember that most people learn practical skills best by doing them repeatedly and by receiving feedback.
- Strike a balance between keeping things moving quickly and letting novices do it for themselves at their own pace.

For coaching sessions the instructor often works at a controllable venue such as a bouldering site, indoor wall or top-roping crag in order to focus on movement and technique without the distractions of a more serious venue (a number of coaching ideas are covered in *5.1.2 Improving technique*, page 36).

## Teaching leading

Introducing climbers to leading for the first time is a serious undertaking. It involves, not only the mechanics of safeguarding novice leaders from a fall but also the responsibility of introducing them to a whole new arena, in which sound judgement and decision making are crucial. It is possible to teach climbers the 'nuts and bolts' of leading without them taking on board the additional

seriousness involved. Aspiring leaders should have sufficient experience to appreciate and accept the additional risks as well as having the appropriate skills. It is important that they want to lead rather than feel it is expected of them. An instructor may find it difficult to judge whether climbers are ready to lead without first having seen them climb in a number of situations. Equally important, but sometimes overlooked, is the competence and reliability of the belayer, who could be required to hold a leader fall for the first time. The instructor can't be in two places at once and will need to concentrate primarily on the leader, so must be happy that the belayer can operate the belay device safely without someone alongside to supervise.

When choosing an appropriate route for a first lead the instructor should consider the following:

- The grade will probably be well below the climber's peak ability.
- Runners should be good quality and closely spaced.
- The belayer should be in sight.
- Sound top anchors are important as the instructor may require a fixed rope.
- It is best to avoid crowded routes and keep out of the way of faster teams.
- Cold, wet and windy conditions will invariably affect safety.

## Methods of safeguarding the leader
### Slack top-rope

As part of a progression or in situations or conditions where it is not appropriate to undertake an actual lead, it can be simulated instead. The aspirant leader climbs on a slack top-rope, whilst at the same time using a practise 'lead' rope. This gives a taste of the insecurity experienced while learning how to get comfortable to place and clip runners. The rope can be arranged as a top or bottom-rope with the instructor watching from above, below or alongside.

### Alongside on a fixed rope

In most cases, and certainly for introducing novices to leading for the first time, the instructor is normally best positioned alongside the leader on a separate fixed rope. This is the best way to ensure the instructor's own personal safety whilst offering maximum security to the leader. The instructor can talk through runner placements, coach movement and if required clip the leader to a point of safety to prevent a fall. The main disadvantage of this system is the time taken to set up the fixed rope. It can also give new leaders a false sense of security, which can be hard to adjust from when they go on to try a route by themselves. It is vital that the instructor paints a realistic picture of how subsequent ascents may feel and give good advice on how to make the next step.

**FIGURE 13.13   TEACHING LEADING**
Photo: Plas y Brenin collection

The instructor must be able to ascend the rope at the same pace the leader is climbing and be close enough to be of immediate assistance but without getting in the way of crucial holds. The instructor's ascending technique must be smooth and practised so their attention can be with the leader and belayer. There are a number of methods to choose from according to the steepness and difficulty of the climb. On easy angled, low-grade climbs the instructor may opt for a fixed rope and one ascender (plus a back-up), which is moved up the rope as required. On steeper and harder climbs the instructor will probably need two ascenders to make progress. Some methods of ascending fixed ropes are outlined overleaf. Whichever combination of devices is chosen the instructor should be familiar with any possible problems and always back up prusiks or mechanical ascenders with a knot such as a clove hitch clipped to the harness that is moved up the rope periodically.

The fixed rope must be arranged to avoid sharp edges, loose blocks and climbers on other routes; the use of rope protectors should be considered. The rope should be rigged to lie alongside the climb, so if the pitch is not straight up it can be re-routed with strategic anchors to allow for changes in direction on the climb. Occasionally the instructor may incorporate a second fixed rope as a back-up and to increase flexibility when safeguarding the leader. However, if there were a real concern about damage to the fixed rope this would indicate an inappropriate choice of route.

FIGURE 13.14   TEACHING LEADING – INSTRUCTOR ASCENDING A FIXED ROPE ON EASY ANGLED GROUND

## Ascending fixed ropes

On easy angled climbs one ascender attached to the harness with a short sling may be sufficient to make smooth progress. The instructor pulls up on the rope with one hand whilst sliding the ascender up with the other or climbs the rock and uses the ascender for safety. A back-up knot, such as a clove hitch that is moved up the rope, is essential here (see Figure 13.14). Alternatively the ascender can be coupled with a belay device which is added below the ascender and also attached to the harness belay loop. This requires a two-handed 'pump' action of moving the devices alternately up the rope. An auto-locking device such as a Grigri can be used effectively here or, if a standard belay device is used, it requires a French prusik above it clipped to the harness belay loop to act as a clutch. These configurations provide an additional point of security and a quick means of changing over to descend if required (see *Figure 13.15*).

When using two ascenders there are a number of devices and ways to arrange them, but a popular method is to attach

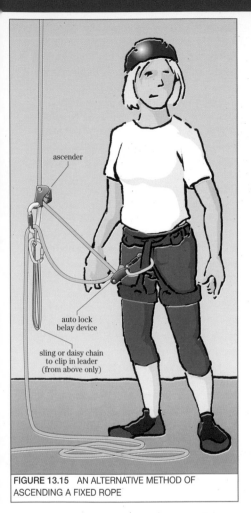

ascender

auto lock
belay device

sling or daisy chain
to clip in leader
(from above only)

**FIGURE 13.15**   AN ALTERNATIVE METHOD OF
ASCENDING A FIXED ROPE

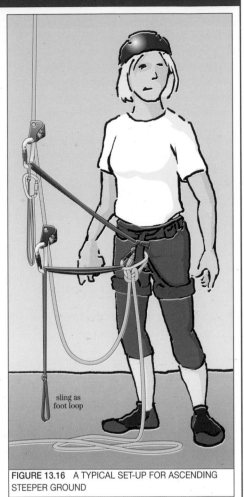

sling as
foot loop

**FIGURE 13.16**   A TYPICAL SET-UP FOR ASCENDING
STEEPER GROUND

the top ascender to the harness and the lower ascender to a foot loop created with a long sling. It is wise to be clipped loosely from the harness to the lower device as additional security or to use a clove hitch back-up as described above (see *Figure 13.16*).

## Protecting a fall

If a leader fall looks likely the instructor must decide whether to let this happen, having first checked the runners and alerted the belayer, or whether to intervene. This is a difficult judgement to make. Short, controlled leader falls onto solid runners can be a valuable experience for new leaders but this must be weighed against the potential risks. Injury to the leader (and/or belayer) is possible even during a short fall and the consequences of a longer fall occurring, due to belayer error or runner failure, could be very serious. In most cases the instructor will attempt to avoid or prevent falls by anticipating where they are most likely to happen and protecting the leader accordingly. However, the possibility of an unexpected fall can never be ruled out; it is essential that leader, belayer and instructor are all aware of this.

The instructor can safeguard the leader in a number of ways including:

- checking or backing up runners and if necessary clipping the rope in to them for the leader;
- extending runners with long slings to provide intermediate runners where they are needed;
- placing and clipping a runner above the leader's head to provide a 'top-rope' past a tricky or unprotected section;
- creating an additional runner by clipping a quickdraw to a knot on the fixed rope to protect blank sections;
- clipping the leader to the fixed rope for a rest; and
- clipping the leader to the fixed rope in case of a fall.

The instructor constantly assesses the level of 'help' and security the leader requires. Over the course of a few days or routes the instructor will hopefully be able to gradually take a 'back seat'. If the leader needs considerable assistance or looks like they might fall at any moment the route is probably too hard or the climber not yet ready for leading. When protecting a fall the instructor must consider carefully how best to attach the falling leader to a fixed rope. Clipping the leader in for a rest or holding a fall from above is unlikely to create an excessive load but it is unwise to catch a fall on an ascender for example. If a leader fall is being held by a 'runner' on the fixed rope, the stretch in the rope can make the fall much longer than expected. Likewise, care must be taken to avoid shock loading tape slings if they are being used to clip in the leader.

## Other methods

The instructor can coach and teach whilst soloing next to a leader but can offer little immediate physical assistance and is extremely vulnerable to being pulled or knocked off. It may be an appropriate technique to use on very easy pitches with reasonably competent climbers but the instructor must consider all of the safety implications carefully and always solo above and out of reach of the leader.

If the leader is confident and experienced it may be appropriate for the instructor to watch and give advice from above with a top-rope at the ready. This assumes that both leader and belayer are competent already but are looking for psychological rather than physical support and a watchful eye. The instructor may have pre-placed a few crucial runners or should at least have climbed the route to be able to give advice on runner placements and tricky moves.

# Descending from multi-pitch crags

THE EASTERN TERRACE DESCENT ON CLOGGY IS NOTORIOUSLY LOOSE AND FUNNELS DEBRIS DOWN
A NUMBER OF POPULAR CLIMBS BELOW

Climbers should keep their wits about them until the descent is safely completed. Descent routes are often loose and require care to avoid dislodging rocks onto parties below, especially if the fall-line sends debris down the crag.

Many descents from multi-pitch crags involve little more than a steep walk. At popular venues there is usually a well-worn footpath to follow, otherwise it is a case of picking a line that skirts the steep ground. It is often worth carrying footwear for the walk off, as rock boots are uncomfortable to walk in and can be lethal on damp grass or muddy paths.

A large number of descents involve some simple scrambling that can be down climbed without the rope. To negotiate steeper sections of scrambling terrain a short abseil can be rigged or techniques can be used that are described in *Chapter 16: Scrambling* on page 173.

## 14.1 Multiple abseils

*Multiple abseil descents* are rarely called for from crags in the UK unless an unplanned retreat is necessary. *In-situ* abseil anchors are the exception rather than the norm so an abseil retreat normally involves leaving behind gear. Although it is tempting to minimise the gear abandoned to save money, the anchors selected must be bombproof. Large threads, spikes and blocks are the easiest to use and require leaving behind only a sling and karabiner at most. A

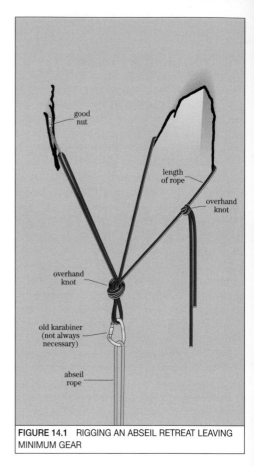

FIGURE 14.1 RIGGING AN ABSEIL RETREAT LEAVING MINIMUM GEAR

### Nylon against nylon

Concerns are often raised about nylon rubbing against nylon due to its low melting point (see also *Dyneema® slings* on page 57).

Abseiling on a rope running directly through a sling is OK because damage to the rope is minimal. However, some damage may occur to the sling when the rope is pulled down very quickly, so it is always worth being suspicious of *in-situ* slings that have been abseiled from without a karabiner. They should be checked thoroughly by rotating the sling to inspect its whole length. Rope slings are less susceptible to damage than tape slings, especially if the sheath is still whole.

piece of tape or rope cut to the required length is cheaper than leaving a sewn sling; a karabiner is not essential but will make the rope easier to pull. Both materials are equally strong but tape has less tendency to roll off spikes and is less bulky to carry. A tape sling should be tied with a tape knot (see *Tape knot* on page 70) and rope with an overhand or double fisherman's knot as normal (see *Reef knot and Double Fisherman's to join two ropes* on page 69).

Where natural anchors are not available one or more pieces of gear are required. It may be possible to leave just a single bombproof nut and karabiner for example but if there is any doubt at all about its quality, another should be added so the load can be shared between them. The number of karabiners left behind can be minimised by tying a length of tape directly to the anchors (see *Figure 14.1*). *In-situ* anchors need checking, with any frayed or faded tape being replaced, and pegs and bolts require careful scrutiny.

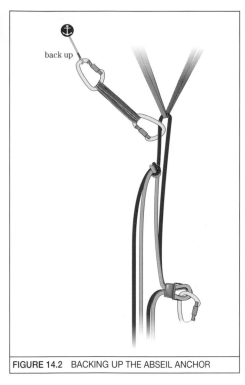

FIGURE 14.2   BACKING UP THE ABSEIL ANCHOR

## 14.2 Rigging the abseil

The method for rigging the abseil is the same as rigging a retrievable abseil on a single pitch crag (see page 98). All abseilers should prepare a cow's tail, which will become the point of attachment at the top and at every subsequent abseil station (see *Lark's foot* on page 70). While abseiling it is kept out of the way by taking it around the waist and clipping it to a gear loop or back to the harness belay loop. Overhand knots can be used to adjust the length.

## 14.3 Backing up abseils

It is sound practise to back up the abseil anchor while the first abseiler descends. If the heaviest person goes first the anchors are effectively tested so the last person can remove the back-up before setting off. To do this a bombproof piece of gear is linked to the abseil rope so there is only a little slack and no weight on it. Should the abseil anchor fail the load will come onto the back-up without a big shock load (see *Figure 14.2*).

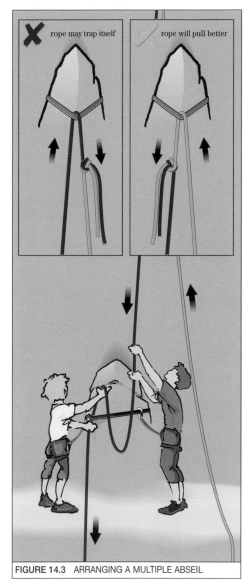

FIGURE 14.3   ARRANGING A MULTIPLE ABSEIL

## 14.4 Sequence

The first abseiler carries the gear in order to rig the next set of anchors and should always use a safety back-up such as a prusik for stopping easily. Often the best line of retreat is to follow the route climbed using the belay stances as abseil stations. Abseiling down an unknown section of cliff is intimidating and may offer a poor selection of abseil points. On locating or selecting the next abseil point the abseiler remains on the rope whilst arranging the anchors and clips in with the cow's tail once it is set up. It is a good idea to tie the ends of the rope to the new anchor as a back-up for the next abseiler especially if the top set of anchors is poor. It is also wise for the first abseiler to hold the ends of the rope as the next abseiler descends. Once the second abseiler is down and clipped to the anchor, the rope is untied and one end fed through the new abseil point while the rope is pulled. When abseiling directly off a sling it is better to arrange it so the rope to be pulled lies on the inside of the sling. This way it is less likely to pinch the sling against the rock thus making retrieval easier (see *Figure 14.3*).

## 14.5 Jammed ropes

Getting the abseil ropes jammed is frustratingly common and can happen in a number of ways. There may simply be too much friction, a crack may trap the knot, the rope can drop behind a flake or the ropes can twist around each other. Extending anchors towards the front of the ledge, careful placing of the ropes and untwisting the ropes before pulling help minimise rope jams. It is also sensible for the first abseiler down to give the ropes a pull to check they are running smoothly and for the last abseiler to move the knot down over the edge if possible.

A jammed rope may be freed by adjusting the pulling position, flicking the rope or occasionally just by pulling harder. The last should be done with caution, as the jam could be the result of a wedged block waiting to be dislodged. Sometimes weighting the wrong side of the rope then releasing this before pulling the right side does the job.

If the rope hasn't budged at all it can be ascended by prusiking on both ropes up to the jam, the ropes are freed and re-positioned before abseiling back down and trying again. If the rope has been pulled part way before jamming leaving only one end in reach, it may be dangerous to ascend the remaining rope in case it frees itself with the climber attached. In this situation the remaining rope can be tied into to lead back up, or the rope can be cut, abandoning the stuck section and continuing in a series of much shorter abseils. In either case this is a difficult and potentially dangerous situation to deal with.

## 13 NOTES FOR INSTRUCTORS Abseiling with

Attempting a multiple abseil descent with a novice has a number of potential problems. Apart from it being extremely intimidating, there is the possibility of the novice freezing part way down, getting something stuck in the device or even unclipping inadvertently from the rope before setting off. In most cases the instructor needs to descend first in order to locate and rig the next abseil point but this leaves the novice unattended at the top. To avoid the possibility of a novice attaching to the abseil rope incorrectly, the instructor can arrange a 'stacked abseil'.

### Arranging a stacked abseil
One or two extra abseilers can be attached to the abseil rope before the instructor sets off. For their comfort it helps to lengthen their abseil devices using a screwgate and quickdraw (see *Figure 14.4*). While the instructor is descending the rope is under load and it is impossible for the next abseiler to set off as they are effectively 'trapped' by the tension in the rope.

The instructor abseils and rigs the next abseil point maintaining weight on the rope at all times, only releasing it when ready to receive the next abseiler. The instructor ensures the abseiler's safety by being ready to pull hard on the rope to control speed or stop a fall. It is a good idea to keep the rope running through the abseil device to ensure this back-up is effective.

The instructor can do little, however, if a confused abseiler detaches inadvertently from the abseil rope. Likewise if an abseiler freezes or becomes stuck part way down this would be a difficult problem to solve. For these reasons the stacked abseil technique is only recommended with

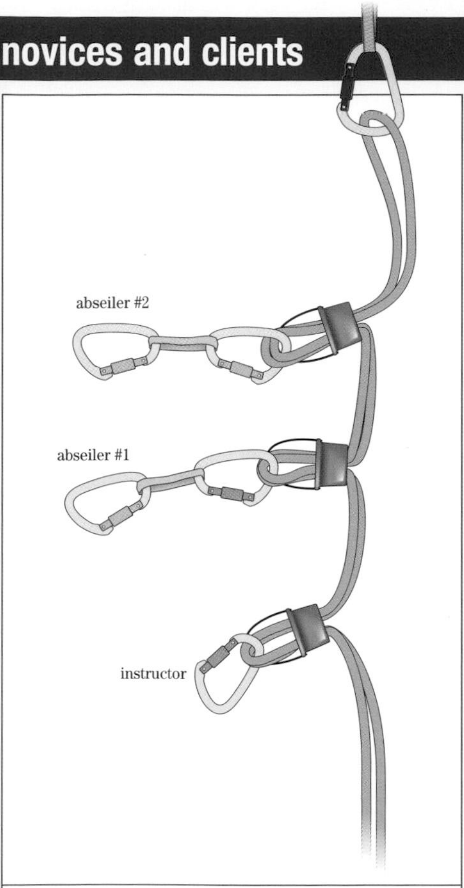

FIGURE 14.4   STACKED ABSEIL SETUP

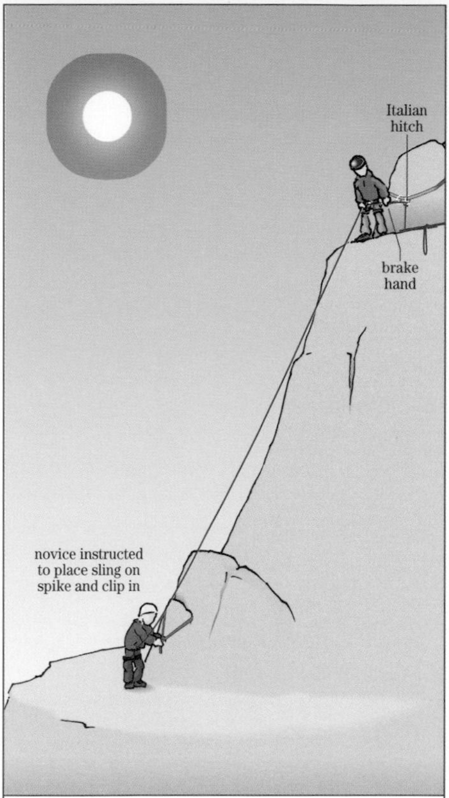

FIGURE 14.5   LOWERING A NOVICE

experienced abseilers and when absolutely necessary.

## Lower and abseil

If it is inappropriate to arrange a stacked abseil the instructor may decide to lower a novice down first and follow by abseil. If there is a clearly visible large ledge and obvious anchor to attach to, the novice can be instructed to do this, but should also remain tied to the rope (see *Figure 14.5*). The instructor then introduces just a little slack in the rope to the novice before abseiling on both ropes, in this way the novice is still safeguarded (see *Figure 14.6*). Two novices can be safeguarded in the same way by lowering one on each rope and then joining the two ropes with long tails to allow a minimum of slack to each novice (see *Figure 14.7*). It is essential they do not move or load the rope, as this will make it impossible for the instructor to descend. One novice can be safeguarded by a counterbalance system. This involves the instructor abseiling on the other side of the rope counterbalancing the novices' weight.

Yet another option is for the instructor to tie two ropes together and lower the novice a longer distance to reach the ground. The instructor can then follow in two abseils or in an emergency abseil on the joined ropes, passing the knot and abandoning them. Lowering and abseiling past a knot is covered in *15.3.1 Lowering* on page 157.

ropes joined away
from ends to
safeguard novices

enough slack to
allow instructor
to abseil

novice safeguarded
by instructor abseiling on
both ropes and by sling

both novices safeguarded on ledge
by instructor abseiling

**FIGURE** 14.6 SAFEGUARDING A NOVICE DURING DESCENT

**FIGURE** 14.7 SAFEGUARDING TWO NOVICES DURING DESCENT

# Multi-pitch problem solving

CAREFUL ROPE-WORK IS CALLED FOR TO AVOID THE ROPE JAMMING BEHIND THE FLAKE ON **MUR Y NIWL** VS 4c, CRAIG YR YSFA

Problems that arise when climbing in a multi-pitch setting, though infrequent, have a potential additional seriousness over the single pitch environment due to scale, environment and remoteness.

15

**This section expands on the simple techniques and solutions to problems highlighted in the single pitch section, in order to equip climbers with the techniques and confidence to get themselves out of trouble on bigger crags.**

The majority of the problems that do occur on multi-pitch routes have a simple origin, such as a jammed rope or the climber falling onto unclimbable ground, but are exacerbated by communication difficulties. At times these can result in a stalemate with neither climber knowing what the problem is or what to do about it. Yet other incidents arise due to going off-route or getting benighted. Most of these are avoidable with preparation and care. However, sometimes things do go wrong and it should be remembered that it is impossible to be prepared for every eventuality or to be able to solve every problem. Some situations require help from others, whether that is neighbouring climbers or an experienced rescue team.

# 15.1 Priorities

In the rare situation of a climber being very badly hurt in a fall or by stonefall for example, it is necessary for their partner to get down to give help and first aid as quickly as possible. This normally involves escaping from the rope system and abseiling or prusiking down to the injured climber. Once first aid has been administered a further plan of action can be developed. This may involve returning to the stance by prusiking back up the abseil rope and then **hoisting** or **descending** as appropriate. In certain situations it may be impossible for one climber to rescue the other without risk of further injury, in this case the priority is for the climber to escape from the cliff by the safest route, up or down, and get help.

An unconscious or badly injured casualty will need to be put in the safest and most comfortable position with particular attention to keeping the airway open – this may be the number one priority. A casualty hanging on a rope may need help staying upright and this can be achieved with an improvised chest harness clipped to the rope. This can be done with a **Parisien baudrier** constructed from a long sling (see *Figure 15.1*).

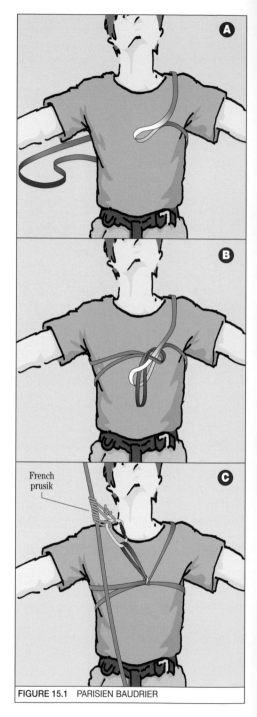

FIGURE 15.1 PARISIEN BAUDRIER

If the casualty has a large chest it is easier to use the method shown in *Figure 15.2*. It is essential the harness can not tighten around or constrict the chest. The chest harness can be clipped

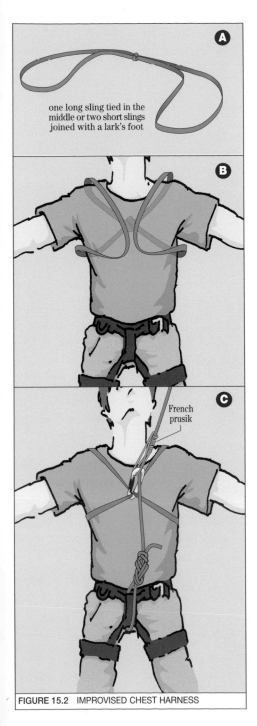

one long sling tied in the middle or two short slings joined with a lark's foot

**A**

**B**

French prusik

**C**

**FIGURE 15.2** IMPROVISED CHEST HARNESS

direct to the rope or better to a short French prusik so the position can be adjusted, ensuring that the casualty's weight is not being held solely by the prusik.

## 15.2 A few basic rules

There aren't many hard and fast rules, remember this is 'improvised' rescue and if an unorthodox system is working and is safe then don't change it. However, the following reminders are worth adhering to:

- **Always look for the easiest option:** shout for help, lower to the ground or get the casualty to take their weight off the rope by standing on a ledge.
- **Escape down in preference to hoisting:** whenever possible.
- **Always back up prusiks:** they can (and do) slip.
- **Keep your options open for as long as possible:** don't start a complicated manoeuvre until you're sure how best to proceed.
- **Use releasable systems where possible, so steps can be reversed:** for example, to get a casualty's weight off a knot requires a hoist but a tied off Italian hitch can be released back onto a prusik.

## 15.3 Escaping down

Making use of gravity is preferable to hoisting, wherever possible. There are a number of ways to evacuate down from a crag that involve lowering, abseiling or a combination of both. A competent climber should always look for the safest option, even if it is not the quickest.

### 15.3.1 Lowering
The simplest option is often to *lower* the injured climber to the ground or a ledge and for the leader to abseil. This a good and quick option providing:
- the injuries will not be made worse;
- the ground or a good ledge will be reached;
- the rope is not running over sharp edges or loose rock; or
- the belayer has good control of the rope and can see what is going on.

If the ground is more than a rope length away it may be possible to lower to a good ledge first. If the injured climber is not able to create an anchor on the ledge the leader must ensure their safety from above (see *Figures 14.5, 14.6* and *14.7* on pages 153–154). By tying two ropes together the ground can often be reached; this involves passing the knot on both the lower and abseil.

### Lowering past a knot

1   Tie the ropes together with an overhand or double fisherman's and reef knot (see page 69 *Overhand to join two ropes* and *Reef knot and Double Fisherman's to join two ropes*).

2   Tie a French prusik to the lowering rope in front of the lowering device and attach this to the anchors with a long (120cm) sling. Ensure the prusik won't be out of reach or rub against the rock when it's loaded.

3   Add a back-up by tying a figure of eight on the bight about 1 metre behind the knot and clipping it to the anchor (see *Figure 15.3*).

4   Lower the climber by holding the French prusik open until the knot is about 50cm from the lowering device and allow the French prusik to take the load, then creep the knot to about 20cm from the lowering device.

5   Take the rope out of the lowering device and replace the lowering device on the rope behind the knot. Release the French prusik so the load comes back on to rope. (If two hands are needed to do this, tie off the lowering device).

6   Take off the French prusik, remove the back-up knot and continue to lower.

### Abseiling past a knot

The abseiler sets up an abseil safety back-up (normally a French prusik) above the abseil device clipped to the harness belay loop. The adjustment must be such that when hanging from the prusik it can be reached easily with a slightly bent arm as it may take some force (and both hands) to release. This is normally the length of a short sling doubled or a 30cm quickdraw.

1   Abseil until the knot is level with the knees (about 50cm below the abseil device), load the prusik and creep down until the knot is about 20cm from the abseil device. (Too close and it'll jam against the abseil device, too far and it'll jam against the prusik.)

2   Pick up the rope hanging below and tie a back-up knot such as figure of eight which is clipped to the harness belay loop with a screwgate.

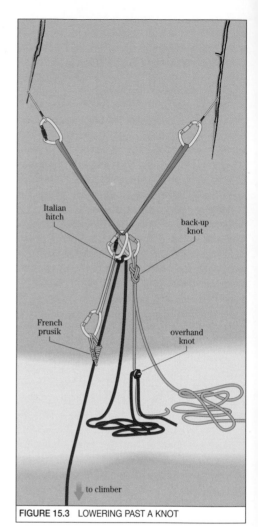

**FIGURE 15.3**   LOWERING PAST A KNOT

3   Remove the abseil device from the rope and replace it below the knot.

4   Add a prusik back-up below the abseil device if needed.

5   Pull down on and release the top prusik, while ensuring no slack feeds through the abseil device. (If two hands are needed the abseil device can be tied off.)

6   Remove the slack top prusik and back-up figure of eight knot and continue descent (see *Figure 15.4*).

*Troubleshooting*

To avoid problems the distance of the prusik above the abseil device must be correct. Too long and it'll be out of arms reach making it difficult to release. Too short and it will jam against the knot.

FIGURE 15.4    ABSEILING PAST A KNOT (**1**) LOAD PRUSIK WHEN KNOT IS ABOUT 20CM BELOW ABSEIL DEVICE
(**2**) ADD A BACK-UP KNOT (**3**) REMOVE ABSEIL DEVICE AND REPLACE IT BELOW KNOT. HOLD DEAD ROPE SECURELY
AND RELEASE PRUSIK (**4**) REMOVE PRUSIK AND BACK-UP KNOT THEN CONTINUE WITH DESCENT

### 15.3.2 Accompanied abseil

If the injured and non-injured climbers are on the same ledge an *accompanied abseil* (where one person controls the rope while they both descend) is a good option. This is explained on page 128 in *Figure 12.3*.

If the injured climber is midway up a pitch it may be possible for the rescuer to escape from the system and abseil on a separate rope, picking up the casualty on the way down. The casualty is clipped to an accompanied abseil set-up and freed from the original rope by cutting or untying it. Cutting is quick but must be done with great care as loaded ropes cut remarkably easily. Always cut away from the rope that you are on. Untying is only possible with the casualty's weight completely off the rope. If there is no ledge to stand on or if the casualty is unconscious a stirrup hoist can be used.

**Stirrup hoist**

1  Ensure that the casualty is secured to the abseil rope either directly to the abseil device or to the rescuer's central harness attachment point. Add a back-up knot on the rope below.
2  Tie a prusik to the casualty's rope.
3  Clip a sling to the casualty's harness belay loop and run it doubled through a karabiner on the prusik (see *Figure 15.5A*).
4  Use the other end of the sling to stand in whilst pulling the casualty up.
5  Keep the weight on the sling until the knot is untied (see *Figure 15.5B*).
6  Release weight from sling gradually so casualty is lowered onto abseil rope.
7  Remove prusik and sling, continue descent (see *Figure 15.5C&D*).

*Troubleshooting*

This technique sounds easier than it is and requires practise!

### 15.3.3 Counterbalance abseil

This system combines abseiling and lowering, enabling the rope to be retrieved for the descent.

1  Escape the system (see *12.2.2 Escaping from the system* on page 128).
2  Clip the live rope (behind the French prusik) through a screwgate at the main anchor point.
3  Attach an abseil device and prusik safety back-up to the rope on the other side of this screwgate and attach a short sling to the harness belay loop in preparation for the 'pick-up.'
4  Remove the Italian hitch back-up, release and remove the French prusik while weighting the rope to counterbalance the weight of second.
5  Clear any extra gear from the belay.
6  Abseil to the second, clip the short sling to the casualty's harness belay loop and continue abseiling. The casualty will remain slightly above the rescuer and is pulled down by the weight of the rescuer via the sling.
7  Re-belay at an appropriate stance and continue descent by lowering or an accompanied abseil (see *Figure 15.6*).

*Troubleshooting*

The main disadvantage of this system is that there are loaded moving ropes running over potentially sharp edges or loose rock. There is also the danger of the ropes jamming in a crack during the descent which would create a very difficult problem to solve. If there is any doubt over the suitability of the terrain this method should not be used.

It is possible to abseil off the end of the rope so the rescuer should either be tied in or tie a knot in the end of the rope.

If the belayer has a clear view of the problem and is at a 'text book' belay (with anchors that are in reach of the belayer and equalised to a central point) it may not be necessary to escape the system first. A French prusik is attached to the live rope and clipped to the anchor. The prusik is loaded so the belay device locking knot can be untied. Slack is taken from behind the device and clipped to a lowering screwgate at the anchor. An abseil safety back-up is added and the belay device clipped through the harness loop in addition to the central rope loop. The rescuer is then ready to go.

# 15.4  Hoisting systems

Hauling an injured climber up a route is rarely the first choice of action; it is always hard work, it may worsen the injuries and the problem of getting off the top of the crag still remains. However, hoists are not as complicated as climbers often imagine. Basic hoisting principles, with a

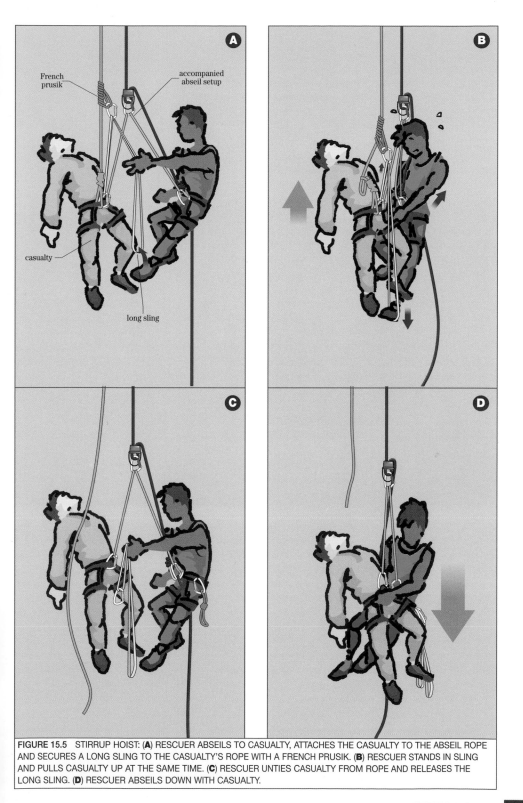

**FIGURE 15.5** STIRRUP HOIST: (**A**) RESCUER ABSEILS TO CASUALTY, ATTACHES THE CASUALTY TO THE ABSEIL ROPE AND SECURES A LONG SLING TO THE CASUALTY'S ROPE WITH A FRENCH PRUSIK. (**B**) RESCUER STANDS IN SLING AND PULLS CASUALTY UP AT THE SAME TIME. (**C**) RESCUER UNTIES CASUALTY FROM ROPE AND RELEASES THE LONG SLING. (**D**) RESCUER ABSEILS DOWN WITH CASUALTY.

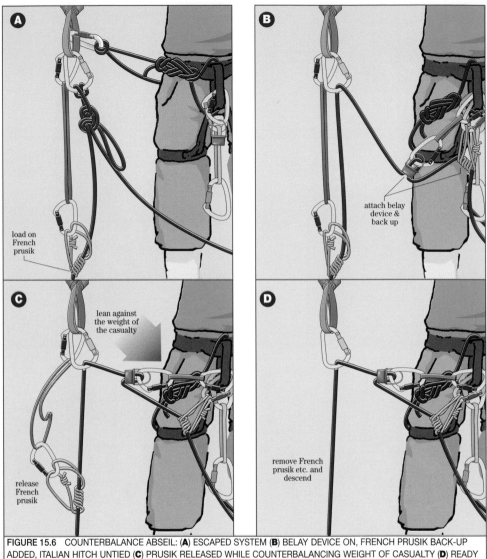

FIGURE 15.6    COUNTERBALANCE ABSEIL: (**A**) ESCAPED SYSTEM (**B**) BELAY DEVICE ON, FRENCH PRUSIK BACK-UP ADDED, ITALIAN HITCH UNTIED (**C**) PRUSIK RELEASED WHILE COUNTERBALANCING WEIGHT OF CASUALTY (**D**) READY FOR DESCENT

few adaptations, can be applied to a number of situations; stuck or injured climbers, a heavy rucksack or haul bag, tensioning tyrolean traverses and also crevasse rescue.

### 15.4.1  Assisted hoist

An assisted hoist is a useful technique if a second is unable to climb a short section of a route but wants to continue with the climb or is slightly injured and needs more than a tight rope. A combination of the second and belayer both pulling and a simple pulley system is very effective.

1  Tie off the belay device (see *Figure 12.4 Tying-off a belay device* on page 129).

2  Tie a French prusik to the live rope in front of the belay device and attach it to the central rope loop or harness belay loop with a short quickdraw (see *Figure 15.7A*).

3  Drop a loop of rope with a screwgate karabiner attached down to the second, who clips it to the central rope loop or harness belay loop, ensuring there are no twists (see *Figure 15.7B*).

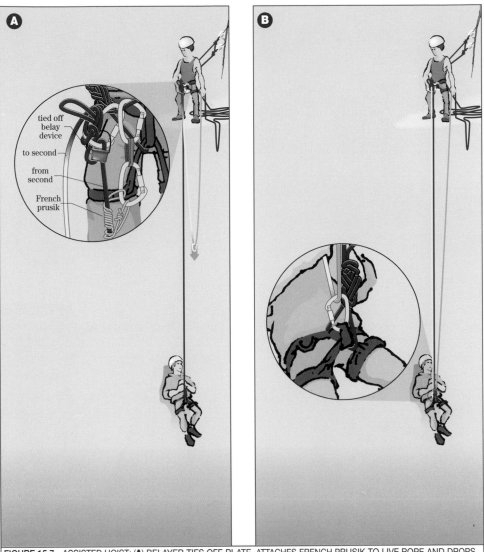

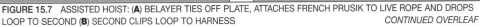

**FIGURE 15.7** ASSISTED HOIST: (**A**) BELAYER TIES OFF PLATE, ATTACHES FRENCH PRUSIK TO LIVE ROPE AND DROPS LOOP TO SECOND (**B**) SECOND CLIPS LOOP TO HARNESS *CONTINUED OVERLEAF*

**4** Untie the belay device locking knot.

**5** The leader pulls on the new rope coming up from the second while the second pulls on the rope travelling downwards (this is the 'brake rope' coming from the belayer's belay device through the prusik), at the same time walking up the rock (see *Figure 15.7C*).

**6** If a rest is needed the second can lean back while the leader makes sure the prusik is biting. The leader can relax but should still keep hold of the brake rope.

*Troubleshooting*

Problems arise if the prusik has too many or too few wraps, it either grips too well and jams up or doesn't grip at all, so this should be tested at the start. If things are too cluttered at the belay device it might not run smoothly. This technique does not work on traverses or when the second is over a third of the rope length away.

### 15.4.2 Unassisted hoist (in the system)

If a stuck second is over a third of the rope length away or is unable to pull on the rope but might be

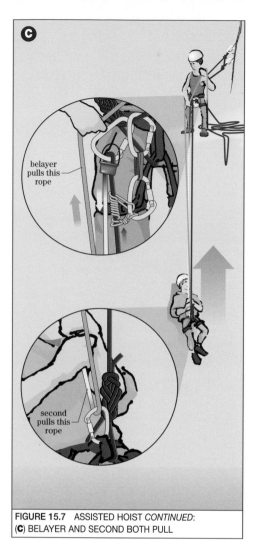

FIGURE 15.7   ASSISTED HOIST *CONTINUED*:
(**C**) BELAYER AND SECOND BOTH PULL

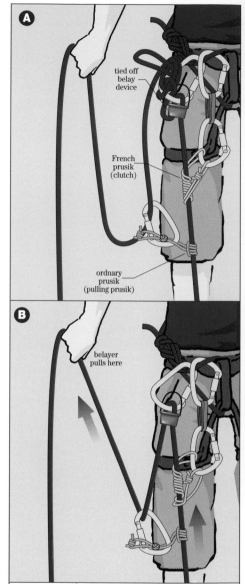

FIGURE 15.8   UNASSISTED HOIST (IN THE SYSTEM):
(**A**) BELAYER TIES OFF BELAY DEVICE, ATTACHES
FRENCH PRUSIK TO LIVE ROPE AND ADDS A SECOND
PRUSIK FOR PULLING (**B**) BELAY DEVICE LOCKING
KNOT IS UNTIED. BELAYER CAN START PULLING

able to assist by walking up the rock, this hoist
may be the answer. The leader stays in the system so it is quick to set up.

1  Repeat Stages 1 and 2 above as for an
   assisted hoist.
2  Tie a second prusik below the French prusik;
   this is a pulling prusik so it needs to bite.
   effectively, an ordinary prusik works well here.
3  Clip the rope from behind the tied-off belay
   device to this prusik and push it as far down
   the rope as possible (using the foot can be
   very effective here).
4  Untie the belay device locking knot and pull
   on the rope coming up from this second
   prusik (see *Figure 15.8*).

*Troubleshooting*

The main problem with this system is that the
pulling is done with the arms from a restricted
stance. It will help provide a super tight rope but
may not be sufficient to haul a very heavy weight.
Two snap-link karabiners on the lower prusik
will reduce the friction.

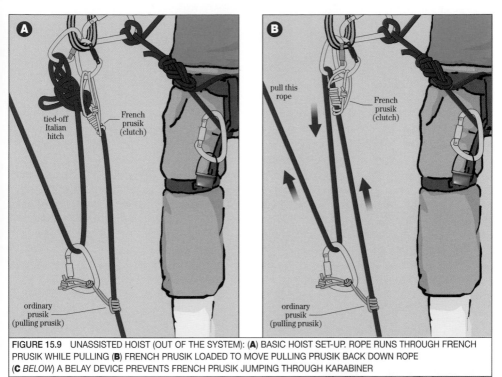

FIGURE 15.9   UNASSISTED HOIST (OUT OF THE SYSTEM): (**A**) BASIC HOIST SET-UP. ROPE RUNS THROUGH FRENCH PRUSIK WHILE PULLING (**B**) FRENCH PRUSIK LOADED TO MOVE PULLING PRUSIK BACK DOWN ROPE (**C** *BELOW*) A BELAY DEVICE PREVENTS FRENCH PRUSIK JUMPING THROUGH KARABINER

### 15.4.3  Unassisted hoist (out of the system)

To haul the full weight of a climber, a hoist can be set up from outside the system that enables the leader to move around and pull more effectively.

The decision to hoist is not made lightly, as it is strenuous and could worsen any injuries. An unconscious climber would be bumped and scraped unless the ground is very steep. A short hoist may be considered if the second is just below the stance, the team is very close to the top of a big crag or above the sea, making descent inappropriate or impossible.

1   Escape the system (see *12.2.2 Escaping from the system* on page 128).

2   Tie a French prusik to the loaded rope and attach it with a screwgate karabiner to the anchors; this acts as the clutch or autobloc.

3   Tie an ordinary prusik below the first one; this is the pulling prusik.

4   Run the loaded rope through a screwgate karabiner at the anchors down to a karabiner on the ordinary prusik.

5   Untie and remove Italian hitch back-up. Start pulling (see *Figure 15.9*).

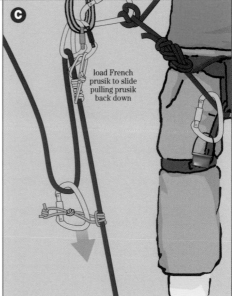

*Troubleshooting*

The leader must be secured on the ledge with enough slack to move around and pull effectively. The pulling rope can be clipped with a clove hitch to the leader's harness to enable pulling with the whole body by bending and straightening the legs.

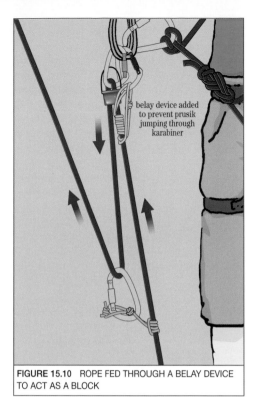

FIGURE 15.10 ROPE FED THROUGH A BELAY DEVICE TO ACT AS A BLOCK

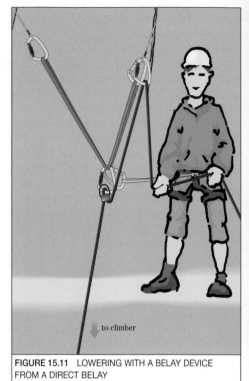

FIGURE 15.11 LOWERING WITH A BELAY DEVICE FROM A DIRECT BELAY

Occasionally the French prusik jumps through the pulley karabiner fouling the whole system. To prevent this the rope can be fed through a belay device, which acts as a block (see *Figure 15.10*). This also means that the hoist can be easily converted into a lowering system by simply removing the prusiks. However, in this situation it is important to ensure the belayer has adequate control of the dead rope by either being positioned behind the belay device or clipping the dead rope through a karabiner behind the belay device (see *Figure 15.11*).

If there is too much friction it is worth trying two pulley karabiners or better a lightweight pulley wheel. Mechanical devices can be used in place of the prusiks to increase efficiency; there are a number of effective lightweight ascenders available but climbers should be completely familiar with their use and limitations, especially with 'skinny' ropes before deciding to carry them.

### 15.4.4 Hip hoist

This variation of an unassisted hoist makes use of the powerful leg muscles and works best on a small stance with high anchors.

1  Attach a prusik to the load rope and clip this direct to the harness belay loop.
2  Run the rope through an alpine clutch (see *Alpine clutch* on page 69).
3  Squat down and slide the prusik as low as possible.
4  Stand up and pull down on the dead rope (on the other side of the clutch) at the same time.
5  Let the clutch take the load and squat back down while moving the prusik down too (see *Figure 15.12*).

*Troubleshooting*
The alpine clutch is the most effective way to minimise slippage but it is not reversible. A pulley karabiner and French prusik autobloc (as described above) can be used but is not efficient.

### 15.4.5 Traverses

Hoists, lowers and abseils work best in a straight line. If an injured and/or stuck climber is on a traverse it may first need to be straightened. This can be done by either moving the casualty to below the stance or by re-belaying above the casualty. It is important to consider the direction

alpine
clutch

belayer stands
to hoist climber
upwards

French prusik
clipped to
harness

fallen
climber

FIGURE 15.12   HIP HOIST

1   Escape the system (see *12.2.2 Escaping from the system* on page 128).
2   Climb, prusik or abseil to the casualty, taking the end or loop of rope to clip to the casualty's harness belay loop (see *Figure 15.13A*).
3   Return to the belay.
4   Belay the original and new ropes with Italian hitches direct to the belay (see *Figure 15.13B*).
5   Pay out the original rope and take in the new rope alternately, tying them off each time if necessary (see *Figure 15.13C*) until the casualty pendulums down and across to below the stance (see *Figure 15.13D*). Lower, abseil, counterbalance abseil or hoist as appropriate (it may first be necessary to retrieve the original end of the rope from the injured climber before continuing).

If the climber is within throwing distance, the belayer doesn't need to escape the system. Instead a loop of rope (taken from the belayer's end of the rope) can be thrown to the second. This new rope is taken-in on an Italian hitch, while the original rope is paid out through the belay device.

Re-belaying above an injured climber is a lengthy procedure and only necessary if it is impossible to descend or continue from the original stance (see *Figure 15.14A*).

1   Escape the system (see *12.2.2 Escaping from the system* on page 128).
2   Climb or prusik along the traverse and arrange anchors to create a belay above the casualty.
3   Attach a French prusik to the rope and connect it to the belay (see *Figure 15.14B*).
4   Return to the original belay, release the tension and lower the casualty onto the new French prusik and belay (see *Figure 15.14C*).
5   Climb across once more back-roping through the original belay to back up the French prusik (see *Figure 15.14D*).
6   Back up the French prusik at the new belay with an Italian hitch tied off (see *Figure 15.14E*).
7   Pull the rope through from the original belay. Lower, abseil, counterbalance abseil or hoist as appropriate.

of load on the anchors, which may well be sideways, and reinforce belays if necessary.

Moving the climber to below the original stance is the simplest option, especially if they are within throwing distance. This can be a useful way to rescue a climber who has fallen and is unable to re-gain the traverse line.

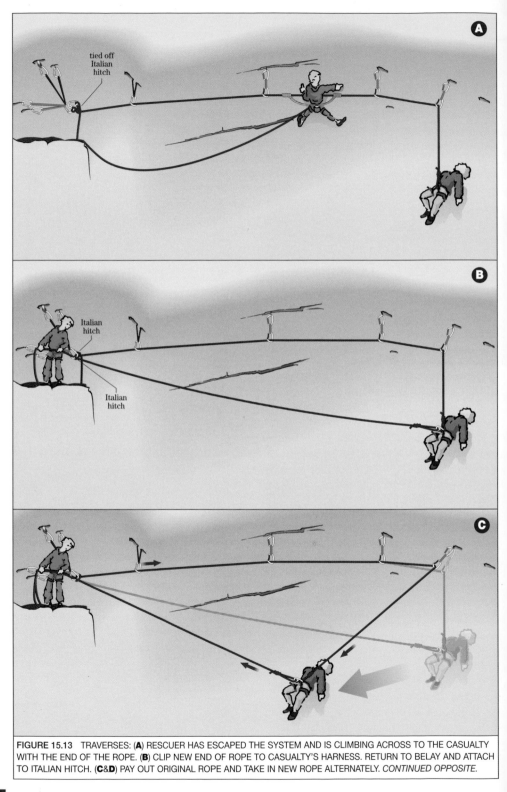

**FIGURE 15.13** TRAVERSES: (**A**) RESCUER HAS ESCAPED THE SYSTEM AND IS CLIMBING ACROSS TO THE CASUALTY WITH THE END OF THE ROPE. (**B**) CLIP NEW END OF ROPE TO CASUALTY'S HARNESS. RETURN TO BELAY AND ATTACH TO ITALIAN HITCH. (**C**&**D**) PAY OUT ORIGINAL ROPE AND TAKE IN NEW ROPE ALTERNATELY. *CONTINUED OPPOSITE.*

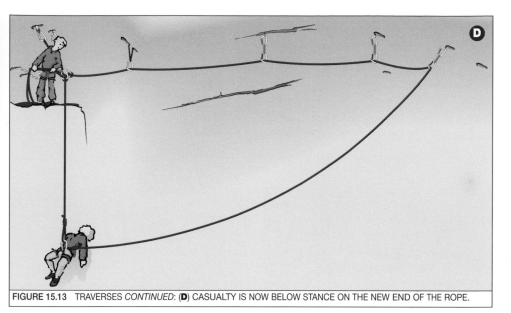

FIGURE 15.13 TRAVERSES *CONTINUED*: (**D**) CASUALTY IS NOW BELOW STANCE ON THE NEW END OF THE ROPE.

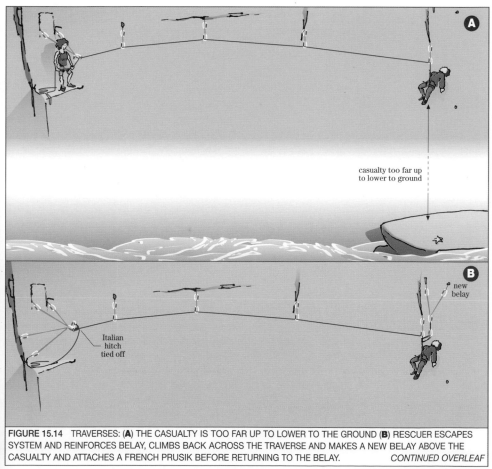

FIGURE 15.14 TRAVERSES: (**A**) THE CASUALTY IS TOO FAR UP TO LOWER TO THE GROUND (**B**) RESCUER ESCAPES SYSTEM AND REINFORCES BELAY, CLIMBS BACK ACROSS THE TRAVERSE AND MAKES A NEW BELAY ABOVE THE CASUALTY AND ATTACHES A FRENCH PRUSIK BEFORE RETURNING TO THE BELAY. *CONTINUED OVERLEAF*

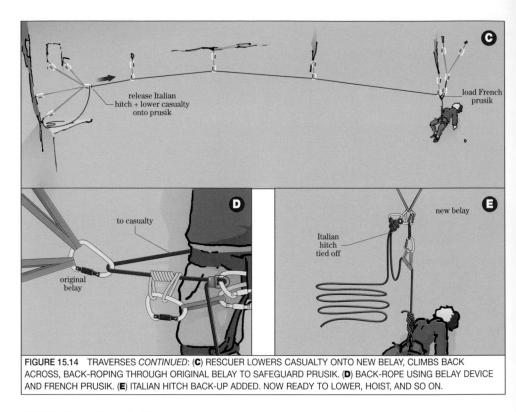

FIGURE 15.14  TRAVERSES *CONTINUED*: (**C**) RESCUER LOWERS CASUALTY ONTO NEW BELAY, CLIMBS BACK
ACROSS, BACK-ROPING THROUGH ORIGINAL BELAY TO SAFEGUARD PRUSIK. (**D**) BACK-ROPE USING BELAY DEVICE
AND FRENCH PRUSIK. (**E**) ITALIAN HITCH BACK-UP ADDED. NOW READY TO LOWER, HOIST, AND SO ON.

## 15.5  Leader falls

If a fallen leader is injured, in most situations it
should be possible to lower directly back to the
ground or the stance and take it from there. If
more than half a rope length has been run out or
if the route traverses above the sea things are
more complicated. In both scenarios the belayer
must escape the system, ensuring there is an
adequate upward-pulling anchor and re-belay
above the injured climber as outlined above,
before lowering, abseiling or hoisting.

## 15.6  Conclusion

Rescue techniques always seem ridiculously
complicated when written down, but they are not
so bad in practise, honest! The answer is to try
out the basic techniques somewhere safe with
the book and plenty of prusiks to hand. A good
place to start is in the living room or on the stairs,
before finding a very short drop to practise dan-
gling a weighted rucksack over; only then is it
time to enlist the help of a 'body'. Always ensure
the anchors are bombproof and always use an
additional back-up rope that both climbers can
clip into.

Textbook solutions won't always fit real life
situations; it is more important for climbers to
have a grasp of the basic principles which can be
applied with common sense and a cool head. It is
only vital to act with speed in a few situations;
otherwise it is better to take a few moments to
consider all the options before committing to a
lengthy and possible risky manoeuvre. The techniques for lowering and hoisting outlined here
are examples of some of the more popular ones
used, but they are not the only methods that are
effective.

By knowing what can go wrong and anticipating problems in the first place the chances of
them occurring are reduced, this is the way forward. (See also *18 Accidents* on page 201.)

ENJOYING THE SOLITUDE OF THE CUILLIN RIDGE, SKYE

# Part V

# Scrambling and other activities

# Scrambling

EXPOSED SCRAMBLING ON CRIB GOCH, SNOWDON

Scrambling has a delightful fluidity which appeals to adventurous walkers and climbers alike. This chapter considers appropriate techniques for protecting the scrambler.

16

Hill walking, scrambling and rock climbing are all aspects of mountaineering but are sometimes considered as separate activities even though there is much overlap. Many walks include sections of scrambling and virtually all scrambles involve some hill walking. The distinction between scrambling and walking depends on how often the hands are used for balance, security and to make progress when moving over steep ground. The difference between scrambling and climbing terrain is even less well defined, as the harder scrambles have much in common with, and in many cases were originally regarded as, easy rock climbs.

Scrambling terrain encompasses ground steep enough to warrant using the hands for more than just the occasional hold as well as exposed ridges, gullies, ghylls and faces where there may be short sections of rock climbing at about Moderate grade. (Rock climbing grades are explained on page 44).

## 16.1 Guidebooks, route selection and route finding

There are many scrambling guidebooks that cover the Lake District, North Wales and parts of Scotland and Ireland. These select notable lines giving information about how to locate the scramble, a route description and grade. Other scrambles are discovered by chance, by careful scrutiny of a map or by following one's nose up an interesting section of hillside.

## Equipment

### Helmet
It is not common practise to wear helmets on classic Grade 1 type scrambles especially as these are often ridge lines with minimal threat of stonefall. However, in the event of a fall from such routes a helmet would undoubtedly reduce the risk of head injury. Much scrambling terrain is loose and in these areas a standard rock climbing helmet is a sensible precaution. Scramblers must make their own judgement according to the terrain and their own experience.

### Harness
If the use of the rope is planned or expected, it makes sense to carry and use a harness. This may be a rock climbing harness or a lighter alpine style harness, which may be a better fit over bulky mountain clothing.

### Boots
Reasonably stiff but light, well fitting and precise boots feel more secure when standing on small holds than loose, bendy walking boots. Approach shoes are a popular alternative and some are designed with friction on rock in mind. It should be remembered though that such low cut footwear offers less protection and support to the ankle on rough terrain.

### Rope
A 50m single rope is adequate for a party of two or three.

### Small rack
Depending on the severity and nature of the route a small rack can be selected from the list below. Easy scrambles can normally be protected adequately with slings and karabiners alone, but if sections of harder scrambling are anticipated a small amount of technical gear is a wise addition.
- Nuts on wire 2,4,6,8,10
- Hexagonal nuts 6 and 8 or camming devices 2 and 3
- Quickdraws × 2
- Long slings × 3
- Short slings × 2
- Snap-link karabiners × 4
- Screwgate karabiners × 4
- HMS karabiner or belay device

# Confidence roping, short roping and moving together

## Confidence roping

Confidence roping is used to safeguard one person with a short length of rope out (about 1–2 metres) while moving on exposed but non-serious terrain. It normally takes place in a hill walking context where a rope is not normally needed but is used by the leader to secure a nervous individual within a group.

## Short roping

Short roping is the planned use of the rope to protect one or two individuals on scrambling type terrain. It incorporates the use of a number of techniques according to the difficulty of the ground and the competence and experience of the individuals. It can be used in ascent or descent and normally tackles difficulties as a series of short pitches with the rope shortened (using body coils) accordingly.

## Moving together

Moving together is an advanced and potentially serious technique (not often called for in the UK) that involves two or more individuals moving at a steady pace and at the same time over exposed alpine type terrain. Runners can be arranged by the leader and removed by the last person but assured and competent movement by all members of the party is crucial to ensure safety.

It is important, when selecting an appropriate route, to consider not only the grade but also how damp conditions, aspect and the time of year affect the scramble. Certain rock types feel less secure in the wet and shady north facing routes are often green and slimy long into the summer.

Route finding can be straightforward if the scramble follows a major feature, but tends to be rather more complex if the route is located on a big open face. Whether following a route description or not, care is required in selecting the best line to take; this should avoid loose sections, excessive difficulties and blind alleys. Slightly harder sections on clean, dry rock are often preferable to easier looking, but vegetated (and therefore less secure) variations. Many scrambles have long approaches and descents, taking in summits or making a mountain journey and these require additional general mountain skills such as navigation.

# 16.2 Protecting scrambles

Scrambles can be protected using a variety of techniques according to their difficulty and taking into account the competence and experience of the party.

Classic ridges, such as the Aonach Eagach in Glencoe, Crib Goch on Snowdon, Striding Edge on Helvellyn and the Beenkeragh-Carrauntoohill ridge in Kerry, are considered to be Grade 1 scrambles. They all have sections of exposed footpath and steep rocky terrain furnished with good holds. There may be isolated tricky steps but they are normally completed without the use of a rope by a confident team in good conditions. Unexpected strong winds, cold, wet, ice or darkness present a very different prospect and many parties might protect steep or exposed sections of these same routes with a rope under such conditions. This emergency or occasional use of the rope is covered in *Hill Walking* (see *Appendix 6: Bibliography* on page 220) and focuses on situations where a rope alone is carried. Winter conditions transform many straightforward scrambles into serious climbs requiring specialist equipment and techniques that are beyond the scope of this book.

Harder scrambles, encompassed by the Grades 2 and 3, are usually more serious and have sections of more continuous and steeper rock that may include pitches of Moderate grade rock climbing. They may also be completed without the use of a rope, but only by experienced scramblers or climbers confident in making tricky moves on exposed ground. Such solo

FIGURE 16.1   USING THE ROPE ON A GRADE 3 SCRAMBLE

ascents are normally made in calm weather when the rock is dry. Damp, vegetated routes with greasy, lichenous rock are considerably harder to climb with security and certainty. Both the extent of the difficulties and the condition of the route are often hard to predict and the consequences of a slip from such exposed terrain would be disastrous. For these reasons it is normal to use a rope on harder scrambles (see *Figure 16.1*).

In addition to scrambling routes such as those described in guidebooks, this chapter also considers the easier sections of mountaineering routes and the scrambling approaches to, or descents from, rock climbs.

FIGURE 16.2  TYING OFF BODY COILS (**A**) SLIDE HAND BETWEEN COILS AND BODY (**B**) PULL BIGHT OF ROPE BACK THROUGH (**C**) WRAP BIGHT OVER COILS (**D**) TIE OVERHAND KNOT AROUND MAIN ROPE (**E**) LEAVE ONLY A SHORT TAIL (**F**) CLIP TAIL INTO SCREWGATE ON CENTRAL ROPE LOOP. PULL ROPE TO CHECK KNOT DOESN'T SLIDE

## 16.2.1  Short roping

Harder scrambles consist of a series of short, tricky steps separated by easier sections and ledges that are often piled with loose rock. Protecting such ground in full rope length pitches is cumbersome, creates rope drag, causes stonefall and makes communication difficult. A more efficient system is to protect the hard sections as *short pitches* and to move at the same time with great care on the easy sections.

The rope is shortened by wrapping coils of rope diagonally around the chest and tying them securely so there is no chance of them tightening around the body in the event of a fall. These body coils should be neat and hang just above the waistline. There are several methods for tying off

the coils, and one popular system is shown here (see *Figure 16.2*). The amount of free rope out between scramblers will be dictated by the terrain but is normally 10–15 metres.

## 16.2.2  Short pitches

A short, steep rock step can be protected in many ways according to the competence of the party and the difficulty of the step. The idea is to strike a balance between speed and safety. At one extreme an experienced climber may climb the step without being belayed or placing runners and bring up a confident partner by adopting a braced stance (see below), taking in the rope hand over hand. This would be quick but offers limited security. A less experienced team on the same step could find an anchor at the base for the second to attach to and belay from. The leader would climb the step, placing runners where necessary and belay the second up from an anchor at the top; in other words they could treat it as a short climbing pitch. When deciding what level of security is required the team should consider difficulty and seriousness of the terrain, likelihood and consequences of a fall or slip and availability of anchors or runners.

# 16.3 Belaying

When scrambling in short pitches it a good idea to make use of anchors at the base of tricky steps. This is particularly important if the ledge is small and there is a chance of the second being pulled off the ledge by a falling leader. If an anchor is not available in this situation, the leader should place a runner instead to protect the whole team. On spacious ledges where there is little possibility of the second being pulled off, an anchor may not be essential.

A confident and competent leader may not require to be belayed by the second, especially on short sections where a fall would only result in landing back on the ledge. However, if there is any doubt about the degree of difficulty or the consequences of a fall, the second should belay the leader using a waist belay (see *Figure 16.8*), an Italian hitch or even a standard belay device if

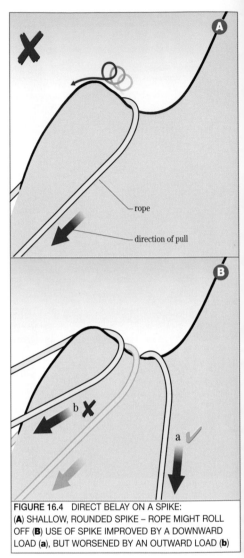

FIGURE 16.4   DIRECT BELAY ON A SPIKE: (**A**) SHALLOW, ROUNDED SPIKE – ROPE MIGHT ROLL OFF (**B**) USE OF SPIKE IMPROVED BY A DOWNWARD LOAD (**a**), BUT WORSENED BY AN OUTWARD LOAD (**b**)

one is carried. Runners are occasionally needed to protect a tricky or exposed step and are placed with the same considerations as on a rock climb.

At the top of a tricky step the leader selects from one of the following belay options:

### 16.3.1 Direct belay around rock

It is sometimes possible to run the rope directly around a solid anchor, normally a rock spike or block which must be bombproof and shaped appropriately to hold the rope without it slipping off or riding up (see *Figure 16.3*). Care must be taken to avoid shallow spikes (see *Figure 16.4*)

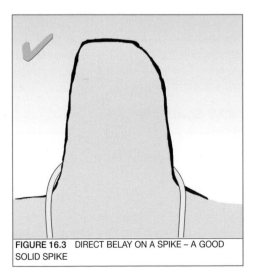

FIGURE 16.3   DIRECT BELAY ON A SPIKE – A GOOD SOLID SPIKE

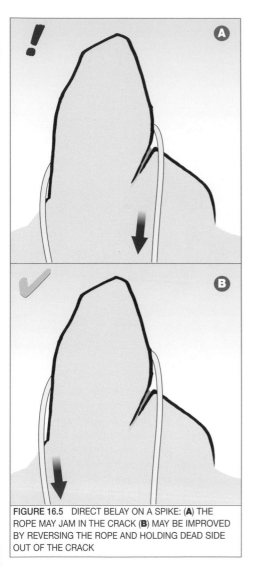

FIGURE 16.5   DIRECT BELAY ON A SPIKE: (**A**) THE
ROPE MAY JAM IN THE CRACK (**B**) MAY BE IMPROVED
BY REVERSING THE ROPE AND HOLDING DEAD SIDE
OUT OF THE CRACK

and those with sharp or rough edges that may
cause damage or constrictions where the rope
may become trapped (see *Figure 16.5*). The
belayer takes the rope in around the anchor
ensuring a secure grip on the dead rope at all
times; gloves will help. It is often best to feed the
rope around the anchor with a hand on each side
and then swap hands on the dead rope (see *Figure 16.6*). Friction created by the rope against
the rock enables the belayer to hold a slip. On a
spacious ledge the belayer does not need to be
attached to the anchor, making it a very quick
system to set up. It is vital to remember that any
resulting force will be taken directly on the

FIGURE 16.6   TAKING IN THE ROPE AROUND A SPIKE

FIGURE 16.7   DIRECT BELAY USING AN ITALIAN HITCH

anchor so sound judgement of the anchor is crucial. If there is any doubt about its suitability it should be used as an indirect anchor.

### 16.3.2  Direct belay (Italian hitch)

If an anchor is not suitable to accommodate the rope alone it may be possible to place a sling around the spike, block or thread. This is used as a direct belay using an HMS screwgate karabiner and Italian hitch. The belayer is attached to the same sling for security if the ledge is small or exposed (see *Figure 16.7*). If natural anchors are not available, one or more pieces of gear are placed and equalised to a central point with a sling. Belaying directly from a single anchor is only appropriate if the anchor is bombproof, as it will take the whole load of a fall. If a marginal anchor can not be backed up it is safer to use an indirect system.

### 16.3.3  Indirect belay

A semi-direct or indirect belay may be necessary if anchors are not good enough to take a direct loading. The belayer ties on and belays from the central rope loop using an Italian hitch or a belay device as in a rock climbing situation. If a waist belay is used whilst tied on from the front of a

harness, it is important to take into account the sideways position. The live rope should be on the same side of the body as the anchor ropes, in other words, if the anchor ropes are on the belayer's left side the live rope is held in the left hand and the right becomes the brake hand. In this way any load twists the belayer onto the anchor rope increasing friction and grip on the rope (see *Figure 16.8A*). If this is set up the wrong way round there is a danger that the belayer may be untwisted from the rope and unable to hold the fall (see *Figure 16.8B&C*).

### Braced stance (hand over hand)

With this method it is possible to hold a minor slip and prevent a fall, but only if the rope is held securely with no slack in the system at all. Weight difference must be taken into account, as while it might be possible for a heavy leader to hold a lighter second, the reverse may be impossible.

The technique requires either a dynamic standing position with one foot forward or a sitting stance with feet braced against something solid. The hands grab the rope alternately and kink the rope maintaining a constant tension and tight rope to the second. The arms are bent and ready to give full support by incorporating the

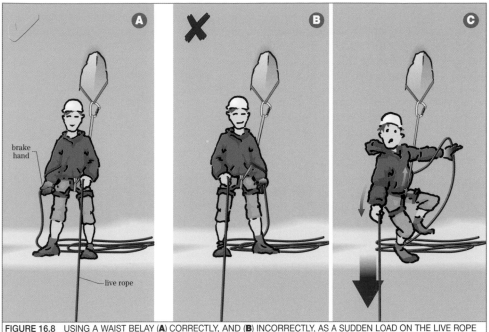

**FIGURE 16.8** USING A WAIST BELAY (**A**) CORRECTLY, AND (**B**) INCORRECTLY, AS A SUDDEN LOAD ON THE LIVE ROPE CAN CAUSE THE BELAYER TO UNTWIST (**C**)

muscles of the arm, shoulder and the strength of the whole body. Gloves with a non-slip finish are a good idea to ensure a firm grip, and by utilising the thumb, a 180° turn can be created on the rope, which would help prevent a friction burn in the case of a slip (see *Figure 16.9*).

Careful judgement is required to determine when it is appropriate to use this technique, as the consequences of it failing are potentially disastrous. It should be considered as a means of supporting weight in the event of a slip and *not* a means of holding a fall. It should not be used where there is any likelihood of a fall occurring. Considerable practise is needed to understand its limitations; this is best done with a willing partner above a very short drop with a safe, soft landing.

**Braced sitting stance (waist belay)**

A sitting stance with the rope running across the ground creates friction, which makes holding a slip easier. A waist belay ensures a firm grip on the rope and incorporates body weight too, with the feet braced against something solid the strong muscles of the legs are used to great effect. This system is more secure than a braced stance but still requires careful judgement. The rope is taken in with a sequence of hand move-

ments to ensure the dead rope is held securely at all times.

# 16.4 Moving together

This technique involves a party moving at the same time whilst roped up. It is used primarily on long, exposed alpine type ridges where speed is important. It can be used by a party of two to four, but requires confident and secure movement by all members of the party. Protection is arranged by weaving the rope around rock spikes or placing and clipping the rope to runners at intervals to ensure there is always at least one point of security. The runners are placed by the leader and removed by the last person.

This is potentially a 'one off, all off' technique, so judgement, practise and caution are all essential and it should only be used on difficult or serious terrain by experienced and confident parties. However, it is a useful method of travelling on the easy scrambling ground between harder sections where a rope for safety is desirable but not essential and when the rope will be needed again later. In other words it is an efficient method of

# Waist belay technique

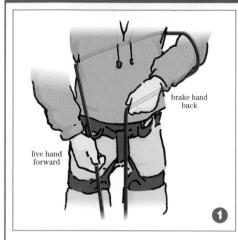

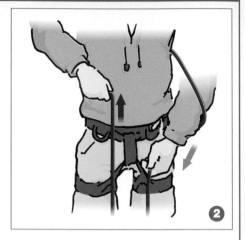

**1** Start position: The rope is flicked over the head to sit around the waist. The live hand is forward and the brake hand is twisted around the dead rope just in front of the waist.

**2** Slack is taken in with a pull-push motion, the live hand pulls back and the brake hand pushes forward.

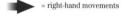 = left-hand movements

= right-hand movements

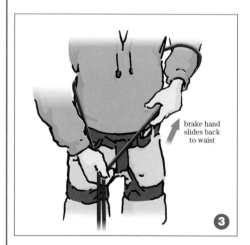

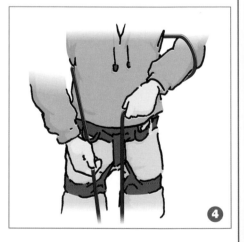

**3** The live hand slides down the rope and pinches the dead rope in front of the brake hand enabling the dead hand to slide back up to the waist.

**4** The live hand releases its pinch on the dead rope and both hands are back to the start position.

FIGURE 16.9   BRACED STANCE: NOTE DYNAMIC BODY POSITION, GLOVES AND SECURE KINKED GRIP ON ROPE

transporting the rope and, if done correctly, offers some security too.

On easy, non-serious terrain, where two hands are not needed for progress and the chances of a slip are remote, the rope is just being transported to the next harder section. A few small coils or laps (folds) of rope are held in the hand to shorten it further. Coils can kink the rope, so lapping or folding the rope into the palm of the hand is often better. Whichever method is used the amount of rope held should not over-fill the hand and the coils should reach no lower than mid-calf to avoid tripping over them. To prevent the coils or laps slipping out of the hand they can be finished with a locking turn of the rope diagonally across the palm of the hand. The person at the front normally holds the coils and everyone moves at the same pace, close together and keeping the rope off the ground (see *Figure 16.10*).

For slightly trickier terrain that is exposed but doesn't warrant pitching, the technique is adapted to increase security. Hand coils are dropped leaving 10–15m of rope out. The leader places runners and the second moves at a pace to ensure slack doesn't develop. There should be at least one point of security at all times; this may be the rope running behind a flake or clipped to a runner. It is not common to use this technique in the UK other than for very short sections, exposed horizontal ground or by competent teams of equal ability moving on terrain well within their capability (see *Figure 16.11*).

## 16.5  Descent

Many people find descending steep ground difficult and intimidating; moving together in descent is therefore only appropriate on very easy terrain. A leader safeguarding a novice stays behind and above, from where the speed and direction of the descent is controlled. From this position, watching and anticipating a slip is made easier as the leader has an unrestricted view down the rope.

FIGURE 16.10    MOVING TOGETHER ON EASY, NON-SERIOUS TERRAIN

FIGURE 16.11    MOVING TOGETHER WITH RUNNERS ON ALPINE-TYPE TERRAIN

Moving together with a novice is a serious undertaking and should only be considered by experienced leaders and even then only on easy or non-serious terrain when it could be considered as confidence roping. The leader holds the coils and stays directly above the novice, maintaining tension in the rope to give security. The arm is slightly bent and the hand kinks the rope for better grip. The arm, shoulder and indeed whole body act as a shock absorber, applying and releasing tension as and when the novice requires more or less support. The rope is held in the downhill hand for maximum control and energy absorption and to prevent the leader being rotated. The distance between leader and novice is as close as possible while still allowing unrestricted movement, normally about 1.5–3m (1–2 arm spans), see *Figure 16.12*.

The limitations of this technique must be fully grasped; it is not for holding falls. A tight rope gives psychological and physical support and slips may be checked. Whether it is possible to hold a slip will depend on the relative weight of leader and second, underfoot conditions and whether the leader is well braced. The leader watches closely, anticipating

**FIGURE 16.12** MOVING TOGETHER ON DRAMATIC BUT NON-SERIOUS TERRAIN

and preventing slips by suggesting better foot placements or holding the rope tight at just the right moment. An experienced leader will be all too aware that it is difficult to hold a slip with slack in the rope, especially if caught unawares or on wet or slippery rock. In poor conditions, unless the terrain is non-serious, it is unlikely to be appropriate to move together. The potential seriousness of this technique cannot be overstated.

The options for descending short, tricky steps include down climbing, abseiling or lowering. Down climbing offers good protection and support for the first person to descend, as they can be belayed from above. The last person should be the most confident and can be either belayed or spotted from below.

Short retrievable abseils can be rigged just as in a climbing situation. It may be possible to avoid leaving any gear behind if there is a solid, well placed spike or block that does not create too much friction to pull the rope. It is useful to carry a length of tape or rope to leave behind thus avoiding leaving more expensive sewn slings. See also *14 Descending from multi-pitch crags*, page 149. To avoid pulling an unnecessary amount of rope through the anchor on short

abseils, one end of rope is lowered just to reach the bottom of the step and then the rest of the rope is dropped, so it hangs off-centre. By pulling on the long end of rope, only the short end passes around the anchor (see *Figure 16.13*).

A lower may be appropriate if one of the party has not abseiled before, in which case the leader lowers the novice to safety before either down climbing or abseiling. On exposed ledges a novice must be safeguarded while the leader descends. It may be possible for the novice to attach to an obvious anchor on the ledge that can be seen and checked from above by the leader. Placing a sling over a spike and clipping to it or wrapping the rope a few times around a spike may be sufficient. In the unlikely event that a safe ledge cannot be found, the novice can be

**FIGURE 16.13**   A SHORT ABSEIL, ROPE ARRANGED OFF-CENTRE

Looking after two novices on scrambling terrain requires the application and practise of additional specialised techniques and is most often undertaken by guides and mountaineering instructors with clients.

The two clients are attached to the rope close together with one tying into the end while the other is tied to a loop about two metres further along the rope. An overhand knot or alpine butterfly is used to create an 'isolation loop', and the client ties to this loop with a re-threaded overhand knot. The tail of this knot should be clipped back to the central loop with a screwgate instead of tying a stopper, which can be cumbersome in this situation (see *Figure 16.14*). It is important that the clients are tied onto the rope rather than clipped on using a screwgate to prevent inadvertent unclipping or a three-way loading on the karabiner.

safeguarded by the rope while the leader abseils; this is explained in *14 Descending from multi-pitch crags*, page 149 and *Figure 16.13*.

# 16.6 Mountaineering routes and approaches to climbs

Mountaineering routes typically involve sections of rock climbing interspersed with easier scrambling sections. To move efficiently on such routes, normal pitched climbing can be alternated with some of the techniques explained above. The rope is kept on the whole time and is shortened with body coils for short roping and moving together. As soon as a section of harder climbing is reached, the body coils are dropped and normal pitched climbing resumes.

Approaches to rock climbs often require the use of scrambling techniques. If double-ropes and a large rack of gear are being carried, just one of the ropes and a few items of gear can be used for the approach and the remainder carried in the rucksack until the climbing starts.

## Safeguarding two clients

Depending on the size of the ledge and the exposure and seriousness of the terrain there are a number of ways of securing two clients on a ledge. A simple and quick method is to place the section of rope between them over a solid spike or flake so counterbalancing each other's weight (see *Figure 16.15*). Alternatively this section of rope can be clove hitched to the anchor thus attaching them both with one knot (see *Figure 16.16*). On a restricted stance however, it is often better to attach them with two separate clove hitches so they are independently secured (see *Figure 16.17*).

FIGURE 16.14   ATTACHING TWO CLIENTS TO A ROPE

FIGURE 16.15   COUNTERBALANCE BELAY

FIGURE 16.16   ONE CLOVE HITCH TO SAFEGUARD BOTH CLIENTS

## Belaying two clients

Maintaining a tight rope to two clients on one rope whilst belaying requires management and briefing from the instructor and co-operation by the clients to move at a similar pace, watching and waiting for each other on tricky moves. In particular it is vital the first client remains below the isolation knot to avoid shock loading the system (see *Figure 16.18*). The second client must pause for the first client to make tricky moves or remove runners so as not to catch up and create slack in the system. The instructor can manage this by belaying in view of the clients.

The likelihood and consequences of holding both clients at the same time must be considered when selecting an appropriate belay method. For example if it is possible (although unlikely) that a slip by one client could result in knocking the other client off, a braced stance in this situation would not be sufficient and one of the more secure methods previously described should be selected.

Managing the rope as the clients arrive at the stance requires careful organisation to avoid leaving someone unprotected. If the anchor is at the back of a large ledge the first client can keep moving towards the anchor and the second client is still protected by taking in the rope until the first client reaches the anchor. If the second client is by now on easy ground it is possible to keep hold of the dead side of the Italian hitch with one hand whilst firmly holding the rope to the second client with the other. However, if the second client is on tricky ground when the first client reaches the anchor greater care is needed. The second client pauses while the first client is secured by either tying off the belay device or clipping to the anchor. The second client can then be belayed with a two handed brace, a waist belay or an Italian hitch as appropriate.

FIGURE 16.17 BOTH CLIENTS ATTACHED TO ANCHOR

to leader/instructor

small exposed ledge

## Lowering two people

There are a number of options for lowering two clients depending on their confidence and experience, the steepness and length of the step and the quality of the anchor. The quickest option is to lower both at the same time but this requires co-operation on their part, and a totally bombproof and appropriate anchor. It should only be considered on fairly easy angled terrain where the clients are supporting much of their own weight.

They can be lowered side by side or one below the other but both systems present problems. Side by side can result in them competing for foot space, knocking together and generally feeling uncomfortable; it is however easier to manage initially because their weight comes simultaneously onto the anchor (see *Figure 16.19A*).

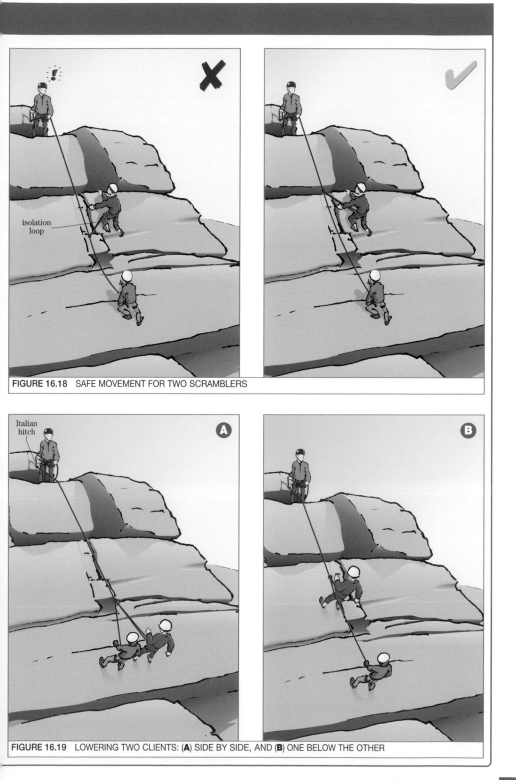

isolation
loop

FIGURE 16.18  SAFE MOVEMENT FOR TWO SCRAMBLERS

Italian
hitch

**A**

**B**

FIGURE 16.19  LOWERING TWO CLIENTS: (**A**) SIDE BY SIDE, AND (**B**) ONE BELOW THE OTHER

One below the other gives each a little space but requires careful management to protect both at the start (see *Figure 16.19B*). The easiest way to achieve this is to arrange a lowering point well back from the edge; this allows the rope to be weighted by both clients before the first client sets off. If the client nearest the instructor stands close to the anchor at the back of the ledge the first client can weight the rope near the front of the ledge. As lowering begins both clients have a tight rope.

On steeper steps the best option may be to lower one at a time. The simplest solution is to tie one client, usually the nearest to the instructor, to the anchor while the first is lowered. Once the first client is safe then the second client is then tied back into the rope and lowered.

KEN PALMER ON THE SECOND PITCH OF THE AMAZING **RAINBOW BRIDGE** E5 6a/b, BERRY HEAD,
BRIXHAM, DEVON

Photo: Mike Robertson

# Sea-level traversing & gorge scrambling

**Sea-level traversing originated in the South of England over a hundred years ago, partly as a method of accessing climbs but also as a form of exploration itself.**

# 17.1 Sea-level traversing

## 17.1.1 History and background

In the early 1900s A W Andrews, who was a prolific Cornish sea cliff explorer, recognised that climbing horizontally avoided loose cliff top finishes. He also embraced the complete sea-level journey, making progress by swimming and lassoing spikes to cross zawns. Sea-level traversing also captivated Menlove Edwards, who once spent a week traversing a Norwegian fjord with his supplies on his back!

In the 1960s, when sea cliff development was at its most popular, traverses were an accepted part of exploration, often giving access to previously unexplored terrain. Rusty Baillie and John Cleare climbed Magical Mystery Tour girdling the Old Redoubt Cliff, Berry Head, which now links one and a half miles of traverse around Torbay.

Today, sea-level traversing is popular with groups looking for a wet weather alternative to climbing or as an adventure activity in its own right. It can be completed dry, as a form of horizontal climbing, or intentionally wet with swims and jumps as an integral part and in this form is known as coasteering. This book considers the traditional dry sea-level traversing which has its roots firmly in climbing.

## 17.1.2 Hazards

*Sea-level traversing* is often viewed as a light-hearted, fun activity ideal for groups of inexperienced youngsters. Indeed on a calm, sunny day at the right location this is true. However, it is one of the most serious climbing environments to operate in, with a myriad of hazards to assess and where the management of risk is highly complex.

The sea presents the most obvious hazard and a sound understanding of tides is essential in order to judge when and for how long a particular traverse is accessible. In addition, the impact of swell and wave patterns coupled with local weather conditions must also be considered. Even then the possibility of being hit by a freak wave or wash from a large vessel must not be discounted.

The rock is often unpredictable, frequently wet or greasy with patches of seaweed and a texture that varies from smooth and glassy to razor sharp and barnacled. Though wave washed rock is normally solid, a watchful eye must be kept on what is above, as cliff tops can be alarmingly loose.

Sea birds, especially at nesting time, can be alarmingly vicious when protecting their young and although dive bombing rarely results in serious injury, it can be unsettling and off-putting.

Many traverses once embarked on are difficult to escape from without completing or reversing the section, in other words they are committing journeys from which evacuation of an injured, tired or cold person would be problematic.

The noise of the sea often makes communication difficult and this is compounded by the lack of opportunities for a group to assemble together. Unexpected immersion in cold water can induce panic and presents a threat of cold injuries or hypothermia, even during the summer months. Weak swimmers if encumbered with clothing and footwear and unaccustomed to a choppy sea may quickly encounter difficulties in even a short stretch of water. Climbing back onto the rock from a sea with a slight swell is difficult to master and scrapes are common.

## Equipment

Assuming a predominantly dry excursion with the emphasis on the climbing, appropriate gear can be selected from the following list:
- Helmet
- Buoyancy aid
- Rock boots or trainers
- Harness
- Double cow's tail
- Rigging ropes and rack
- Throw-line

Repeated exposure to salt water is damaging to climbing equipment so it is preferable to use a dedicated set of gear. Low stretch ropes are the best choice for fixed lines and tyrolean traverses. It is a good idea to carry the climbing gear on a bandolier so it can be ditched quickly if required.

FIGURE 17.1   A TYROLEAN TRAVERSE                                    Photo: Nigel Shepherd

### 17.1.3 Unroped traverses

Traversing above the sea unencumbered by ropes and gear has a delightful flow and feeling of freedom. Much ground can be covered in a short time, but there is always the possibility of a slip or fall, which may result in bumps, scrapes and a soaking. Even a short fall can result in an awkward landing amongst boulders or onto submerged ledges. Spotting awkward sections is an option but not always possible and often difficult

Protecting a group on a tricky or exposed traverse is best done with a fixed rope along which the group protect themselves with a double cow's tail. The rope must be positioned at an appropriate height to prevent landing in the water but also at a height that allows the easiest line to be climbed. The rope is tied off at regular intervals to anchors that are solid and multi-directional or well above the traverse line and extended down to prevent them being lifted out (see *Figure 17.2*). The tension in the rope must be judged to allow for ease of movement but keep slips to a minimum. Tricky sections of climbing may require a taut rope that can be used like a handrail. This is sometimes referred to as a Hinterstoisser traverse and with encouragement even the most timid group member can be coaxed to scuttle crab-like across seemingly blank sections of rock.

It may be possible for a group with two instructors, one rigging at the front and one de-rigging at the back, to move along at a steady pace. The instructors must consider how to feed out or retrieve the rope without it ending up in the water. One method is to coil the rope around the chest so a few coils at a time are dropped or taken in. In this case shorter lengths of rope (25–30m) are more convenient to carry than a full 50m rope. An alternative is to carry the rope in a caving style rope bag clipped to the harness or folded into a rucksack so it feeds out as required. It is obvious that instructors fixing traverses in this style must be operating within their 'comfort zone'. A fall into the sea, encumbered with so much gear and rope, could be very dangerous.

The group move along the traverse, *via ferrata* style, clipping passed the anchors by moving one link at a time (see *Figure 17.3*). The lead instructor must make it clear when it is safe for the group to follow on and there should only be one person between anchors at a time, so the group must wait accordingly.

Sections of down climbing or ascent must be considered carefully as a fixed

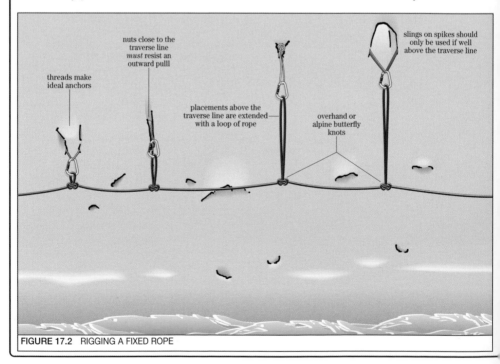

threads make
ideal anchors

nuts close to the
traverse line
*must* resist an
outward pulll

placements above the
traverse line are extended
with a loop of rope

overhand or
alpine butterfly
knots

slings on spikes should
only be used if well
above the traverse line

FIGURE 17.2   RIGGING A FIXED ROPE

rope alone will not prevent a fall. It may be better to protect such sections with a top-rope and, if the climbing is tricky, a fixed knotted hand-line or sling for aid alongside. Lengthy down climbing sections may be best managed with a lower. Judgement, experience and familiarity with a venue, along with a degree of inventiveness with rope systems, will allow instructors to provide groups with a challenging, exciting and flowing journey.

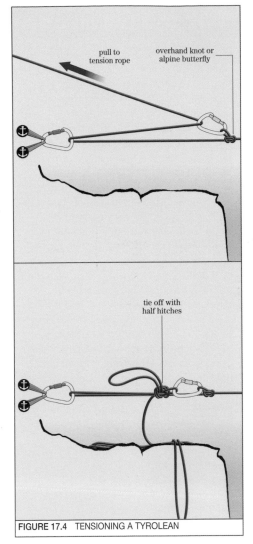

FIGURE 17.4   TENSIONING A TYROLEAN

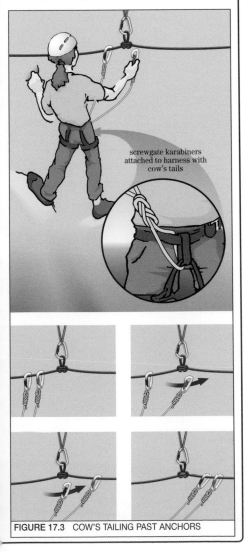

FIGURE 17.3   COW'S TAILING PAST ANCHORS

for a spotter to get into position from where assistance can be given. Unroped traversing is a good option for competent parties of equal ability, on simple sections where a slip is very unlikely or where the consequences of a slip are non-serious, perhaps where the water is shallow and there is easy access out of it.

### 17.1.4  Roped traverses

A climbing pair may choose to tackle a sea level traverse as pitched climbing, establishing belays and placing runners. However, it is very difficult to prevent a fall into the water unless high and closely spaced runners are placed strategically. If a fall into the water occurs the easiest way back

In a group situation it is a good idea to have a back-rope that can be controlled from both ends (a 'push-pull' rope) (see *Figure 17.5*). This can be arranged by clipping the ends of two separate ropes or a knot in the middle of one rope to the harness. It is best to avoid attaching the push-pull rope to the pulley or karabiner on the tyrolean as it tends to cause twisting and impedes smooth running.

In some situations a second tyrolean rope, incorporated as a back-up, is a good idea. The set-up is identical to a single rope system and the two ropes can either be tensioned together as one or independently. Some instructors prefer to leave the back-up rope slackly tensioned, the idea being that if the other rope was to snap the person crossing would drop into a deeper but less force generating 'V' of rope. Specialist pulleys or a figure of eight descender threaded onto the rope instead of karabiners can be used to facilitate smooth running and a faster ride. Hair and clothing must be tucked away to avoid becoming trapped in the moving pulley or karabiner and hands must be kept well clear to avoid pinching and friction burns. Attaching to the tyrolean with a cow's tail is a good option; it provides something to hold onto and allows onward clipping to the next traversing rope.

Rescuing someone stuck on a tyrolean is problematic and should be avoided by thorough preparation and briefings. Ease

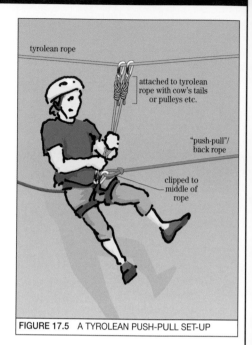

tyrolean rope

attached to tyrolean rope with cow's tails or pulleys etc.

"push-pull"/ back rope

clipped to middle of rope

**FIGURE 17.5** A TYROLEAN PUSH-PULL SET-UP

of take-off and landing at the far side should be considered when the rope is being positioned and tensioned. Up-hill exits can be tricky and strenuous to negotiate and downhill tyroleans must be judged carefully to ensure that there is sufficient of a 'V' in the rope to slow people down before the far side is reached. The push-pull obviously helps here, but care must be taken to ensure it is not damaged by rubbing across the tyrolean rope while under tension.

may be for the belayer to take in and lock the rope off so the swimmer can hand over hand until good holds or a ledge are reached.

### Tyrolean traverses

*Tyrolean traverses* are crossings made on a suspended horizontal rope. They may be required to cross a zawn, access a sea stack or simply as a grand finale to a fun day out. A true committing tyrolean first requires a swimmer to take the rope across but in a planned group activity this part is

usually 'cheated'! Once there is a rope spanning the gap it is secured and tensioned to provide a fixed line along which the party slide; it is best if the traverse runs slightly downhill (see *Figure 17.1*).

Solid and multi-directional anchors that can withstand a downward and outward pull at both sides of the gap are essential. It is normal to equalise several anchors to a central point with slings or a rigging rope. At one side of the gap the end of the rope is attached with a figure of eight

**FIGURE 17.6**   A TYPICAL GORGE SCRAMBLE

on a bight and the other side it is arranged so tension can be applied and released. It makes life easier if there is deep ledge on the tensioning side so clipping on or off can be done without interference from the tensioning system. Tensioning can be done by one person using a basic *Z pulley* (see *Figure 17.4*). Low-stretch ropes are easier to manage and require less of an overlap on the Z section. Even these may require re-tensioning after use by the first few people to cross. If there are several people available to tension the rope a simple method is to attach a prusik or ascender to the rope and pull on this while someone takes the slack in through an Italian hitch at the anchor, which is then tied off and the prusik removed.

The forces generated when a rope is tensioned and loaded are considerable. Over-tensioning, which is possible when mechanical devices are used or if more than one person is involved in pulling tension into the rope, can result in extremely high loads on the anchors, ropes and associated equipment. High strength and corrosion resistant steel karabiners may be advisable in this situation. Care must also be taken to prevent the rope running over sharp edges.

### 17.1.5  Safety

In a climbing situation it is normal to use one rope for the tyrolean and a second rope as a back-rope in case the climber needs pulling back. The climber attaches to the tyrolean rope with a screwgate attached to the harness belay loop and clips or ties to the other rope, which is also clipped to the tyrolean rope. To retrieve a tyrolean rope after use it must be converted to a continuous loop that can be untied and pulled through.

## 17.2  Gorge scrambling

### 17.2.1  Background and environmental considerations

*Gorge* or *ghyll scrambling* is a climbing-based activity, which may or may not involve getting wet and normally involves ascending the chosen route. Canyoning and river running are wet activities where gorges are descended using a combination of abseiling, jumping and swimming and require additional specialist skills that are not considered here.

Stream beds, ghylls and gorges are appealing natural and direct lines to follow up a mountainside. Many are steep sided and graded in a series of tricky steps that provide interesting scrambling in an enclosed and unique environment. Protected from grazing animals and with an abundant water supply gorges are rich in wildlife and often shelter rare species. The ecosystems are fragile and easily damaged and many gorges are designated SSSIs or NNRs. Moss covered boulders are soon scraped clean by scrabbling feet or chaffing ropes and plants clinging precariously to isolated pockets are easily disturbed.

### 17.2.2 Hazards

The rock in and at the edges of streams is normally smooth and glassy or covered in weed or moss. Either way it can be extremely slippery, especially if wet. Even a slip on the flat can result in a hard impact so helmets are essential. Deep pools and fast flowing water present obvious hazards. The strength of the current can be hard to predict and there is often little time to react before being washed towards a drop or obstacle. Sites that could cause entrapment such as submerged tree branches or where the water flows under a boulder must be identified and avoided. Even a foot becoming lodged between two rocks in shallow water can cause a problem.

The possibility of flash flooding must be considered as the effects of rising water are compounded in the confines of a gorge. Streams that are controlled by a dam must be researched thoroughly to ensure there is no possibility of an unexpected release of water. Limestone landscapes can conceal natural underground reservoirs, which can empty dramatically on reaching a critical level causing surges down stream. Familiarity with the wider terrain and setting as well as the gorge itself is important, particularly after heavy rainfall.

The noise of thundering water is magnified in an enclosed space making communication difficult and at times impossible. This should be pre-empted with appropriate briefings beforehand to avoid confusion. Signs of hypothermia following immersions must be watched for and it should be remembered that escape and rescue from a gorge is often difficult as the sides are normally steep, vegetated and may be of poor or broken rock.

### 17.2.3 Techniques and equipment

The techniques of protecting tricky sections are very similar to those described and used in sea level traverses and the equipment needed is therefore the same. Sections may be climbed unroped, protected with fixed lines and cow's tails or topropes; tyrolean traverses can be set up to cross the gorge. Additional care must be taken in protecting pitches or arranging abseils next to waterfalls to avoid the possibility of a pendulum into the flow of water. It is important for the leader to have a clear view down the pitch or abseil and releasable abseil systems should be used.

Jumping into pools should be considered carefully and only take place following a careful inspection. Brown, churned up floodwater can conceal submerged boulders and other hazards.

PATCH HAMMOND ON THE BOLD AND SCARY **CANNIBAL** E4 5c, LEFT HAND RED WALL, GOGARTH

# Part VI

# Accidents and the law

NEIL GRESHAM 'OFF' HIS OWN **AIRDRAWN DAGGER** E8 6c, BOX ZAWN, PEMBROKE          Photo: Mike Robertson

# Accidents

**Climbing has inherent risks.
This chapter examines the nature
of accidents and how rescues
are organised.**

# 18.1 Accidents and rescue

## 18.1.1 Organisation of rescue

The responsibility for search and rescue in the UK and Ireland falls to the area chief of police who enlists the help of voluntary civilian and military rescue teams. The RAF rescue teams are on standby to support military personnel and can become involved in civilian mountain rescue if they are not required for a military operation. There are 28 rescue teams covering Scotland, 11 in Ireland and nearly 60 in England and Wales which are organised into regional groups and co-ordinated by mountain rescue councils or associations. Each team is responsible for recruiting and training their own members to agreed standards, they are also financially independent and must secure the majority of their own funding. With annual running costs at £15,000–£70,000 per team, fund raising requires much effort and donations are always welcomed.

The majority of the rescue teams were established in the 1950s and 1960s but the first co-ordinated efforts took place in the 1930s through the First Aid Committee of Mountaineering Clubs, later to become the Mountain Rescue Committee (with separate branches in Scotland and Ireland), which oversaw the establishment of rescue posts. Placed at strategic locations on the hill, these boxes housed stretchers and first aid supplies including for many years morphine based drugs. It is sad but not surprising that they were regularly ransacked and often found empty, in England and Wales they have largely been phased out. The Search and Rescue Dogs Association (SARDA) established in 1965 plays an important part in locating lost or injured casualties. The reliable and effective service provided by the rescue teams is free to all that require help.

## 18.1.2 Nature of incidents

Incident reports from the rescue teams illustrate who gets injured and how; many teams have their own website where such information can be accessed. The MRCs publish annual rescue statistics, also available on their websites, which give an overall picture of the numbers involved. Such reading, though slightly morbid, is a useful way to learn from mistakes other people have made.

For example, in 2002 there were 655 mountain-related incidents in England and Wales involving 824 people. Over two thirds of these occurred to fell walkers and resulted from a simple slip. One hundred people were involved in rock climbing or scrambling incidents, half of whom sustained injuries of some sort, largely fractures or lacerations to the head, back, neck, lower leg and foot. Scrambling incidents resulted in four fatalities and the MRC comments that injuries to scramblers are exacerbated by long, unroped falls without helmets.

Other trends show an increase in mountain biking incidents and a continued increase in call outs initiated by mobile phones, which now account for 30% of call outs. Mobile phones have certainly saved lives and reduced the seriousness of injuries in the mountains by reducing the time taken to get help and allowing the caller to remain with the casualty. However, mobile phones also encourage inappropriate calls made at the first sign of trouble or in situations that could be resolved without a rescue team.

Anecdotal evidence suggests there has been a worrying increase in bad climbing falls, often where the leader has hit the ground on a well protected route. These have been as a result of poor runner placements, rope-work, belaying or a combination of all these. In other words the accidents were avoidable and resulted largely through lack of relevant experience.

## 18.1.3 Getting help

There are no hard and fast rules about what type of incident warrants a rescue team call out. Amongst climbers and mountaineers there has always been a tradition of self-reliance, in other words, if it is possible to limp back to safety the climber should choose this option. Likewise it may be possible to enlist the help of some neighbouring climbers or nearby walkers. Serious injuries or an incident in a remote setting or on a crag are likely to require specialist medical or technical help and assistance with evacuation.

## International distress signal

The internationally recognised *distress signal* is six blasts/flashes repeated at one-minute intervals.

The recognised *reply* is three blasts/flashes repeated at one-minute intervals.

Getting help may be as simple as delving for the mobile phone, making a 999 call and asking for the police who co-ordinate the rescue service. It should be noted that emergency calls made from a mobile phone may result in a delay. (See *18.2 Procedure in the event of an accident* overleaf.) When this is not an option someone must raise the alarm by heading for the nearest phone. If the whole party is crag fast or the casualty too badly injured to leave alone, it may be possible to attract the attention of someone nearby by shouts, whistle blasts or torch flashes.

### 18.1.4 Crag incidents

Accidents on a crag are always unique so the response will be likewise. Climbers should use common sense and work within the limits of their experience to minimise further injury. A few situations will require a quick response such as if the fallen climber is unconscious and hanging on a rope in which case the airway may be blocked.

Trying out a complicated improvised rescue manoeuvre for the first time with a seriously injured casualty is rarely appropriate. A confident and competent climber may be able to evacuate an injured partner to the ground or a safe ledge without worsening injuries but this is normally a complex procedure. If help is on the way and there is no threat from stonefall or falling further and the injured person is reasonably comfortable, it may be best simply to wait. (See also *15 Multi-pitch problem solving*, page 155.)

RAF or coastguard helicopters are involved in about a fifth of evacuations, greatly improving the odds for badly injured individuals. They are particularly useful in climbing incidents where the injuries may be severe and where the evacuation involves crossing difficult, dangerous or complex terrain. In certain situations it may be possible to pluck the casualty direct from the cliff but this requires considerable expertise and confidence on the rescuers' part. Normally the casualty must be moved to a safe position slightly out from the base of the crag from where the helicopter can winch more easily.

Helicopters are extremely noisy and create an enormous amount of downdraft so it is important to secure all loose clothing and equipment. Bivvy bags blowing around for example will make a pilot very twitchy and they will more than likely pull away from the incident until they consider the area safe. Never approach a helicopter unless

FIGURE 18.1   EVERY RESCUE TEAM HAS A NUMBER OF EXPERIENCED MEDICS AND FIRST AIDERS

Photo: Blizzard/Ray Wood

FIGURE 18.2   HELICOPTERS SUCH AS THIS RAF SEA KING ARE OFTEN USED TO RESCUE INJURED CLIMBERS

specifically requested to do so by a member of the crew, and then only from the direction indicated which will be in full view of the pilot. Never go around the rear of the aircraft, almost all have a tail rotor! Usually a crewmember will be winched down and it is they who will take control of the situation. Do not attempt to reach out for them or belay them unless they specifically request assistance. To attract attention raise both arms to create a V, one arm raised and one down by your side will indicate "no help required". Helicopters will normally approach in to the wind and invariably drop a smoke bomb to indicate what the wind is doing just above the surface; they do fly in darkness and in such cases are equipped with night vision equipment so never point your torch directly at them! It would be much more useful to point your torch either down at the casualty or on someone alongside you to help them focus and judge distance. Keep the entire group together in one place so the pilot can see all those involved, and keep all others well away from the area.

### 18.1.5  Waiting for help to arrive
An injured person and the rest of the party require monitoring, reassurance, shelter and warmth but the party should also be conspicuous so the rescuers can spot them easily; bright clothing can help with this. It is important the party remains where they are once a location has been reported.

### 18.1.6  First aid training
Basic first aid training is a pre-requirement of all the leader and instructor awards and is recommended for anyone taking part in climbing and mountaineering. There are a great number of courses available, the majority are designed for accidents that take place in or near homes or buildings so help and shelter are never far away. Those that are tailored to the outdoors are more relevant as they include additional problems of exposure to the elements and remoteness.

# 18.2  Procedure in the event of an accident

- Assess the situation. (Take a moment to look at what has happened and why.)
- Check for hazards.
- Approach the casualty carefully. (On a crag this could be difficult to do safely. If it is a climber and they are still on the rope ensure they can't fall any further etc.)
- Give first aid as appropriate.

- If injuries are minor and help is to hand it may be possible to assist the injured climber back to the road.
- If assistance is required from a Mountain Rescue Team follow the procedure below.
- Decide how to raise the alarm. This may be using a mobile phone or getting to the nearest land line phone.
- If someone needs to go for help consider: where is the nearest point of help, who should go for help and who should stay with the casualty, can the casualty be safely left alone. These are not always easy decisions to make but consider the options logically until the best solution is reached.

### 18.2.1  Making a 999 call from a mobile phone
First make a note of all relevant details including:

- Location (this should include a 6 figure grid reference from an OS map if possible).
- Name, sex and age of casualty.
- Nature of injuries.
- Number of people in party and intended destination if appropriate.
- The number of the mobile phone in use.

Then do as follows:

1  Dial 999 and ask for the Police.
2  Make sure you tell the operator where you are so they can put you through to the appropriate area police.
3  When connected to a police control room, check that it is the right one. If it is not, then make sure that the information will be passed on.
4  Explain the nature of your call, giving details previously prepared.
5  Do NOT change your position until contacted by Rescue Team, who will agree future protocol for use of phone.
6  If you have to make a further 999 call, use ALL the above procedure again.

Making a 999 call from a landline should be simpler as there is no potential confusion about your location. You should have the same information ready when making the call. You will probably be asked to wait at the phone for the police to arrive.

# The law & risk management

BEN BRANSBY ON THE SERIOUS AND COMMITTING **DEATH TRAP DIRECT** E6 5c, MOUSETRAP ZAWN, SOUTH STACK, GOGARTH

**Climbers should be aware of the risks involved with climbing and their responsibilities towards others.**

# 19.1 Climbers and the law

Climbers have a responsibility to do their best to prevent harm to their climbing partners as well as other neighbouring climbers. Every individual person owes a duty of care not to injure their neighbours by their negligent acts and omissions. If a payment is involved there are additional potential contractual responsibilities. This duty of care involves protecting climbing partners, group members or clients and other climbers from foreseeable risks and taking all reasonable steps to ensure an appropriate level of care. Climbing is an activity with an inherent amount of risk and it is impossible to remove the risk completely. Everyone taking part in climbing activities should be made aware of the possible risks so that they recognise their own responsibilities and can take part in the decision making process to manage the risk.

In the case of any group activity it is unwise for clients or participants to be led to believe that by hiring an instructor or guide their safety can or will be 100% guaranteed.

Instructors (or anyone in a position of responsibility who takes their role seriously) do their best to ensure the safety of clients and this includes having appropriate and up-to-date experience for the activity. Gaining a climbing qualification or award, although not a legal requirement, is an accepted method for instructors to ensure they have the relevant skills and experience necessary to take others climbing. (Mountain Leader Training awards are explained in *Appendix 3* on page 214.)

Civil liability insurance should be considered by climbers on a personal level (if a climber knocks a rock down onto another climber who then claims for damages). It is also essential for those working professionally or acting in a position of responsibility (if a group member or client is injured while under the instructor's care and makes a claim). Civil liability insurance is often included for recreational climbers in Mountaineering Council membership. Professional civil liability insurance can be arranged either by an employer or organising body or by the individual. However, it is the instructor's responsibility to ensure this cover is in place.

## 19.1.1 Climbing with young people

Anyone climbing with under-18s has a greater responsibility and duty of care. Whilst acting *in loco parentis* (in place of the parent), the instructor must look after young people with the level of care a parent would expect. Parental consent is vital, as is ensuring that non-climbing parents are themselves fully aware of the nature of the activity and any risks involved.

Young people are not expected to understand fully the risks involved in climbing activities or make decisions about taking those risks onboard for themselves, so the instructor must protect them fully against such eventualities. Dangerous places, such as those with a high stonefall risk for example, are not appropriate places to be with young people. High-risk activities, such as leading routes, must be considered very carefully.

Commercial organisations working with young people must hold a current licence issued by the Adventure Activities Licencing Authority and any organisation working with young people should have a child protection policy in place.

In addition to the legal responsibilities of looking after young people, those working and climbing with children should be aware of injuries they are more susceptible to such as over-use injuries that could have a long-term damaging impact on a growing youngster. Anyone involved in training young people should be up-to-date with the latest research into appropriate levels of activity for different age groups.

Equipment used with children should be chosen and fitted carefully. Helmets should be the appropriate size to ensure a snug fit and harnesses must have sufficient adjustment to make sure they don't simply slip down off the hips. Full body harnesses are often a good choice with young children. Climbing hardware should be selected with small, weak fingers in mind.

Venues for climbing with children should have the minimum objective hazards and should be selected with the following in mind:

- Minimum threat of stonefall
- Easy access and short approach
- Free from hazards around the base and top of the crag such as hidden drops, awkward boulder fields, mine shafts.

# 19.2 The management of risk

Rock climbing and mountain activities, however safely organised, carry a certain amount of risk. Those taking part should be aware of these risks in order to both minimise them and accept them. Experienced climbers and mountaineers will already be aware of many of the possible risks but novices may not and it falls to the more experienced climber to take on a role of responsibility here. In the case of groups or individuals under instruction this is even more clearly defined. Any supervisor, leader or instructor in the realm of climbing and mountaineering must fully grasp the process of risk management, which involves balancing the potential risks against the benefits of adventure, excitement and enjoyment.

## 19.2.1 Hazards

Hazards are defined as any source of risk or danger. In the context of rock climbing and scrambling these are many-fold and impossible to list exhaustively but the main ones include:

- Terrain encountered on approaches to or descents from climbs, such as steep and slippery mud, grass or scree, unstable boulder fields, exposed drops, tidal sea-level zones and other water hazards.
- Condition of the rock itself, including inherently unstable rock that may lead to major rock-fall, as is often found in quarries and on some cliff tops. Also stonefall from above, loose holds on the route and wet, greasy or vegetated rock.
- Extreme weather conditions are also likely to increase the feeling of insecurity, especially when encountered on high, long or committing routes.
- Water hazards associated with gorges and sea cliffs.

## 19.2.2 Risk

Risk is the possibility of suffering harm or being affected by a hazard. These may be both physical, resulting in injury, loss of health or death, and emotional, resulting in loss of self-esteem or credibility in the eyes of peers and so on.

## 19.2.3 Judgement

Judgement involves collecting information and selecting a course of action to solve a problem. Accurate judgement is dependent on the quantity and the quality of past experience.

## 19.2.4 Risk management

Risk management involves:

- Recognising and identifying the *hazards*.
- Assessing the *risk* by identifying who might be affected by them.
- Making a *judgement* about the level of risk, and what safety measures are required to reduce risks to an acceptable level.
- Taking a deliberate course of *action* and constantly reviewing or re-assessing the whole process.
- Identifying what steps need to be taken in an emergency.

Successful risk management requires combining technical, leadership and people skills on the part of the climber or instructor in an on-going process of decision making. It is widely accepted that any instructor requires a high level of technical skill. These skills need to be thoroughly learned and practised so they are no longer compartmentalised in order that the instructor can switch between them easily, selecting appropriate techniques for the situation.

The emotional needs of a group or individual are perhaps less obvious and certainly less well defined but equally important. An inexperienced instructor may be focusing so hard on physical safety issues that these are missed.

One of the key qualities for instructors to possess in this respect is empathy. Being able to recall how it felt to be really scared, stressed, tired etc helps the instructor understand how a novice faced with a first abseil or a climber about to lead for the first time may be feeling. An instructor who has never experienced those feelings will find it harder to empathise. It is a mistake to assume that confronting a challenge will have a positive outcome for everyone. If the outcome is negative, in other words falling off a route or backing off an abseil, the participant may experience considerable stress.

Pitching the activity at just the right level is a crucial skill; choosing an appropriate venue, length of abseil or grade of route requires not only careful planning but also on-going monitoring to ensure that enjoyment, excitement and interest are balanced successfully against stress, discomfort or anxiety. This balance is particularly difficult to achieve within a large group where some will be cruising and possibly even bored, while others are over-stretched and stressed. An inexperienced instructor may press on with the session regardless and end up providing an unsatisfactory day for everyone, whilst an instructor with greater experience would hopefully recognise the early signs that things weren't going well and quickly adjust the session. Rigging a different selection of routes or focusing on something different, like bouldering, would be two of the strategies for dealing with this problem.

### 19.2.5 Risk assessment

A formal risk assessment recorded on paper may be a requirement of the employer, authority or organisation and much advice exists to assist with these such as local authority guidance, DfES 'HASPEV' (Health and Safety of Pupils on Education Visits) and HSE 'Five steps to risk assessment'.

Practical, on-going or 'dynamic' risk assessments are undertaken throughout the course of the day as the instructor makes appraisals and adjustments to a basic plan based on observation. These 'judgement calls', sometimes obvious but often subtle, are vitally important and it is here that the instructor's experience plays a big role. The following example highlights the nature of such practical risk assessments:

An instructor has been hired for a day by two new clients who want to experience multi-pitch climbing and 'be stretched'. They have spoken on the phone and the instructor knows they have climbed indoors and once at Stanage, a single pitch gritstone crag and have their own gear.

On meeting the clients the instructor spends 15 minutes talking through their climbing experience, the day ahead and checking their gear. One harness looks old and tatty so the instructor changes it for one in good condition.

Within a 100m of leaving the road, one client is slipping frequently on greasy rock. The instructor makes a mental note of this and adjusts the approach to avoid the boulder field and takes a more circuitous but easier route on grass. This approach skirts beneath a steep, vegetated cliff that is not climbed on but often has sheep and goats moving around on it, so although they are not yet at the base of their crag they stop and put on helmets.

On arrival at the crag they can see that the route the instructor had in mind has a team on pitch two. Although the other climbers are far enough up not to get in the way, the instructor knows there is loose rock on the ledges and so selects a different climb to avoid stonefall risk.

Whilst gearing up the instructor notices the weather is colder and looks less settled than forecast and recommends an additional warm layer despite the clients being warm from the walk-in. The instructor also decides to carry a light rucksack with waterproofs and gloves for them all just in case the weather worsens.

At the top of pitch one, having watched them both climb, the instructor realises one of the clients is not very confident or climbing well enough to manage the crux pitch ahead. Rather than risk a negative experience for the client, the instructor decides to abseil off and start another climb instead.

The clients have both abseiled before, say they are happy without a safety rope and want to try out a French prusik auto-bloc instead. The instructor lets them try a prusik but insists on a safety rope as well, having never actually seen them abseil before.

The second route goes smoothly and on the descent there is an opportunity for a second abseil. This time the instructor allows the clients to abseil without a safety rope so they can be confident in the French prusik.

The weather is now very cold and a little damp, one client has uncomfortably cold fingers and toes, so rather than attempt a harder climb as originally planned, the instructor suggests they climb an easy route/scramble on which they can move quickly, wear comfortable boots and warm clothing. They complete a journey to the summit of the crag before finding a gentle walk-off that once again avoids awkward bouldery ground.

In this brief account, the instructor has changed plan more than a dozen times in the light of further observation and this is the essence of dynamic risk assessment.

# Appendices

JAS HEPBURN ON **PRESUMPTION** HVS, THE SECOND GEO, SHEIGRA IN THE FAR NORTH WEST OF SCOTLAND
Photo: Allen Fyffe

# A.1 Glossary

**Anchor:** A solid attachment point. Can be a tree, boulder, bolt, stake or a piece of gear placed in a crack.

**Belayer:** The person who is safeguarding the rope for the climber.

**To belay/belaying:** To safeguard the rope while another person climbs. Also used to describe the process of setting up the belay.

**The belay:** The stance (*see below*), anchors and attachment system.

**Belay device:** Friction device used by the belayer to help control the rope

**Bombproof/bomber:** A runner that is absolutely secure.

**Bottom-roping:** Climbing a route without first having led the climb. The rope is arranged so the belayer is positioned at the bottom.

**Brake hand:** The hand that holds the dead rope – responsible for holding falls. Also called the control hand.

**Cam stop:** The load bearing stop which prevents the cams on a camming device from over-rotating. Enables them to be used passively, like a chock.

**Central rope loop:** Loop created by tying on to the end of the rope through a harness.

**Chalk-up:** Dipping the fingers into a chalk bag to coat them with magnesium carbonate in order to improve grip by soaking up any sweat or moisture.

**Chock:** A collective name for the wedges used in cracks as runners or anchors.

**Chockstone:** A boulder or rock wedged in a crack.

**Dead rope:** The side of rope after it goes through the belay device that doesn't lead to the climber.

**Direct belay:** A belay system where the load goes directly onto the anchor.

**Flash:** Climbing a route first go without falls or rests.

**Ground anchor:** An anchor at the base of a cliff or wall that will resist an upward direction of pull.

**Hanging belay:** A belay where there is no ledge so the belayer must commit all their weight to the anchors and find the best footholds to stand on. Most common on steep multi-pitch sport routes.

**Harness belay loop:** Webbing loop that normally encloses waist belt and leg loops used to abseil from and to belay from if the belayer is not tied to the rope, such as in a climbing wall.

**Head-point:** To practise moves on a top-rope prior to attempting a lead, usually done on routes with little or no protection possibilities where a fall is not a viable option.

**Indirect belay:** A belay system where the belayer takes part of the load in a fall.

**Leader:** Person who climbs first without a rope from above, placing runners as a safeguard.

**Live rope:** The side of rope that goes from the belay device to the climber.

**Maillon:** Steel or aluminium alloy locking connectors designed to take multi-directional loads. Used to link anchors or a lower-off to a central point. Can be used to create a central attachment point on a harness for abseiling or belaying from.

**On-sight:** To lead or solo a route without practising the moves beforehand.

**Paying out:** How the belayer feeds out rope through the belay device.

**Pitch:** Section of climbing between belays. Can be ground to the top, ground to a ledge, ledge to ledge or ledge to the top. The first is a single pitch and the latter three are multi-pitch.

**Pumped:** When the muscles are over-worked the blood flow is impaired resulting in pain and loss of strength.

**Red-point:** To climb a route, ground up but after practise (usually on the lead), with no falls or rests. The protection equipment will usually be in place; bolts are the norm for this style. Whether the quickdraws are in place or not on a red-point is a matter for heated ethical debate!

**Runner:** Protection point for the lead climber linked to the rope by a karabiner. The rope runs freely past the runner but in a fall it enables the fall to be arrested in conjunction with a belay system. An abbreviation of running belay.

**Second:** Person who follows up after a leader with a rope above them.

**Semi-direct belay:** A belay system where the load is transferred to the anchor via the belayer's central rope loop.

**Semi-hanging belay:** A belay on a small ledge where the belayer needs support from the anchors in order to stay on the ledge.

**Shake-out:** A temporary rest, such as a good hold, on a route which allows the arms to be relaxed, normally one at a time. Gentle shaking and flexing of the hand and arm can off-set the effect of being pumped.

**Skinny ropes:** Refers to the thinnest ropes in their category (9.4mm single ropes or 8mm half-ropes for example).

**Solo:** Climbing without ropes.

**Stacked abseil:** A way of organising an abseil in order to safeguard one or two abseilers. Used by instructors and guides on multi-pitch descents.

**Stance:** Ledge or place to stop and belay at the top of a pitch, normally on a multi-pitch climb.

**Taking in:** How the belayer takes up slack rope. This includes taking in slack hand over hand before belaying and feeding it through the belay or friction device whilst belaying.

**Topping-out:** Reaching the top of a pitch or route.

**Top-roping:** Climbing the route with a rope from above without first having led the climb. The belayer is positioned at the top.

# A.2 Access legislation

## A.2.1 Current legislation on access

| | Recent legislation | Code | Access | Natural Heritage |
|---|---|---|---|---|
| **Scotland** | Land Reform (Scotland) Act 2003 | Scottish Outdoor Access Code | Scottish Natural Heritage | Scottish Natural Heritage |
| **Northern Ireland** | The Access to the Countryside (Northern Ireland) Order 1983 | Northern Ireland Country Code | Northern Ireland Countryside Access and Activities Network (CAAN) | Environment and Heritage Service |
| **Wales** | Wales Countryside and Rights of Way Act 2000 | Country Code *Under revision* | Countryside Council for Wales | Countryside Council for Wales |
| **England** | Countryside and Rights of Way Act 2000 | Country Code *Under revision* | Countryside Agency | English Nature |
| **Republic of Ireland** | Occupiers Liability Act 1995 *This is not a specific act regarding access, but includes access issues* | Mountaineering Council of Ireland 'Good Practice Guide for Walkers and Climbers' | Mountaineering Council of Ireland | The Heritage Council |

You can find out more by visiting the following websites:

## Scotland
**Scottish Natural Heritage**
www.snh.org.uk

**Scottish Outdoor Access Code**
*Current*
www.snh.org.uk/index/i-frame.htm
*Once the SOAC is approved*
www.access-scotland.com

**Legislation for Scotland**
www.scotland-legislation.hmso.gov.uk/
legislation/scotland/acts2003/20030002.htm

## England
**English Nature**
www.english-nature.org.uk

**Countryside Agency**
www.countryside.gov.uk/access

**Legislation for England and Wales**
www.legislation.hmso.gov.uk/acts/
acts2000/20000037.htm

## Wales
**Countryside Council for Wales**
www.ccw.gov.uk

**Legislation for England and Wales**
www.legislation.hmso.gov.uk/acts/
acts2000/20000037.htm

## Northern Ireland
**Environment and Heritage Service**
www.ehsni.gov.uk

**Countryside Access and Activities Network**
www.countrysiderecreation.com

**The Country Code for N Ireland**
www.countrysiderecreation.com/publications/
pubdetails.cfm?id=92

**Legislation for N Ireland**
www.ehsni.gov.uk/natural/country/
Access_countryside1983.doc

## Republic of Ireland
**The Heritage Council**
www.heritagecouncil.ie/

**The Mountaineering Council of Ireland**
www.mountaineering.ie/

**Good Practice Guide**
www.mountaineering.ie/mci/
MCIGoodPractice.doc

**Legislation for the Republic of Ireland**
www.irlgov.ie/oireachtas/frame.htm

## UK
**Dept of Environment, Food and Rural Affairs**
www.defra.gov.uk/wildlife-countryside

**Joint Nature Conservation Committee**
www.jncc.gov.uk/

**Her Majesty's Stationary Office**
www.legislation.hmso.gov.uk/

# A.3 Mountain Leader Training Awards

The awards administered by Mountain Leader Training and are valid throughout the United Kingdom and Ireland. All have the same stages and begin with the assumption that candidates are already committed climbers who wish to lead and/or instruct others. With sufficient personal experience candidates can register on the appropriate scheme and receive a logbook in which to record their relevant experience. The next stages would be attendance on a training course, completion of a consolidation period then attendance on an assessment course. For extremely experienced candidates there is the possibility of receiving exemption from the training part of the scheme. All candidates at assessment must hold a valid First Aid Certificate and after gaining the award must continue to log relevant personal and leadership experience.

## A3.1 Single Pitch Award (SPA)

This award enables holders to supervise people on single pitch crags and climbing walls. The courses, which have a minimum of 20 hours contact time, are run by approved Course Providers and cover personal climbing, safe group management, indoors and out, crag etiquette, environmental responsibilities and more.

The registration requirements are that candidates are a minimum of 18 years old and have 12 months climbing experience. They must be members of a mountaineering council or an affiliated mountaineering club. To attend a training course candidates must have led a minimum of 15 outdoor routes of any grade, using leader placed protection. After training there is a consolidation period before attendance at an assessment which will include personal climbing, group supervision and the use of climbing walls. Candidates must have led an absolute minimum of 40 climbs outdoors on leader placed protection. Some of these must be at least Severe grade and should be on a variety of rock types. For further details contact any home nation Mountain Leader Training.

## A3.2 Mountaineering Instructor Award (MIA)

This scheme trains and assesses people in the skills required for instruction of mountaineering, including all aspects of rock climbing. Prior to registration candidates must hold the Mountain Leader Award. Registration requirements include extensive multi-pitch rock climbing experience at VS 4c or above and substantial group leading experience since passing the ML award. Candidates attend nine days of training and five days of assessment. Personal climbing skills, teaching of leading, improvised rescue, the mountain environment and mountain scrambling are covered at both training and assessment. For further details contact MLTUK.

## A3.3 Mountaineering Instructor Certificate (MIC)

This scheme trains and assesses people in the skills required for instruction of mountaineering, both summer and winter, including snow, ice and rock climbing. Registration requirements for MIC are MIA and Winter ML, winter climbing experience at Grade III and group leadership experience in winter. Candidates attend 5 days of training and 4 days of assessment. Personal winter climbing skills, teaching of all aspects of winter mountaineering and general mountaineering skills are covered and candidates should hold a current First Aid certificate. For further details contact MLTUK.

## A3.4 IFMGA Mountain Guide

This scheme trains and assesses experienced mountaineers in the skills required for the provision of instruction and guiding services in climbing, skiing and mountaineering on rock, ice and snow in all conditions and all seasons at BMG and IFMGA international standards. The award is administered by the British Association of Mountain Guides and is valid world-wide.

Candidates should register with the BMG and have gained substantial experience of United Kingdom and alpine mountaineering. Registration requirements for this scheme are broad and include 50 rock climbs at E1 5b, 50 winter climbs at Grade IV/V, alpine experience at TD and skiing experience that includes off-piste and touring terrain. For further details contact BMG (www.bmg.org.uk or 01690 720386).

# A.4 High Ropes Courses

Ropes courses are designed to be either 'low' (a few feet off the ground) so that stepping or jumping off the obstacle is always an option, or 'high' where they may be 5m plus. Both types of course require careful management but the high courses, which are becoming increasingly popular, carry with them the potential for serious injury. Most of the original high ropes courses were built in trees but many now use poles (like telegraph poles) instead and some are even suspended from high ceilings. Courses may consist of a number of individual elements that are safeguarded by a bottom-rope, such as 'Jacob's Ladder' where the participant climbs a ladder of poles with each rung being further away from the last. These elements may be combined with, or linked by, a high level journey (sometimes described as an 'aerial trek'), where safety is arranged by clipping in with a double cow's tail system to either a wire cable (like a via ferrata), or to a sliding trolley on a metal beam.

## A4.1 Equipment

Equipment needed for high ropes courses includes a helmet, stout footwear, and clothing with long sleeves and legs to minimise abrasion injuries in slips from the obstacles. Due to the frequency and nature of falls occurring full body harnesses or combined sit and chest harnesses are the norm. (A combi sling is a popular way to link a sit and chest harness.) Occasionally the attachment may be at the rear of the full body harness; otherwise a high front attachment is used. Double-rope cow's tails with two karabiners are attached to the harness for clipping in to safety points. Steel karabiners are normally used to minimise damage to the karabiners by the wire cables (which cut through alloy karabiners at a

disturbing rate). These are either screwgates or industrial double-action snaps to decrease the possibility of them being inadvertently unclipped. There should be a readily available 'rescue bag' tailored to the individual ropes course. This normally consists of a rope configured to hoist and lower, knife with a shielded blade (gardening secateurs also work well) and prusiks.

## A4.2 Techniques

On individual elements of the course the most frequently used safety system is a bottom-rope. The belay device can be attached directly to a ground anchor (if there is a solid placement), but it is more common for the device to be attached to a belayer. The belayer is normally clipped to a ground anchor with a sling adjusted to the correct length. This set-up may also be used to belay participants up to the course in the first place, which may be a ladder or a section of climbing wall. Bottom-ropes require single (full-weight) ropes that are often cut to the appropriate length. The choice of belay device should take into account ease of handling, suitability in a direct belay and the ability to hold falls and lower smoothly.

Linear features are protected by a double cow's tail. Courses built in trees normally require the participant to clip past anchored sections of wire cable at the trees. There may be a possibility of 'double unclipping' (when both cow's tails are removed at the same time) at these points, so close supervision is essential. Purpose built pole courses are often designed in a continuous loop to avoid the need to clip past anchors. Participants clip on at the start, under supervision, and then complete the 'journey', often with supervision from below.

## A4.3 Hazards

Participants and staff should be aware of potential problems or hazards with high ropes courses in general and of problems particular to the individual course. These include:

- falls with a high potential fall factor;
- double unclipping;
- awkward falls resulting in abrasions or rope burns;
- uncontrolled swinging or sliding, especially on high speed elements;
- entanglement in safety netting;
- trapped fingers, hair and so on in zip wires;
- falls at points where immediate lowering to the ground is not possible;
- injuries to shoulders during leaps;
- environmental conditions affecting safety such as high winds, cold and wet; and
- damage to the course through heavy use, wind damage and possibly even vandalism.

## A4.4 Good practise

All staff involved with high ropes course should be familiar with appropriate operating procedures, which may include:

- familiarity with the whole circuit;
- checking the course before each session;
- adequately supervising participants both on and nearby the course;
- use of a low practise cow's tail course;
- buddy system, one person on the ground partnered with one person on the course to look out for and point out errors;
- use of colour coding to make it really obvious where to clip to next;
- avoiding fiddly gear that may be difficult to operate with cold hands;
- warming up before leaps;
- no access to the course without supervisor; and
- familiarity and practise with the rescue procedure from all parts of circuit.

Staff training should ideally include site specific training and any accreditation should be site specific and dependent on running regular sessions on that course. Technical advice may come from various sources including Mountaineering Instructors with high ropes experience, arboreal experts, engineers and cable manufacturers.

Course inspections should be carried out regularly by appropriate specialists and before every session or at the start of the day by the instructor in charge.

## A4.5 Other Information

HSE Information sheets. Entertainment sheet 14: Supervision of high ropes courses. Entertainment sheet 15: Maintenance of high ropes courses. See HSE website.

AALA guidance and advice. Collective interpretation 6.05 on ropes courses. See AALA website. www.AALA.org

# A.5  Useful contacts

## A5.1  Climbing sites

www.ukclimbing.com
www.planetfear.com
www.climbinfo.co.uk
www.ukbouldering.com

### Irish Climbing
www.climbing.ie
www.irishclimbing.com

## A5.2  Weather sites

www.met-office.gov.uk
www.metcheck.com

## A5.3  Books and Maps

### Cordee
Tel: 0116 254 3579
www.cordee.co.uk

### Cicerone Press
Tel: 01539 562069
www.cicerone.co.uk

### Stanfords Ltd
www.stanfords.co.uk

## A5.4  Rescue

### Mountain Rescue Committee of England and Wales
www.mountain.rescue.org.uk

### Irish Mountain Rescue Association
www.imra.ie.eu.org

### Mountain Rescue Committee of Scotland
www.mrc-scotland.org.uk

### National Search and Rescue Dogs Association
www.nsarda.org.uk

## A5.5  Environment

### RSPB
www.rspb.org.uk

### Countryside Council for Wales
www.ccw.gov.uk

### The Countryside Agency
www.countryside.gov.uk

## A5.6  Mountain Leader Training

### Mountain Leader Training England
MLTE,
Siabod Cottage, Capel Curig, Conwy LL24 0ET
Tel: 01690 – 720 314
Fax: 01690 – 720 248
E-mail: info@mlte.org
www.mlte.org

### Mountain Leader Training Northern Ireland
MLTNI,
Tollymore MC, Bryansford,
Newcastle, Co Down BT33 0PT
Tel: 02843 – 722 158
Fax: 02843 – 726155
E-mail: admin@tollymoremc.com

### Mountain Leader Training Scotland

MLTS, Glenmore, Aviemore,
Inverness-shire PH22 1QU
Tel: 01479 – 861248
Fax: 01479 – 861249
E-mail: smltb@aol.com
www.mltuk.org

### Mountain Leader Training Wales
### Hyfforddi Arweinwyr Mynydd Cymru

MLTW, Capel Curig, Conwy, LL24 0ET
Tel: 01690 – 720361
Fax: 01690 – 720248
E-mail: info@mltw.org
www.mltw.org

### Mountain Leader Training UK

MLTUK, Capel Curig, Conwy LL24 0ET
Tel: 01690 – 720272
Fax: 01690 – 720248
E-mail: info@mltuk.org
www.mltuk.org

Each home nation board is made up of represen-
tatives drawn from a variety of interested groups
such as the governing bodies for mountaineering,
the providers of education, the voluntary youth
organisations, the mountain rescue organisations,
the military, the professional associations of
mountain instructors, guides and leaders, and
local authorities. MLTUK is made up of members
from each of the home nation training Boards
and mountaineering councils with observers
from the professional organisations and the
national mountain centres.

## A5.7 Mountaineering councils

### Association of British Climbing Walls

www.abcclimbingwalls.co.uk

### British Mountaineering Council

BMC, 177–179 Burton Road,
Manchester M20 2BB
Tel: 0870 – 010 4878
Fax: 0161 – 445 4500
E-mail: office@thebmc.co.uk
www.thebmc.co.uk

### Mountaineering Council of Ireland

Sport HQ, 13 Joyce Way, Park West Business
Park, Dublin 12, Ireland
Tel: 00 3531 – 625 1115
Fax: 00 3531 – 625 1116
E-mail: mci@eircom.net
www.mountaineering.ie

### Mountaineering Council of Scotland

MC of S, The Old Granary, West Mill Street,
Perth PH1 5QP
Tel: 01738 – 638227
Fax: 01738 – 442095
E-mail: info@mountaineering-scotland.org.uk
www.mountaineering-scotland.org.uk

## A5.8 Professional associations and government agencies

### Adventure Activities Licensing Authority

17 Lambourne Crescent, Llanishen,
Cardiff CF4 5GG
Tel: 02920 – 755 715
E-mail: info@aala.org
www.aala.org

### Association of Mountain Instructors (AMI)

AMI, Capel Curig, Conwy LL24 0ET
Tel: 01690 – 720 314
www.ami.org

### British Mountain Guides (BMG)

BMBG, Capel Curig, Conwy LL24 0ET
Tel: 01690 – 720 386
www.bmg.org

### Health and Safety Executive

Rose Court, 2 Southwark Bridge,
London SE1 9HS
E-mail: hseinformationservices@natbrit.com
www.hse.gov.uk

# A.6 Bibliography

## A6.1 Climbing environment and history

BMC (1997) *History of the BMC* British Mountaineering Council

BMC (2000) *Tread Lightly* British Mountaineering Council

HMSO (1978) *Britain Before Man*

Wilson K (1981) *Classic Rock, Hard Rock, and Extreme Rock* Granada

Wilson K (1978) *The Games Climbers Play*

Rhind P and Evans D (2001) *The Plant Life of Snowdonia* Gomer

Meyer K. *How to Shit in the Woods* Ten Speed Press

MC of S *Where to 'go' in the Great Outdoors*

## A6.2 Background and technical

BMC (2001) *Care and Maintenance*

BMC (1999) *Climbing Rock, Classic Climbs, Essential skills*

BMC (1997) *Knots*

BMC (1998) *Ropes*

Creasey M (1999) *The Complete Rock Climber*

Hill P and Johnston S (2000) *Mountain Skills Handbook* David and Charles

Long S (2003) *Hill Walking: The official handbook of the Mountain Leader and Walking Group Leader schemes* The MLTUK

Fyffe A and Peter I (1990) *The Handbook of Climbing* Pelham Books.

Richardson A *Rock Climbing for Instructors*

Shepherd N (1998) *A Manual of Modern Rope Techniques and Further Modern Rope Techniques* Constable

## A6.3 Coaching and training

*Sports Coach UK* and *Coachwise Solutions* produce a Coaching Essentials series available from Coachwise1st4sport (Tel 0113 – 201 5555 or visit www.1st4sport.com). Publications include: *How to Coach Sports Effectively, How to Coach Disabled People in Sport, How to Coach Children in Sport.*

Goddard D and Neumann U (1993) *Performance Rock Climbing* Cordee

Hurn M and Ingle P (1988) *Climbing Fit* Crowood

Bollen S (1994) *Training For Rock Climbing* Pelham Books

Syer J and Connolly C (1987) *Sporting Body Sporting Mind.* Simon and Schuster

BMC (2003) *Performance Training*

## A6.4 Group management, leadership and supervision

Graham J *Outdoor Leadership. The Mountaineers* (ISBN 0-89886-502-6)

Mortlock C (1994) *The Adventure Alternative* Cicerone

MLTUK (2004) *National Guidelines*

Ogilvie K (1993) *Leading and Managing Groups in the Outdoors* N.A.O.E

Priest and Gass: *Effective Leadership in Adventure Programming. Human Kinetics* (ISBN 087322-637-2)

Smith A. (1987) *Working out of doors with young people.* ITRC

## A6.5 Scrambling, sea-level traversing etc.

CCPR *Group Safety at Water Margins*

HSE Information sheets. ***Entertainment sheet 13:*** *Combined water and rock activities.* ***Entertainment sheet 14:*** *Supervision of high ropes courses.* ***Entertainment sheet 15:*** *Maintenance of high ropes courses.*

## A6.6 Accidents and rescue

Mountain Rescue Committee *The Mountain Rescue Handbook*

MacInnes H *International Mountain Rescue Handbook*

Various publications available from Emergency Response Publications. www.emergencyresponse.co.uk

# A.7 Index

## A

abseil rescue 95
abseiling 96
  alternatives to ~ 96, 97
  anchors 98
  attaching to the rope 101
  backing up the abseil anchor 151
  brake-hand 101
  checklist 99
  counterbalance abseil 160
  environmental considerations 96
  equipment 96
  group abseils 104
  in a single-pitch environment 96
  jammed ropes 152
  lower and abseil 153
  multiple abseils 150
  past a knot 101, 158, 159
  releasable abseil 102
  retrievable abseil 98, 99
  rigging an abseil 98, 150, 151
  safety back-up 101, 151
  safety rope 102
  sequence 151
  single rope 96, 99
  stacked abseil 152
  throwing the rope 99
  two ropes 96, 99
  with a belay device 98
  with groups 104
  with novices and clients 152, 154
access 7, 212
  choice of venue 12
  group size 12
  parking 11
accidents 202
  crag incidents 203
  first aid training 204
  getting help 202
  nature of incidents 202
  procedure in the event of an ~ 204

accompanied abseil 127, 160
  tying off a belay device 127
aid climbing 44
anchors 43, 56, 58, 81, 178
  3 anchor essentials 82–83
  attaching to 82–84
    with two ropes 135
  equalising 56, 85
    self-equalising 84
    with slings 82
  selection 58, 91, 137
  testing 58– 59
  types 58–59
ascend a fixed rope 126, 146
Association of British Climbing Walls 106
avoiding problems 126
  TLC 126

## B

back and footing 33
backing off 117
belaying 84, 86, 113, 137, 139, 142, 178
  belay devices 53, 54, 86, 127, 128
    'auto-blocking' 54
    'auto-locking' 53, 54
    'grabbing' 53
    'intermediate' 53
    'slick' 53
    'standard' 54
    Sticht plate 53
    tying off a ~ 129
  belay position 137
  belay systems 63
  belayer attached to ground anchor 92, 94, 113
  belaying a leader 113
  belaying at the top 117
  bell-ringing 93
  brake hand 87
  double-ropes 135
  escaping from the system 128

# G

gorge scrambling 197
  equipment 198
  hazards 198
  techniques 198
grades 44
  adjectival 44
  sport 44
  technical 44
guidebooks 14

# H

handholds 26
  closed crimp 26
  extended grip 26
  jug handles 26
  layaway 26
  open crimp 26
  palming 26
  side pull 26
  smear 26
  undercut 26
head-pointing 18
High Ropes Courses 216
history of rock climbing 13
hitches – see knots 64
hoisting systems 160

# I

improving technique 36
  balance 38
  climbing style 36
  flexibility 38
  footwork 38
  games for children 38
  mental/psychological skills 39
  motivation 40
  point and go 38
  sewing-machine leg 38
  speed climbing 37
  strength 36
injury avoidance 22, 37
  RICE method 22, 24
instructing climbing 143, 144, 146, 148
international distress signal 202

# J

jugs 26

# K

karabiners 55, 120
  auto-locking 55
  cross-loaded 56, 101
  failure 48, 55
  forces on ~ 47, 56
  gate-open strength 48, 55
  HMS 55
  karabiner brake 67
  locking 55
  snap-links 55
  strength markings 55
  wire gate snap-links 55
knots 64
  alpine butterfly 68, 186
  alpine clutch 69
  bowline 66
  clove hitch 67
  double fisherman's 69
  figure of eight 64
    double ~ on a bight 65
    re-threaded ~ 65
    re-threaded ~ on a harness 65
    ~ at an anchor 66
    ~ on a bight 64
  French prusik 68–69, 101–102, 126, 129–130, 146, 160, 164–166, 169–170, 208
  Italian hitch 53–54, 63, 67, 88, 90–93, 98, 102–103, 128, 142, 157, 178, 180, 188
  karabiner brake 67
  Klemheist 69
  lark's foot 70
  ordinary prusik 68
  overhand knot 64, 82, 84–85, 91, 99, 151, 186
  overhand to join two ropes 69
  reef knot 69
  stopper 67
  tape knot 70

# L

law, the
  access legislation 212